PUBLIC SPACES, PRIVATE LIVES

PUBLIC SPACES, PRIVATE LIVES

Beyond the Culture of Cynicism

HENRY A. GIROUX

With an Afterword by Douglas Kellner

ROWMAN & LITTLEFIELD PUBLISHERS, INC.
Lanham • Boulder • New York • Oxford

ROWMAN & LITTLEFIELD PUBLISHERS, INC.

Published in the United States of America
by Rowman & Littlefield Publishers, Inc.
4720 Boston Way, Lanham, Maryland 20706
www.rowmanlittlefield.com

12 Hid's Copse Road, Cumnor Hill, Oxford OX2 9JJ, England

Distributed by NATIONAL BOOK NETWORK

British Library Cataloguing in Publication Information Available

Library of Congress Cataloging-in-Publication Data
Giroux, Henry A.
    Public spaces, private lives : beyond the culture of cynicism /
Henry A. Giroux.
        p.   cm.—(Culture and politics)
    Includes bibliographical references and index.
    ISBN 0-7425-1553-2 (alk. paper)
    1. Social problems—United States.   2. Group identity—United
States.   3. Social values—United States.   4. Common good—
United States.   5. Public interest—United States.   6. Political
participation—United States.   7. Free enterprise—United States.
8. Privatization—United States.   I. Title.   II. Series.
    HN65.G53   2001
    361.1'0973—dc21   2001019528

Printed in the United States of America

♾ ™ The paper used in this publication meets the minimum requirements of American
National Standard for Information Sciences—Permanence of Paper for Printed Library
Materials, ANSI/NISO Z39.48-1992.

For Susan, again and again

CONTENTS

ACKNOWLEDGMENTS

This book represents an attempt to understand and address not merely the crisis of politics but the *rearticulation* of politics in light of the mutually dependent and often changing relations between the public domain and the spheres of private life. It was written out of a sense of public outrage at what was happening in this country to people of color, the poor, and others who came from families and neighborhoods like the one in which I grew up in as a working-class youth in Providence, Rhode Island. But the book was inspired by more than outrage; it was also motivated by the example set by young people on campuses across the country dedicated to fighting the increasing corporatization of higher education, as well as those who marched in Seattle; Washington, D.C.; Philadelphia; and in other cities protesting the actions of the World Trade Organization, the World Bank, and the overall injustices perpetrated by global capitalism. Within the period in which this book was written, more intellectuals appeared to be waking up from their sleepwalking within discourses that appeared to isolate them completely from any sense of social responsibility and public politics. In addition, various youth mobilization groups began talking about moving away from an exclusive emphasis on confronting power to developing educational and political strategies that aimed at gaining power and developing a prodemocracy movement.

Like many of my projects in the past, the idea for this book did not start in the abstract realm of theory, but in the heated and crisis-ridden experiences of the everyday that link the private and the public, the abstract and the concrete. Writing has never been easy for me, and each book that I write carries with it a context of struggle, joy, and sometimes anxiety. Though it is difficult to argue that writing is not a social endeavor, particularly since one always draws from the store of the social through the use of language, memories, histories, and resources, I always feel alone at that moment when one puts ink to the page, when ideas begin their laborious journey to coherency and, ideally, to insight itself. This task was made considerably easier through the help of friends and colleagues who listened to me over the phone, received e-mail attachments, and talked with me in coffee shops throughout this country. In my case, there are a number of people to thank: Susan Searls, Eric Weiner, Paul Youngquist, Ralph Rodriguez, Arif Dirlik, Jackie Edmundson, Stanley Aronowitz, Doug Kellner, Roger Simon, Ken Saltman, Jeff Nealon, Paul Bove, Keith Gilyard, Evan Watkins, Lynn Worsham, Barry Kanpol, Cheryl Glenn, David Goldberg, Lawrence Grossberg, Sut Jhally, Donaldo Macedo, Kostas Myrsiades, Amitava Kumar, Lee Quinby, Robin D. G. Kelley, Carol Becker, Micaela Amato, Don Schule, Ralph Page, Norman Denzin, Nick Coudry, Peter Trifonas, Ted Striphas, and Pat Shannon. Special thanks go to Susan Searls, my partner, for reading the entire manuscript and for helping me think through many of the ideas expressed here. Without her support during a trying time, I would never have been able to complete this book. I also want to thank my children, Brett, Chris, and Jack, for their patience, joy, and spirit. I am deeply appreciative of the support provided by my editor, Dean Birkenkamp. In its current form, this book would not have been written without his strong and unfailing encouragement. Sue Stewart, my administrative assistant, has been invaluable in helping me tie up various details in finishing this manuscript. I am enormously grateful to Dr. Steven Ludwig at the Hershey Medical Center for successfully operating on my back and giving me the freedom once again to be able to sit, pain-free, at my computer. I always appreciate having Grizz, my aging canine companion, around. While writing this book, earlier versions of some of these chapters were published in *Boundary 2, JAC, College Literature, New Art Examiner,* and *Third Text.*

INTRODUCTION

Collective Hopes in the
Age of Privatized Visions

There is a growing sense in American life that politics has become corrupt. Those traditional public spheres in which people could exchange ideas, debate, and shape the conditions that structured their everyday lives increasingly appear to have little relevance or political importance. Emptied of any substantial content, democracy appears imperiled as individuals are unable to translate their privately suffered misery into public concerns and collective action. Civic engagement now appears impotent, and public values are rendered invisible in light of the growing power of multinational corporations to privatize public space and disconnect power from issues of equity, social justice, and civic responsibility. Political exhaustion and impoverished intellectual visions are fed by the increasingly popular assumption that there are no alternatives to the present state of affairs.[1] Within the increasing corporatization of everyday life, market values replace social values, and people appear more and more willing to retreat into the safe, privatized enclaves of the family, religion, and consumption. The result is not only silence and indifference, but the terrible price paid in what Zygmunt Bauman calls the "hard currency of human suffering."[2]

As those public spaces that offer forums for debating norms, critically engaging ideas, making private issues public, and evaluating judgments disappear under the juggernaut of neoliberal policies, it becomes crucial for progressives to raise fundamental questions about what it means to revitalize a politics and ethics that takes seriously "such values as citizen participation, the public good, political obligation, social governance, and community."[3] The call for a revitalized politics grounded in an effective democracy substantively challenges the dystopian practices of neoliberalism—with their all-consuming emphasis on market relations, commercialization, privatization, and the creation of a worldwide economy of part-time workers—against their utopian promises. Such an intervention confronts progressives with the problem as well as challenge of developing those public spheres—such as the media, higher education, and other cultural institutions—that provide the conditions for creating citizens who are capable of exercising their freedoms, competent to question the basic assumptions that govern political life, and skilled enough to participate in shaping the basic social, political, and economic orders that govern their lives.

For many young people and adults today, the private sphere has become the only space in which to imagine any sense of hope, pleasure, or possibility. Market forces focus on the related issues of consumption and safety. Reduced to the act of consuming, citizenship is "mostly about forgetting, not learning."[4] And as social visions of equity cede from public memory, unfettered brutal self-interests combine with retrograde social policies to make security a top domestic priority. One consequence is that all levels of government are being hollowed out, reducing their role to dismantling the gains of the welfare state as they increasingly construct policies that now criminalize social problems and prioritize penal methods over social investments. Increasingly, notions of the public cease to resonate as a site of utopian possibility, as a fundamental space for how we reactivate our political sensibilities and conceive of ourselves as critical citizens, engaged public intellectuals, and social agents. The growing lack of justice in American society rises proportionately to the lack of political imagination and collective hope.[5] We live at a time when the forces and advocates of neoliberalism not only undermine all attempts to revive the culture of politics as an ethical response to the demise of democratic public life, but also aggressively wage a war against the very possibility of creating noncommodified public spheres and forums that provide the conditions for critical education, link learning to social change, political agency to the defense of public goods, and intellectual courage to the refusal to surrender knowledge to the highest bidder. Understood as both a set of economic policies and an impoverished notion of citizenship, neoliberalism represents not just a series of market-driven programs but also a coherent set of cultural, political, and educational practices.

Unlike some theorists who suggest that politics as a site of contestation, critical exchange, and engagement has either come to an end or is in a state of terminal arrest, I argue in *Public Spaces, Private Lives* that the current, depressing state of politics points to the urgent challenge of reformulating the crisis of democracy as part of the fundamental crisis of vision, meaning, education, and political agency. Politics devoid of a democratic vision degenerates into either cynicism or appropriates a view of power that appears to be equated only with domination. Lost from such accounts is the recognition that democracy has to be struggled over—even in the face of a most appalling crisis of political agency. There is also little attention paid to the fact that the struggle over politics and democracy is inextricably linked to creating public spheres where individuals can be educated as political agents equipped with the skills, capacities, and knowledge they need not only to actually perform as autonomous political agents but also to believe that such struggles are worth taking up. Central to my argument is the assumption that politics is not simply about power, but also, as Cornelius Castoriadis points out, "has to do with political judgements and value choices,"[6] indicating that questions of civic education—learning how to become a skilled national and global citizen—are central to both the struggle over political agency and democracy itself. Finally, there is the widespread refusal among many progressives and critical theorists to recognize that the issue of civic education—with its emphasis on critical thinking, bridging the gap between learning and everyday life, understanding the connection between power and knowledge, and using the resources of history to extend democratic rights and identities—is not only the foundation for expanding and enabling political agency, but that such education takes place across a wide variety of public spheres through the very force of culture itself.

This book challenges the assumptions that any viable notion of politics is dead by arguing that critical knowledge grounded in pressing social problems offers individuals and groups some hope in shaping the conditions that bear down on their lives. It also links the production of such knowledge to the urgent call to revitalize the language of civic education as part of a broader discourse of political agency and critical citizenship in a global world. *Public Spaces, Private Lives* represents an attempt, however incomplete, to link democracy to public action and to ground such a call in defense of militant utopian thinking as a form of educated hope. Utopianism in this context suggests that any feasible notion of the political must address the primacy of pedagogy as part of a broader attempt to revitalize the conditions for individual and social agency while, simultaneously, addressing the most basic problems facing the prospects for social justice and global democracy.

Throughout this book, I draw upon scholarly and popular sources and use theory as a critical resource to name particular problems, make connections between the political and the cultural, and break what Homi Bhabha has called "the continuity and the consensus of common sense."[7] As a resource, theory also becomes important as a way of critically engaging and mapping the important relations among language, texts, everyday life, and structures of power as part of a comprehensive effort to understand the conditions, con-

texts, and strategies of struggle that will lead to social transformation. The
tools of theory emerge out of the intersection of the past and present and
respond to and are shaped by the conditions at hand. It is the contention of
this book that we need new theoretical tools—a new vocabulary—for linking
hope, democracy, education, and the demands of a substantive democracy.
While I believe we need a new vocabulary for connecting how we read critically to how we engage in movements for social change, I also think that
simply invoking the relationship between theory and practice, critique and
social action will not do. Any attempt to give new life to a substantive democratic politics must also address how people learn to be political agents and
what kind of educational work is necessary within what kind of public spaces
to enable people to use their full intellectual resources both to provide a profound critique of existing institutions and to struggle to create, as Stuart Hall
puts it, "what would be a good life or a better kind of life for the majority of
people."[8] As progressives, we are required to understand more fully why the
tools we used in the past often feel awkward in the present and fail to respond
to problems now facing the United States and other parts of the globe. More
specifically, we need to understand the failure of existing critical discourses
to bridge the gap between how the society represents itself and how and why
individuals fail to understand and critically engage such representations in
order to intervene in the oppressive social relationships they often legitimate.
This book, I hope, makes a small contribution toward providing the outlines
of such a new discourse.

The growth of cynicism in American society may say less about the reputed
apathy of the populace than it might about the bankruptcy of the old political
languages and the need for a new language and vision for clarifying our intellectual, ethical, and political projects, especially as they work to reabsorb
questions of agency, ethics, and meaning back into politics and public life.
Along these lines, Sheldon Wolin has recently argued that we need to rethink
the notion of loss and its impact on the possibility for opening up democratic
public life. Wolin points to the need for progressives, theorists, and critical
educators to resurrect and raise questions about "What survives of the de-
feated, the indigestible, the unassimilated, the 'cross-grained,' the 'not wholly
obsolete.'"[9] He raises an issue discussed in the last chapter of this book—that
"something is missing" in an age of manufactured politics and pseudo-pub-
lics catering almost exclusively to desires and drives produced by the commercial hysteria of the market. What is missing is a language, movement, and
vision that refuses to equate democracy with consumerism, market relations,
and privatization. In the absence of such a language and the social formations
and public spheres that make it operative, politics becomes narcissistic and

caters to the mood of widespread pessimism and the cathartic allure of the spectacle. In addition, public service and government intervention are sneered upon as either bureaucratic or a constraint upon individual freedom.

This book aims to make a small contribution to resurrecting a language of resistance and possibility, a language that embraces a militant utopianism, while constantly challenging those forces that seek to turn such a hope into a new slogan or punish and dismiss those who dare look beyond the horizon of the given. Hope, in this instance, is the precondition for individual and social struggle, the ongoing practice of critical education in a wide variety of sites, the mark of courage on the part of intellectuals in and out of the academy who use the resources of theory to address pressing social problems. But hope is also a referent for civic courage and its ability to mediate the *memory* of loss and the *experience* of injustice as part of a broader attempt to open up new locations of struggle, contest the workings of oppressive power, and undermine various forms of domination. At its best, civic courage as a political practice begins when one's life can no longer be taken for granted. In doing so, it makes concrete the possibility for transforming hope and politics into an ethical space and public act that confronts the flow of everyday experience and the weight of social suffering with the force of individual and collective resistance and the unending project of democratic social transformation.

PUBLIC SPACES, PRIVATE LIVES

1

CULTURAL STUDIES AND THE CULTURE OF POLITICS

Beyond Polemics and Cynicism

We expect [people] brutally exploited and intolerably poor to rest and be patient in their misery, because if they act to end their conditions it will involve the rest of us, and threaten our convenience or our lives. . . . We have identified war and revolution as tragic dangers, when the real tragic danger, underlying war and revolution, is a disorder which we continually re-enact.

—Raymond Williams

CYNICISM AND THE CULTURE OF POLITICS

If the dominant media and its army of professional pollsters are to be believed, the American public is increasingly embracing a culture of cynicism.[1] This growing phenomenon casts doubt upon both the validity of public commitment and civic engagement and the legitimacy of investing in a vibrant culture of politics in order to educate people to struggle for the development of a radical democratic society that makes good on its promises of equality, social rights, freedom, and justice. Cynicism has always occupied a prominent place in American political culture. In the last few decades it has moved from ironic satire to a mocking posture of distrust and disbelief and emerged as a "culture of antipolitics" that dismisses as futile both the discourse of critique and the call for social transformation.[2] Political and social agency appear to have limited currency in the face of a massive rise in corporate power, increasing economic inequalities, a long-term decline in real wages, a massive defunding of public services, and a full-fledged assault on the welfare state by the forces of neoliberalism. Neoliberalism, associated with the rise of the Reagan and Thatcher governments in the early 1980s, refers, as Robert McChesney writes, to those policies "that maximize the role of markets and profit-making and minimize the role of nonmarket institutions. . . . [N]eoliberalism . . . posits that society works best when business runs things and there is as little possibility of government 'interference' with business as possible."[3] Neoliberalism, in this instance, refers to a political, economic, and cultural formation that construes profit making as the essence of democracy and consuming as the only operable form of citizenship and provides a rationale for a handful of private interests to control as much of social life as possible in order to maximize their personal gain and profit.

Signs of exhaustion appear to be everywhere, and the loss of political commitment in an age of political cynicism cuts across ideological, class, and generational lines. For example, Carl Boggs argues that American society in the 1990s has "become more depoliticized, more lacking in the spirit of civic engagement and public obligation, than at any time in recent history with the vast majority of the population increasingly alienated from a political system that is commonly viewed as corrupt, authoritarian, and simply irrelevant to the most important challenges of our time."[4] Roberto Unger and Cornel West convincingly argue that Americans increasingly harbor a distrust of collective solutions and institutional interventions to solve major social problems.[5] This distrust is evident in the growing refusal on the part of many people to participate in social movements and political parties, or to invest in the power of the government to implement social, economic, and political reforms. A national survey of college freshmen conducted in 2000 found that political engagement among first-year students had reached an all-time low. "Only 28.1 percent of incoming college students expressed an interest in keeping up to date with political affairs."[6] Political indifference is also born out in the widespread refusal on the part of many adults and young people to vote or participate in the political system. For instance, voter turnout in the 1996 presidential election was the lowest of any election since 1924. Moreover, in the mid-term elections of 1998, little more than 12.2 percent of 18- to 24-year-olds voted, compared with 19 percent in 1994.[7]

Of course, political cynicism is not simply about the refusal of large sections of the population to vote. Socially engaged citizenship as the refusal of political cynicism is about the willingness of people to participate individually and collectively in administering the basic institutions that shape their lives and to exercise control in wielding power over organizations as diverse as the government, workplace, home, and school. Crucial to any viable notion of social citizenship, thriving public dialogue, and an expansion of critical thinking is the project of developing social movements that can both challenge the subordination of social needs to the dictates of the "free" market in every sphere of society and that offer alternative models of radical democratic culture, rooted in social relations, that take seriously the democratic ideals of freedom, liberty, and the pursuit of happiness. As Nancy Fraser and Linda Gordon point out, social citizenship combines traditional notions of individual rights, equal respect, and public participation in public life with the "entitlement to social provision—the guarantee of a decent standard of living." This notion of citizenship provides individuals and groups "with institutions and services designed for *all* citizens, the use of which constitutes the *practice* of social citizenship: for example, public schools, public parks, universal health insurance, public health services."[8] In its more substantive forms, citizenship provides the conditions for public participation and engagement within a vastly changing set of historical conditions.[9] Undermining this conception of citizenship, cynicism becomes both an ideological weapon and a symptom of those cultural and institutional forces that subvert the individual and collective dimensions of political life and social transformation.

According to Kevin Mattson—a self-described spokesperson for Generation X—irony, detachment, and indifference are the hallmark characteristics of his generation. He alleges that many young people have lost faith in the culture of politics and that they now believe that what was once possible for previous generations is out of reach for their own. In Mattson's view, rapacious neoliberalism and its market-driven conservative ideology—buttressed by the death of liberalism after the 1960s and the current absence of a viable left movement—offer young people few oppositional discourses with which to critically engage the cynicism that permeates almost every aspect of American culture, a cynicism that defines the social life of those he labels Generation X.[10] In the eyes of many young people, politics as a sphere of concrete possibility appears to have given way to an unregulated and all-powerful market that models all dreams around the narcissistic, privatized, and self-indulgent needs of consumer culture. For many young people, a waning sense of civic engagement and public responsibility is matched by a sharply declining knowledge about history, public affairs, government, and social issues.[11] Generational stereotypes aside, the young increasingly bear the burden of a society that offers them an impoverished sense of politics; a future filled with low-paying, temporary jobs; and a growing gap between what is learned at all levels of education and the knowledge and skills of citizenship that they will need to address the most pressing social and economic problems of a troubled world.

The eminent sociologist Zygmunt Bauman argues that, as the bridges between private and public life are dismantled, major industrial societies—such as the United States—become increasingly incapable of both translating private troubles into public issues and understanding how public life affects private experience. One consequence is a politics that, in Bauman's words, "lauds conformity and promotes conformity."[12] In an age that declares that ideology and history have reached their ultimate liberal democratic expression, politics increasingly means that "citizens" no longer need to bother themselves with "any coherent vision of the good society [or] of having traded off the worry about the public good for the freedom to pursue private satisfaction."[13] If Bauman is right, we are quickly moving toward a period in American history in which society has stopped questioning itself and, in doing so, not only ignores its most pressing social problems but produces a politics that offers nothing but more of the same.

The lack of political imagination that permeates mainstream culture is matched both by a lack of collective outrage against glaring material inequities and by the growing belief that today's culture of investment and finance makes it impossible to address major social problems such as inadequate health care, education, and housing, on the one hand, and, on the other, the growing inequality of wealth, generational entitlements, and racial apartheid characteristic of inner cities.[14] Michael Walzer, among others, has argued that such forces have drastically undermined the faith of the poor in either the possibility of politics or the sense that they have any power to change the direction of their lives.[15] More and more people are dropping out of the middle rungs of society or are barely making it due to factors such as the growing unequal distribution of income, the continued reduction of the state to its policing functions, and the permanent state of insecurity caused by the policies of neoliberalism. For many poor people, repression now replaces social investment as the state's central activity; public spending recedes as the market is increasingly deregulated; and, as industries simultaneously merge and downsize, thousands of workers are laid off or are faced with temporary employment. For those who occupy the poorest rungs on the social ladder, the threat of job insecurity—along with worsening economic opportunities—has displaced hope with a growing sense of apathy, resignation, and political indifference.[16] The failure of the poor to participate in the culture of politics is, however, only one index of the failure of social justice and, all too often, is cited extensively by liberals as a way of overlooking the complicity of the middle and upper classes in undermining social justice and political agency. The poor are not solely responsible for the growing culture of cynicism; yet, more than any other group, they often bear the consequences of a devalued notion of social citizenship and its effects on social policy and public life.

The evisceration of political culture is especially evident in a post-Littleton, post-Lewinsky climate in which the vast majority of the nation's populace feel removed from a culture of politics whose impact seems to be most strongly felt in the dominant and the tabloid media while it is largely absent from social life. As columnist Eric Alterman observed in *The Nation,* if the 1970s was the "age of the investigative reporter, then the late nineties may go down in history as the age of the blowjob reporter. . . . Ever since the word 'Lewinsky' entered the lexicon, nothing makes an editor's pencil perk up quite so much as the word 'oral' next to the word 'sex.' "[17] The dominant media has carpet bombed audiences with endless stories about oral sex, cigars, and presidential sexual indiscretions—not to mention the prime coverage given to Reverend Jerry Falwell's melodramatic announcement that Tinky Winky, a whimsical doll figure from *Teletubbies* (a popular children's animated television show), is gay and hence a menace to society. At the same time, the media has had little to say about the decline of democracy itself—a decline characterized by the growing gap between the rich and the poor, the shameful increase in child poverty, the accelerating violence being waged against people of color and gays, and the diminishing access that the poor and the working class have to a political culture increasingly dominated by multinational corporate interests. In this scenario, politics becomes a matter of spectacle, voyeurism, and cheap thrills.

Millennial politics signals its own exhaustion, when the only choice is, as Russell Jacoby says, "between the status quo or something worse. Other alternatives do not seem to exist."[18] Coupled with the general public's increasing loss of faith in public government, public institutions, and the democratic process, the only form of agency or civic participation offered to the American people is consumerism rather than substantive forms of social citizenship.[19] As Robert W. McChesney argues:

> To be effective, democracy requires that people feel a connection to their fellow citizens, and that this connection manifests itself through a variety of nonmarket organizations and institutions. A vibrant political culture needs community groups, libraries, public schools, neighborhood organizations, cooperatives, public meeting places, voluntary associations, and trade unions to provide ways for citizens to meet, communicate, and interact with their fellow citizens. Neo-

liberal democracy, with its notion of the market *uber alles,* takes dead aim at this sector. Instead of citizens, it produces consumers. Instead of communities, it produces shopping malls. The net result is an atomized society of disengaged individuals who feel demoralized and socially powerless.[20]

The erasure of democratic politics from the cultural arena can also be seen in the suppression of dissent across a wide variety of public spheres—including the media, universities, and public schools—that are increasingly coming under the control of megacorporations or are being corporatized.[21] As conglomerates, such as Disney, Viacom, Time Warner, and Bertelsmann, gobble up television networks, radio stations, music industries, and a host of other media outlets, it becomes more difficult for stories that are critical of these concentrated industries to see the light of day. When Viacom acquired CBS, most of the stories covering the event in the dominant media focused on the personalities of the top CEOs involved in the deal. With the exception of a few reports in the *Boston Globe, New York Times,* and *Chicago Tribune,* the threat that the deal posed to the free flow of information and the implications it might have for undermining a healthy democracy were largely ignored in the dominant media. Concentrated corporate control does not welcome stories or investigative reports that are critical of corporate culture and its policies and practices. For example, soon after Disney bought ABC, Jim Hightower—a popular radio talk show host—was fired for making remarks critical of the Telecommunications Act of 1996 and the Disney corporation. Similarly, in 1998 David Westin, president of Disney-owned ABC, refused to air a 20/20 segment by Brian Ross investigating instances of pedophilia at Disney World and the hiring of employees who had previous criminal records (including sexual misconduct), a failure that resulted in Disney's refusal to do adequate background checks. Fairness & Accuracy in Reporting, a liberal, national media watchdog group advocating independence and criticism in journalism, claims that Westin also "killed a story about the sweatshop factories producing ABC personality Kathie Lee Gifford's clothing line" and that one ABC producer argued that reporters are constantly trying "to avoid news stories that might displease Disney . . . because no one wants to piss off the bosses."[22] Similar examples can be found in all of the major networks.

Moreover, as higher education is increasingly corporatized, it also becomes subject to policies and practices that limit dissent and the pursuit of knowledge. For example, progressive and leftist intellectuals find it increasingly difficult to protect either their existing appointments or to get hired. The attack on the democratic principles of academic freedom and intellectual diversity are further exacerbated by the moral panics created in the media by conservative politicians, academics, and policy makers—such as William Bennett, Pat Buchanan, Roger Kimball, Charles J. Sykes, Roger Shattuck, Lynne Cheney, and William Kristol—with the help of an endless amount of financial backing from such conservative sources as the John M. Olin Foundation, the Harry Bradley Foundation, the Smith Richardson Foundation, and the Richard Scaife Foundation, to name only a few.[23] These conservative public intellectuals are far outside of the mainstream of popular opinion on many issues. Yet, they are regularly hosted in the dominant media as celebrities, and they are unwaveringly dedicated to bashing progressive academics and offering instant sound bites about the decline of civility, the corruption of Western values, and the growing need to purge the universities of dissenting voices, especially if they come from the left. Clearly, progressive positions that might offer a challenge to such views are conspicuously missing from the dominant media.

Such an assault on the culture of democratic politics is further strengthened as schools divorce themselves from pedagogies and models of learning that address important social issues, interrogate how power works in society, or engage crucial considerations of social justice as constitutive of the interrelationship between cultural practice and democratic politics in the name of standardization and testing. In short, the ascendancy of corporate culture in all facets of American life has tended to uproot the legacy of democratic concerns and rights that has historically defined the stated mission of higher education.[24] Within the neoliberal era of deregulation and the triumph of the market, many students and their families no longer believe that higher education is about higher learning. Instead they believe it is about gaining a better foothold in the job market. Colleges and universities are perceived—and perceive themselves—as training grounds for corporate berths. Corporate culture has also reformulated social issues as largely individual or economic considerations, while canceling democratic impulses by either devaluing or absorbing them into the imperatives of the marketplace. This suggests a dangerous turn in American society, one that both threatens the democracy that is fundamental to our freedoms and removes the ethical referent from the meaning and purpose of higher education.

As corporations become more and more powerful in the United States, democratic culture is increasingly replaced by corporate culture, while educational leadership is stripped of its ethical and political obligations and is redefined primarily as a matter of management, efficiency, and cost-effectiveness. In the name of efficiency, educational consultants all over America advise their clients to act like corporations, selling products and seeking "market niches" to save themselves. In this corporatized regime, management models of decision making replace faculty governance. Once constrained by the concept of "shared" governance, in the past decade, administrations have taken more power and reduced faculty-controlled governance to an advisory status. Given the narrow nature of corporate concerns, it is not surprising that, when matters of accountability become part of the language of school reform, they are divorced from broader considerations of social responsibility. Missing from much of the corporate discourse on schooling is an analysis of how power works in shaping knowledge, how the teaching of broader social values provides safeguards against turning citizenship skills into training skills for the workplace, or how schooling can help students reconcile the seemingly contradictory needs of individual freedom and democratic community so as to forge a new conception of public life. In the corporate model, knowledge becomes capital—a form of investment in the economy—but appears to have little value when linked to the power of self-definition or the capacities of individuals to expand the scope of freedom. Nor does such a language provide the pedagogical conditions for students to critically engage knowledge as deeply implicated in issues and struggles concerning the production of identities, culture, power, and history. Hence, the corporate view of schooling has no way of recognizing that education must be more than simply a form of training. When education capitulates to the market, not only does training replace education but the idea of higher education as a public good is surrendered to the logic of the bottom line.

Although most commentators argue that political culture has been on the decline since Watergate, there is little understanding of the dialogical relationship between culture and democracy. Typically, conservatives believe that American culture is in crisis and the problem is democracy (except when it provides new markets). In this discourse, democracy promotes unpatriotic dissent, moral relativism, the dumbing down of schools, welfare, and the lowering of standards, most of which can be traced to the upheavals of the 1960s.[25] Such sentiments are echoed in the halls of Congress by majority whip Tom DeLay, who believes that the culture of politics has been corrupted by the breakdown of religious values, the power of big government, and the bodies of welfare recipients who allegedly drain the national treasury.[26] In DeLay's view, moral righteousness is the defining postulate of civic virtue and is considered far more important than the democratic principles of liberty, freedom, and equality. Furthermore, these principles, more often than not, give rise to forms of dissent that in Anthony Lewis's opinion, undermine the true believers' faith in "certainty" and "their absolute conviction [that] they are right."[27] Such views can also be found in high-profile conservatives such as former 2000 presidential hopefuls Pat Buchanan and Gary Bauer. In this discourse, morality is invoked as a way of controlling individual behavior and of drawing public attention away from issues of economic and social justice.

For many liberals, in contrast, the crisis of political culture is presented in somewhat different terms. In the liberal perspective, democracy is in crisis and the problem is culture. Yet, culture is less a problem for its lack of moral principles than it is for its proliferation of cultural differences, its challenge to patriarchal authority and racial exclusions, its refusal to offer a unified homage to the dictates of the market, and its spread of violence and incivility through popular culture. In this model of liberalism, radical cultural politics threatens the dominant image of the public sphere as male, middle-class, and white; it also undermines the liberal notion of consensus and challenges the market-crazed celebration of instant gratification and the endless pursuit of getting and spending. In this view, the public sphere undermines the freedom associated with private gain and resurrects a notion of the social marked by political differences and the allegedly antagonistic calls for expanding democratic rights. Liberalism, in its more "compassionate" strains, advocates a culture of gentility and civility, one that dismisses the democratic impulses of mass culture as barbaric and the ethos and representations of an electronically based popular culture as irredeemably violent, crude, and tasteless.[28] Both positions share a cynicism toward and a condemnation of national popular culture, perceiving it as impure, sullied, and corrupted by the logic and discourse of difference. In addition, both positions condemn democratic, nonmarket, noncommodified forces that often provide a critical vocabulary for challenging the self-serving notion that the free market and corporate domination of society represent the ultimate expression of democracy or that the neoliberal view of society represents humanity at its best. Neither position offers any hope that America's future will be any different from its present.

Finally, there is the notion—largely held by an orthodox, materialist left— that culture as a potential sphere of political education and change undermines the very notion of politics itself; this point of view is often reduced to battles over material issues rather than struggles that accentuate ideology, language, experience, pedagogy, and identity.[29] Left anticulturalists posit their concerns with class and economic justice against a cultural left largely organized around issues of race, sex, and gender. For instance, Micaela di Leonardo argues in *Exotics at Home* that a radical anthropology undermines any notion of critical politics to the degree that, as Sherry Ortner observes, it emphasizes culture "instead of the hard, objective realities of political-economic forces impinging on people's lives."[30] Similarly, Eric Alterman dismisses the "racism/sexism/homophobia crowd" as political losers because they have no sense of the primacy of class politics in American history.[31] Todd

Gitlin echoes the "culture versus class" position by claiming that cultural studies is primarily about choosing sides, mistaking the academy for the larger society and undermining public engagement because its practitioners fail to stress the primacy of class and the materiality of power.[32]

This position appears frozen in time, collapsing under the burden of its own intellectual weariness and political exhaustion. Weighted down in a nineteenth-century version of class struggle and domination, contemporary scholarship from the orthodox left often refuses to pluralize the notion of antagonism by reducing it to class conflicts and further undermines the force of political economy by limiting it to a ghostly economism.[33] In addition, orthodox left criticism mirrors the increasing cynicism and despair exemplified in its endless invocation of such terms as "real politics" and its call for a return to materialism—a call premised on the elitist assumption that the average person is incapable of engaging in serious debates about political and cultural issues—just as it buttresses the notion that a pedagogy of persuasion has no role to play in opening up a space of resistance and political struggle. As such, its rhetoric largely appears as high-minded puritanism ("the only true members of the church") matched only by an equally staunch anti-intellectual populism ("radical social critique emanating from the universities is politically worthless"), and an ideological rigidity that barely conceals its contempt for notions of difference, cultural politics, and social movements that do not focus exclusively on class and economic justice. In one of the more devastating critiques of what she calls majoritarian left politics, Ellen Willis argues that the alleged opposition between class/capitalism and cultural politics constructed by left conservatives is simply wrong. She writes:

> People's working lives, their sexual and domestic lives, their moral values are intertwined. Capitalism is not only an economic system but a pervasive social and ideological force: in its present phase, it is promoting a culture of compulsive work, social Darwinism, contempt for "useless" artistic and intellectual pursuits, rejection of the very concept of public goods, and corporate "efficiency" as the model for every social activity from education to medicine. In every sphere, Americans face the question of whether they will act, individually and collectively, in behalf of their own desires and interests, or allow established authority to decree what they must do, what they may not do, what they deserve, what they have a right to expect. If they do not feel entitled to demand freedom and equality in their personal and social relations, they will not fight for freedom and equality in their economic relations.[34]

Willis is right in arguing against a left-oriented materialism that claims "we can do class or culture, but not both."[35] But there is more at stake than the refusal to connect economic and cultural issues; there is the broader rejection of engagement in a political struggle that recognizes consciousness, agency, and education as central to any viable notion of politics. And it is this issue that links the material left to liberals and conservatives who also refuse to reform the basic institutions of civil society as part of a wider struggle to expand democratic identities, values, and social relations. What all of these ideological positions share is a widespread public cynicism regarding the need to develop schools and other educational sites that prepare young people and adults to become active agents of democratic politics; to develop vigorous social spheres and communities that promote a culture of deliberation, public debate, and critical exchange; and to encourage people to organize pedagogically and politically across a wide variety of cultural and institutional sites in an effort to develop democratic movements for social change. At stake here is both the need to register the crisis of political culture and recognize the important role that cultural studies might play in addressing such issues. In part, this means acknowledging that many of the current attacks on cultural studies can be understood as part of a broader attack on the culture of politics and the attempt to undermine any linkage between culture, politics, pedagogy, and power, on the one hand, and on the other, the discourse of social criticism and social change.

In what follows, I want to argue that the spate of recent attacks on cultural studies might best be seen as symptomatic of a broader attack on cultural politics in public life. Such a recognition allows cultural studies theorists to view such attacks as more than forms of academic sniping or as simply symptomatic of the self-reflexive character of debate that cultural studies generates both within and outside of its ranks. In "The Cultural Studies' Crossroad Blues," Lawrence Grossberg insightfully argues that the attack on cultural studies should be understood as part of a broader assault on the viability of the political as a crucial sphere for investing in social change, on the courage to imagine the possibility of workable political communities, and on the theoretical necessity for articulating a theory of critical agency that does not focus exclusively on individual agency.[36] If Grossberg is right, and I think he is, it becomes necessary to provide a sustained response to such attacks—particularly those waged in the mainstream media—in ways that are productive rather than simply defensive. I am referring in this case not to those critiques of cultural studies that are thoughtful, well-argued, risk-taking, and are intended to expand the possibilities of critical exchange and social engagement.[37] Cultural studies has always been self-reflective about its own motivating questions, theoretical projects, and political formations.[38] On the contrary, I am referring to a species of argument that condemns, provides no room for equal discussion, collects proof of the other side's guilt, and treats an interlocutor as a suspect or as an enemy who must be eliminated. The distinctiveness of such assaults leads to my second point.

Responding to such polemics provides cultural studies theorists and its many practitioners with the opportunity to make clear how cultural studies might be useful for producing the knowledge, skills, pedagogies, modes of collaborative association, and forms of social engagement that might be helpful in addressing a range of problems and public conversations that are shaping what Grossberg calls "the politics of policy and public debate."[39] At stake here is the opportunity for cultural studies theorists to illuminate and defend the importance of cultural politics and the role it can play in expanding radical democratic struggles. In this instance, cultural studies theorists would seize on the primacy of the relationship between culture and politics by emphasizing the point that any viable notion of political and economic transformation involves connecting learning to social change, bridging the gap between broader, systemic forces and those contexts where people actually live out their daily lives, and cultivating notions of social struggle that recognize the futility of separating economics and class-based issues from other forms of antagonism and cultural considerations. Cultural studies advocates need to articulate those elements of a political project—however unstable and provisional—that shape its own practices in opposing the evisceration of politics while simultaneously intervening, pedagogically and politically, in the shaping of public life. Of course, there is a need for cultural studies theorists to engage in both short- and long-term projects—projects that undertake diverse approaches toward producing and engaging theoretical discourses, as well as developing knowledge more directly tied to social change. At the same time, to recognize this issue, it is imperative that these diverse approaches require what Ellen Willis calls formulating a radical democratic vision "of what kind of society we want and agitating for that vision, in every inventive way we can, wherever we find ourselves."[40]

If such a vision can move on the ground, it should not be mistaken for the irresponsible demand to develop what Derrida calls a political project whose object is the "logical or theoretical consequences of assured knowledge (euphoric, without paradox, without aporia, free of contradiction, without undecidabilities to decide)."[41] Nor should the call for such a project suggest that cultural studies work cannot assume multiple forms, directions, and expressions. On the contrary, such a project—while grounded in a compelling vision of a society that provides the greatest degree of security and justice for all of its citizens—would be anticipatory, not messianic. It would hold democracy responsible to its promises and provide the groundwork for an ongoing political debate—marked by multiple forms of intervention—regarding the urgency of politics and the crisis of public life within the context of global capitalism. While cultural studies prides itself on being a politics that offers no guarantees, this does not relieve its practitioners of mapping existing relations of power, providing resources for engaging in acts of resistance, and confronting the dystopian forces at work in shaping our entry into the new millennium. In fact many cultural studies theorists have been doing this for some time, but such work needs to gain more visibility within broader public spheres.

CULTURAL STUDIES AND THE POLITICS OF POLEMICS

In the current dystopian climate, there are increasingly frequent attempts on the part of theorists occupying various positions on the political spectrum not simply to engage cultural studies in a critical dialogue but to write its obituary.[42] Cultural studies becomes an easy target in the current historical conjuncture. Yet, in contrast to the pervasive cynicism that cuts across the ideological spectrum, cultural studies theorists often work to further both a language of critique and possibility. Many of its practitioners view the relationship between culture and politics as pivotal to understanding and connecting the complex relations between theory and practice, power and social transformation, and pedagogy and social agency. Within these diverse traditions, culture is a site of struggle over material resources, communication, politics, and power. As Cary Nelson, Paula Treichler, and Lawrence Grossberg have pointed out, cultural studies is perceived as dangerous because "its practitioners see [it] not simply as a chronicle of cultural change but as an intervention in it, and see themselves not simply as scholars providing an account but as politically engaged participants."[43] In the ideologically diverse and excessive rhetorical flourishes that dismiss cultural studies as politically radical, nihilistic, faddish, or unscholarly, there are not only the residues of anti-intellectualism, but also an attack on the basic presupposition that cultural politics can play a role in shaping democratic public life. For many critics, it seems unimaginable that cultural studies might play a crucial part in challenging the popular disinterest in the culture of politics by reenergizing the role that academics and other cultural workers might play as oppositional public intellectuals, addressing multiple audiences and drawing attention to the important role that cultural pedagogy and politics can play in forging alliances between academics and various groups outside of the university. But before I address what I think cultural studies theorists might do in response to the ongoing criticisms they are facing vis-à-vis the broader attempt to expand the possibilities of a radical cultural politics, I want to highlight some representative examples of such critiques and show that they are symptomatic of both a particular style of polemics and a part of a broader culture of depoliticization and despair that has become the hallmark of the present historical era.

The first commentary comes from Jeffrey Hart, one of the senior editors of the conservative magazine *The National Review*. Hart positions his commentary on cultural studies in response to the question "What is a liberal-arts education suppose to produce?" He answers,

> Select the ordinary courses. I use ordinary here in a paradoxical and challenging way. An ordinary course is one that has always been taken and obviously should be taken—even if the student is not yet equipped with a sophisticated rationale for so doing. The student should be discouraged from putting his money on the cutting edge of interdisciplinary cross-textuality [cultural studies]. . . . If the student should seek out those ordinary courses, then it follows that he should avoid the flashy come-ons. Avoid things like Nicaraguan Lesbian Poets. Yes, and anything listed under 'Studies,' any course whose description uses the words "interdisciplinary," "hegemonic," "phallocratic," or "empowerment," anything that mentions "keeping a diary," any course with a title like "Adventures in Film". Also, any male professor who comes to class without a jacket and tie should be regarded with extreme prejudice unless he has won a Nobel Prize.[44]

According to Hart, cultural studies is the enemy of higher education because it raises questions outside of existing disciplinary boundaries and attempts to be self-reflexive about "ordinary" knowledge with respect to its historical construction, ideological interests, and assumed truths. Equally disturbing to Hart is the role that cultural studies plays in challenging not only how canon formation might be used to secure particular forms of authority but also its refusal to uphold the traditional sartorial style of male authority and professionalism. Of course, what disturbs Hart the most about cultural studies is that, while often disguised under the rubric of "ordinary courses," it legitimates critical pedagogical practices that are self-consciously political, upholds the university as a space for dissidents to produce critical knowledge, and focuses on how power shapes and is reinvented in the interaction among texts, teachers, and students. Embodying the belief that what teachers, students, and other cultural workers do actually matters as part of a broader attempt to expand the possibilities of democratic values, identities, and relationships, cultural studies invokes the unimaginable, if not subversive, practice of making problematic that which precisely parades under the ordinary, commonsensical, and universal. Adding to the unpopularity of cultural studies is the recognition that it does not define itself as a technique but as a pedagogical and performative practice that unfolds in a wide range of shifting and overlapping sites of learning. Central to such a pedagogy are strategies of representation, engagement, and transformation that are used to investigate the complex contours of political and social agency and how such investigations translate into providing the conditions for students and others to address in the most rigorous way possible the more urgent and disturbing issues facing them in the current historical conjuncture.

In Hart's view, cultural politics has no place in the academy because it poses a clear threat to conservative assumptions about teaching, culture, and authority. The second commentary comes from Roger Shattuck, the former president of a conservative group, the Association of Literary Scholars and Critics. In *Candor and Perversion: Literature, Education and the Arts,* Shattuck rails against Cary Nelson and me in particular, and the field of cultural studies in general, for challenging the assumption that pedagogy is neither disinterested nor innocent and is always implicated in questions of ideology, power, and authority. Shattuck views any notion of education and pedagogy that is associated with politics, transformation, or social change as a betrayal of the more noble conservative educational goal of "transmitting traditional knowledge and skills and . . . teaching as dispassionately as possible the history of our institutions."[45] In opposition to the notion that pedagogy is a moral and political practice, rather than merely a method or technique, Shattuck posits a notion of pedagogy that banishes issues of self-reflexivity and critique by refusing to address the different ways in which knowledge, power, and experience are produced under specific conditions of learning. Shattuck reduces teaching to the transmission of facts. In this discourse, as Aronowitz points out, the teacher "becomes the instrument of the approved intellectual and moral culture, charged with the task of expunging destructive impulses."[46] Shattuck adamantly denies that education always presupposes a vision of the future, or that pedagogy cannot escape its ideological role as an interventionist practice designed to produce and legitimate particular forms of knowledge, identifications, values, and social relations. For Shattuck, cultural studies pedagogy is dangerous because it would "transform our schools and colleges into seedbeds of revolution."[47] Lost here is even the slightest understanding of how pedagogy works to put particular subject positions in place.

Rather than define the process of schooling and learning as integral to creating centers of critical learning and the production of socially engaged citizens, Shattuck defines schools as assimilation factories. As a consequence, Shattuck views the emergence of multiple cultures and differences within the university as a sign of fragmentation and a departure from, rather than an advance toward, democracy. Shattuck is indifferent to the Western-based, culturally bound arrogance of this view of the curriculum and refuses to engage or trouble the historical origins of the perceptions it embodies, and as Susan Bordo puts it, "the social relations that sustain them, [or] the system of thought in which they are embedded."[48] In this discourse, schools are unproblematically defined as regulatory agencies, requiring intellectual and discursive assimilation as a condition for students to participate in both the process of schooling and the pedagogical practices that ground it. Hence, it comes as no surprise when Shattuck argues that "schools will serve us best as a means of passing on an integrated culture . . . and the vital process of education [should continue] to concern itself more with tradition than with change . . . more with the discovery of human universals than with the interests of rival groups."[49] Based upon what Willis characterizes as a faith in "old-fashioned authoritarian pedagogy, indoctrination in morals, official inspirational versions of history, great books for the elite, [and] vocational training for the masses,"[50] Shattuck displays both a retrograde notion of pedagogy and a disdain for critical forms of education that enable teachers and students to recognize antidemocratic forms of power and to learn the knowledge and citizenship skills necessary to fight substantive injustices in a society founded on deep inequalities.

Viewing pedagogy as transmission and schooling as a conservative force for social and cultural reproduction, Shattuck has little to say about what higher education should accomplish in a democracy and why such forms of education seem to be failing. Nor does he appear bothered by the increasing corporatization of the university and how his own views become complicitous with such a process, especially his attempts to cleanse higher education of its critical and emancipatory functions. Shattuck is alarmed by the notion that cultural studies theorists believe that the defining purpose of education is not to train students to take their place in either the corporate order or the existing society, but to encourage human agency as an act of social intervention. He wants to mold human behavior rather than provide the educational conditions for it to unfold. In the end, he confuses training with education and organizes his defense of educational training in the name of enduring values and an attack on the alleged evils of political correctness.

Shattuck can't imagine a pedagogy designed to criticize the very foundation it puts into place; nor can he imagine a pedagogical practice that is about transforming knowledge rather than simply processing it. Hence, it comes as no surprise when he condemns Nelson for opposing "the reading of literature as literature in English department offerings and favors the 'unashamed advocacy' of social reform."[51] Nor does it come as a surprise when he claims that I have "betrayed an honorable profession by trying to plunge it into a vindictive politics of race," because I have troubled his view of educational assimilation by raising questions about how racism operates both within and outside of the academy.[52] But betrayal means more than simply warranting critique and generating debate; Shattuck actually suggests that I should be dismissed from my university position.[53] When it comes to attacking cultural studies' theorists, the conservative claim to civility appears to have been stretched to the limit.

The third type of criticism aimed at cultural studies, as I mentioned earlier, often comes from some members of a materialist left who argue that the study of culture is both uncritical and unpolitical. According to this position, cultural politics is opposed, if not inimical, to the study of materiality and power. This position dismisses as a form of populism, or shoddy scholarship, or as not counting as "real politics," the examination of the imbrication of power and symbolic forms; the study of representations, discourse, images, audiences, popular culture; and the analysis of the relationship between cultural forms and their history, practice, and transformation.[54] In this discourse, cultural studies allegedly not only trivializes the meaning of politics but also undermines the possibilities for building social movements around the primacy of a class-based politics sustained by a rigorous assault on the foundations of a capitalist social order. At its worst, this type of critique can be found in the work of Todd Gitlin, who urges cultural studies theorists to free themselves of the burden of imagining that they engage in a political practice by struggling over and within public sites such as the university, media, or public schooling.[55] Gitlin believes that politics takes place largely in the streets through consolidated demonstrations; through social movements organized around class-based labor struggles; or through political struggles aimed at dismantling the most pressing "concrete" problems produced by capitalist social relations. For Gitlin and others, the notion of "real politics" can only be embraced through the primacy of a materialism defined primarily through struggles over class, labor, and capital. Culture, in this view, has no politics, nor does it offer a site through which to understand, deploy, resist, and organize power. Some theorists argue that, because cultural studies does not provide a systematic critique of capitalism and the market, it has, in McChesney's words, "become a joke in some universities in that it has become an ongoing punch line to a bad joke. It signifies half-assed research, self congratulations, and farcical pretension."[56]

The materialist position is locked into a simple binarism that pits culture against a political economy perspective. As a result, it fails to make important connections and distinctions regarding how power is experienced within diverse social forms and how culture, in turn, deploys power to reproduce, mediate, resist, and transform such forms. Moreover, by universalizing class as the central category of politics, struggle, and agency, such critiques do more than ignore how class is lived through the modalities of sexual orientation, race, and gender.[57] They also fail to acknowledge the multiple dimensions of oppression and how such antagonisms expand the meaning and nature of pedagogical, political, and democratic struggles.[58] Equally important is the failure of such critiques to understand how agency, identities, and subject positions are constructed through the pedagogical force of culture and what this suggests for engaging and struggling over and within those institutions and public spheres that articulate between everyday life and material formations of power.

All of these critiques, which extend from the left to the right of the political spectrum, mirror what has become a standard, almost generic, type of attack on cultural studies. In some cases, they combine a residue of anti-intellectualism with what Foucault has called the "sterilizing effects of polemicism."[59] That is, lost in these critiques of cultural studies is any attempt to persuade or convince, or to produce a serious dialogue.[60] What largely remains are arguments buttressed by an air of privileged insularity that appear beyond interrogation, coupled with forms of rhetorical cleverness, built on the model of war and unconditional surrender, that are designed primarily to eliminate one's opponent. However, these arguments have little to say about what it means to offer alternative discourses designed to prevent the democratic principles of liberty, equality, and freedom from being put into practice in our schools and other crucial spheres of society.[61] As Chantal Mouffe argues, this is the Jacobin model of scholarship in which one attempts "to destroy the other in order to establish [one's] point of view and then not allow the other the possibility of coming back democratically. That's the struggle among enemies—the complete destruction of the other."[62] In short, the avoidance principle at work in political culture often finds its counterpart—both within and outside of the academy—in forms of social criticism that do little more than instrumentalize, polemicize, obscure, or insulate. Of course, this discourse and pedagogy typically threatens no one. Foucault has argued that such polemics rarely offer new ideas or provide any constructive possibility of an equal discussion.[63]

I want to modify Foucault's position on polemics by suggesting that much of what appears to be a polemical attack on cultural studies should be read as a broader attempt to promote a culture of political avoidance; that is, to undermine the very possibility of politics. I also want to argue that one way of responding to such attacks is to demonstrate how cultural studies practitioners might live up to the historical responsibility that they bear for bridging a relationship between theoretical rigor and social relevance, social criticism and practical politics, and individual scholarship and public pedagogy as part of a broader commitment to put new visions into place that are grounded on radical democratic traditions. This suggests taking seriously Pierre Bourdieu's admonition that "[t]here is no genuine democracy without genuine opposing critical powers. [It is the obligation of such intellectuals to be able] to make their voices heard directly in all the areas of public life in which they are competent."[64]

BEYOND THE CULTURE OF CYNICISM

In opposition to the positions I have outlined above, struggles over culture and pedagogy are not a "betrayal of enduring values" or a weak substitute for a "real" politics. They are central to forging relations between discursive and material relations of power, between theory and practice as they pertain to the relationship between education and social change. In addressing this position, I want to offer a rebuttal to the contemporary politics of cynicism by making a more substantial case for both the politics of culture and the culture of politics—as well as the primacy of the pedagogical as a constitutive element of a democratic political culture that links struggles over identities and meaning to broader struggles over material relations of power. In what follows, I address what it might mean to theorize cultural studies as a form of politics and pedagogy in which the performative and the strategic emerge out of a broader project informed by the shifting and often contradictory contexts in which popular politics and power intersect. At stake here is the necessity of reinvigorating the intellectual life necessary to sustain a vibrant political culture, one that puts, as Elizabeth Long suggests, "knowledge in the service of a more realized democracy."[65]

The regulatory nature of culture and its power to circulate goods, discipline discourses, and govern bodies suggests that the nervous system of daily life is no longer to be found in the simple workings and display of raw industrial power—the old means of production—but in the wired infrastructures that compute and transmit information at speeds that defy the imagination. As it becomes increasingly clear that the politics of culture is a substantive and not a secondary force in shaping everyday and global politics, the culture of politics provides the ideological markers for asserting the ethical and public referents to think at the limits of this new merging of technology and politics. No longer relegated simply to the Olympian heights of high culture, or summarily dismissed simply as a reflection of the economic base, culture has finally gained its rightful place, institutionally and productively, as a crucial object of debate, a powerful structure of meaning making that cannot be abstracted from power, and a site of intense struggle over how identities are to be shaped, democracy defined, and social justice revived as a serious element of cultural politics.

As the interface between global capital and new digital technologies refigure and reshape the face of culture, the importance of thinking through the possibilities and limits of the political assumes a new urgency. What constitutes both the subject and the object of "the political" mutates and expands as the relationship between knowledge and power becomes a determining force in producing new forms of wealth, increasing the gap between the rich and the poor, and radically influencing how people think and act. Culture as a form of political power becomes a formidable force in producing, circulating, and distributing information while transforming all sectors of the global economy. Moreover, it has ushered in a veritable revolution in the ways in which meaning is produced, identities are shaped, and historical change unfolds within and across national boundaries. For instance, on the global and national levels, the foreshortening of time and space, as Bauman points out, has radically altered how the power and wealth of multinational corporations shape the cultures, markets, and material infrastructures of all societies, albeit with unevenly distributed results.[66] As wealth accumulates in fewer hands, more service jobs command the economies of both strong and weak nations. Furthermore, Westernized cultural forms and products erode local differences, producing increasingly homogenized cultural landscapes. Finally, as state services bend to the forces of privatization, valuable social services—such as housing, schools, hospitals, and public broadcasting—are abandoned to the logic of the market. For many, the results are far-reaching: an increase in human poverty and suffering, massive population shifts and migrations, and a crisis of politics marked by the erosion and displacement of civic values and democratic social space.[67]

Increasingly within this new world order, the culture-producing industries have occupied a unique and powerful place in shaping how people around the globe live, make sense of their contexts, and shape the future, often under conditions not of their own making. Stuart Hall succinctly captures the substantive nature of this "cultural revolution" when he argues that the domain constituted by the activities, institutions and practices we call "cultural" has expanded out of all recognition. At the same time, culture has assumed a role of unparalleled significance in the structure and organization of late-modern society, in the processes of development of the global environment and in the disposition of its economic and material resources. In particular, the means of producing, circulating and exchanging culture have been dramatically expanded through the new media technologies and the information revolution. Directly, a much greater proportion of the world's human, material and technical resources than ever before go into these sectors. At the same time, indirectly, the cultural industries have become the mediating element in every other process.[68]

On the one hand, culture has become the primary means through which social practices are produced, circulated, and enacted; on the other, culture is given meaning and significance. Culture becomes political as it is mobilized through the media and other institutional forms; these institutional forms, as is well known, operate pedagogically and politically to secure certain forms of authority, offer sanctioned subject positions, and legitimate specific social relations. In addition, culture is political to the degree that it gives rise to practices that represent and deploy power, thereby shaping particular identities, mobilizing a range of passions, and legitimating precise forms of political culture. Culture, in this instance, becomes productive and is inextricably linked to the related issues of power and agency. As Grossberg points out, the politics of culture is foregrounded in "broader cultural terms [of how] questions of agency involve the possibilities of action as interventions into the processes by which reality is continually being transformed and power enacted. . . . Agency involves relations of participation and access, the possibilities of moving into particular sites of activity and power, and of belonging to them in such a way as to be able to enact their powers."[69] What Grossberg is suggesting here regarding the possibilities for critical agency has important implications for engaging culture in both political and pedagogical terms.

Culture has now become the pedagogical force par excellence, and its function as a primary educational condition for learning is crucial to making forms of literacy operational within diverse social and institutional spheres through which people define themselves and their relationship to the social world.[70] The relationship between culture and pedagogy in this instance cannot be abstracted from the central dynamics of politics and power. Broadly conceived, culture is always tangled up with power and becomes political in a double sense. First, questions of ownership, access, and governance are crucial to understanding how power is deployed in regulating the images, meanings, and ideas that frame the agendas that shape daily life. Second, culture can be used to deploy power through the institutional and ideological forces it uses to put certain forms of subjectivity in place. That is, the cultural sphere, in its diverse locations and productions, offers up identifications and subject positions through the forms of knowledge, values, ideologies, and social practices that it makes available within unequal relations of power to different sectors of the national and global communities. As a pedagogical force, culture makes a claim on certain histories, memories, and narratives. As James Young has noted in a different context, it tells "both the story of events and its unfolding as narrative"[71] in order to influence how individuals take up, modify, resist, and accommodate themselves to particular forms of citizenship, to present material relations of power, and to specific notions of the future.

Cultural studies theorists can respond to their critics by making clear that the current crisis of cultural politics and political culture facing the United States is intimately connected to the erasure of the social as a constitutive category for expanding democratic identities, social practices, and public spheres. In this instance, memory is not erased as much as it is reconstructed under circumstances in which public forums for serious debate are eroded. The crises of memory and the social are further amplified by the withdrawal of the state as a guardian of the public trust and by its growing lack of investment in those sectors of social life that promote the public good. Moreover, the crisis of the social is further aggravated, in part, by an unwillingness on the part of many radicals, liberals, and conservatives to address the importance of formal and informal education as a force for encouraging critical participation in civic life. There is scant attention given to how pedagogy functions as a crucial cultural, political, and moral practice for connecting politics, power, and social agency to the broader formative processes of democratic public life. Such concerns are important because they not only raise questions about the meaning and role of politics and its relationship to culture, but also because they suggest the necessity of rethinking the purpose and function of pedagogy in light of the calls by diverse ideological interests to corporatize all levels of schooling.

In short, the demise of politics as a progressive force for change within the cultural sphere is particularly evident in the recent attempts to corporatize higher education, which, while offering one of the few sites for linking learning with social change, is increasingly being redefined in market terms as corporate culture subsumes democratic culture and critical learning is replaced by an instrumentalist logic that celebrates the imperatives of the bottom line, downsizing, and outsourcing. Obsessed with grant writing, fund raising, and capital improvements, higher education increasingly devalues its role as a democratic public sphere committed to the broader values of an engaged and critical citizenry. Private gain now cancels out the public good, and knowledge that does not immediately translate into jobs or profits is considered ornamental. In this context, pedagogy is depoliticized and academic culture becomes the medium for sorting students and placing them in into an iniquitous social order that celebrates commercial power at the expense of broader civil and public values.[72]

Under attack by corporate interests, the political Right, and neoliberal doctrines, pedagogical discourses that define themselves in political and moral terms—particularly as they draw attention to the operations of power and its relationship to the production of knowledge and subjectivities—are either derided or ignored. Reduced to the status of training, pedagogy, in its conservative and neoliberal versions, appears completely at odds with those versions of critical teaching designed to provide students with the skills and information necessary to think critically about the knowledge they gain and what it might mean for them to challenge antidemocratic forms of power. All too often, critical pedagogy, both inside and outside of the academy, is either dismissed as irrelevant to the educational process or is appropriated simply as a technique for "encouraging" student participation. The conservative arguments are well known in this regard, particularly as they are used to reduce pedagogical practice either to the transmission of beauty and truth or to management schemes designed to teach civility—which generally means educating various social groups about how to behave within the parameters of their respective racial, class, and gender-specific positions. Missing from these discourses is any reference to pedagogy as an ideology and social practice engaged in the production and dissemination of knowledge, values, and identities in concrete institutional formations and relations of power.

Similarly, those liberal and progressive discourses that do link pedagogy to politics often do so largely within the logic of social reproduction and refuse to recognize that the effects of pedagogy are conditioned rather than determined and thus are open to a range of outcomes and possibilities. Lost here is any recognition of a pedagogy without guarantees, a pedagogy that, because of its contingent and contextual nature, holds the promise of producing a language and a set of social relations through which the just impulses and practices of a democratic society can be experienced and related to the power of self-definition and social responsibility.[73] In contrast, neoliberalism—with its celebration of the logic of the market—opts for pedagogies that confirm the autonomous individual rather than empower social groups, pedagogies that celebrate individual choice rather than those that support plurality and participation. In the eyes of too many neoliberals and conservatives, excellence is about individual achievement and has little to do with equity or providing the skills and knowledge that students might need to link learning with social justice and motivation with social change.

The decline of democratic political culture is also evident in the current attempts of conservatives and liberals to hollow out the state by withdrawing support from a number of sectors of social life that, in their deepest roots, are moral rather than commercial and that provide a number of services for addressing pressing social problems, particularly as they affect the poor, excluded, and oppressed. The shrinkage of democratic politics is also visible in the ongoing legislative attacks on immigrants and people of color, in the containment of political discourse by corporations that increasingly control the flow of information in the public sphere, and in the shrinking of noncommodified public spheres that provide opportunities for dialogue, critical debate, and public education.

TOWARD A PRACTICAL CULTURAL POLITICS

Central to any practical politics of cultural studies is the need to reinvent power as more than resistance and domination, as more than a marker for identity politics, and as more than a methodological referent for linking discourse to everyday life and its underlying institutional formations.[74] All of these notions of power are important, but none adequately signifies the need for cultural studies to foreground the struggle over relations of power as a central principle that views cultural politics as a civic and moral practice linking theory to concrete struggles and knowledge to strategies of social engagement and transformation. As such, the reinvigoration of political culture becomes a strategic and pedagogical intervention that has a purchase on people's daily struggles and defines itself partly through its (modest) attempts to keep alive a notion of engaged citizenship as a crucial performative principle for activating democratic change. Toward this end, cultural studies must be guided by the political insight that its own projects emerge out of social formations in which power is not simply put on display but signifies the struggle to expand the practice of social citizenship, to enlarge the commitment to social equality, and to broaden of the possibilities for social justice and human freedom. Cultural studies is important because it has a crucial role to play in analyzing and interpreting events in a larger political and historical context. Similarly, it provides an opportunity to open up spaces inside and outside of the university in which teachers and students can find ways to connect knowledge to social change, while restoring, as Paul Gilroy has suggested, an ethical dimension and critical vocabulary for shaping public life as a form of practical politics.[75]

Part of the challenge that cultural studies theorists face is not only the increasing cynicism and despair that have taken over national political life in the United States but also the growing academicization and institutionalization of cultural studies. Cultural studies advocates and practitioners must be attentive to the ways in which the processes of accommodation and incorporation of cultural studies contribute to the atrophy of the discourse of democracy and ethics among progressive cultural workers and educators. Cultural studies, like education itself, increasingly appears to have little influence in producing the knowledge and skills that are necessary for students and others to extend the critical impulse of what they are taught so as to keep alive a sense of politics, social responsibility, and urgency regarding the ongoing acts of oppression being waged nationally and internationally against youth; the poor; workers; people of color; and women who fall victim to abuse, poverty, violence, illiteracy, and disease. In part, this might be ascribed, as some conservative theorists suggests, to the bad faith of careerism or the obscure discourse of hermetic academics. However, I think there is a more serious problem confronting the field of cultural studies. In a time of unparalleled neoliberal and neoconservative domination over economic and public life, there are numerous forces that threaten and undercut the possibility for cultural studies theorists to speak to students and a broader public about important political, economic, and social issues. Clearly, such conditions—largely promoted by the increasing vocationalization of the university, the right-wing attack on critical work, and the shrinking of public spaces for intellectuals to take a critical stand—must be addressed and resisted through an organized struggle to defend the university as a democratic public sphere.

Given the importance that cultural studies places on the everyday and the significance of addressing the historical and relational contexts of particular struggles, it appears crucial that cultural studies practitioners redefine what it means to address cultural politics as a realm of concrete possibilities. Clearly, this effort involves more than producing new theoretical discourses, however important this task is. I am not suggesting that cultural studies theorists and practitioners refuse a rigorous critique and debate among themselves and with others, nor that we reject the need for multiple and diverse forms of counter-hegemonic struggles. I am simply suggesting that we give more thought to how these crucial and diverse approaches reclaim cultural studies as both a dislocating intervention and a politics of social transformation. At the same time, cultural studies theorists must be more clear about what we have in common that will enable us to organize and use our collective resources to further fight against the increasing depoliticization of daily life. Cultural theorists as diverse as Grossberg and Aronowitz address this issue, in part, by arguing for the development of a more systemic critique of capitalism and the market within cultural studies, one that is not reducible to questions of ownership and labor relations.

What is also at issue is the ability of cultural studies theorists to contextualize and politicize their intellectual practices by being able to speak to multiple audiences and actively engage, where possible, in broader public conversations, especially as these might affect policy decisions. What might it mean for cultural studies advocates inside and outside of the university to take seriously their role as oppositional public intellectuals who believe that what they say and do can make a difference in creating strategies of understanding, engagement, and transformation? Such a position would suggest that cultural studies practitioners attempt to understand and engage how capital works pedagogically to secure its political interests, how it uses cultural politics precisely as an educational force in shaping a new generation of accommodating intellectuals. It would also show how capital legitimates the dismantling of the gains of the welfare state and eliminates those public spaces that provide the conditions for social movements to organize and spread their messages. Additionally, cultural studies requires greater attentiveness to linking studies about the ownership of the media to how the media functions pedagogically as a form of cultural politics; how the decline of the military-industrial complex has given rise to a prison-industrial complex buttressed by a politics of race and identity politics that permeate the cultural institutions of everyday life[76]; and how cultural work in the academy might articulate with and play a role in expanding the possibilities of radical democratic struggles. This focus requires, in part, that cultural studies practitioners help strengthen and build social movements and organizations capable of addressing and mobilizing against the numerous forms of violence and oppression that increasingly are being waged against large segments of the global population.

Publicizing the myriad forms of political work that are attempting to reclaim public space and expand democratic relations should be made available not only among politically similar allies but in the larger public sphere. Such work provides a concrete opportunity to challenge the culture of political cynicism and indifference. There is little doubt in my mind that this work goes a long way in challenging the culture of political avoidance while demonstrating that, as Bourdieu succinctly puts it, democracies cannot exist "without genuine opposing powers."[77] It is particularly crucial that cultural studies theorists engage what Bourdieu calls "the function of education and culture in economies where information has become one of the most decisive productive forces."[78] Because it is precisely through such cultural and institutional formations that cultural studies practitioners—in conjunction with broader social movements—can produce analyses, questions, ideas, and pedagogical practices that the media both ignore and offer the conditions through which people might be mobilized. Evidence of such work can be found in the writings of Stanley Aronowitz, Carol Becker, Evan Watkins, Susan Bordo, Rey Chow, Arif Dirlik, Michael Dyson, Nancy Fraser, Paul Gilroy, Lawrence Grossberg, Stuart Hall, Joy James, Robin Kelley, Angela McRobbie, Toby Miller, Meaghan Morris, Chantal Mouffe, Edward Said, Michele Wallace, Cornel West, and Ellen Willis, and many others too numerous to name. It can also be found in the struggles of young people today—many of them in higher education—who are breaking down the boundaries between academic life and public politics. Such a struggle was visible in the actions of thousands of college students participating in the campus anti-sweatshop movement as well as in the activities of those brave students from the University of California at Berkeley, who in April 1999 demonstrated and went on hunger strikes to save the Ethnic Studies department.[79] It was also on display in 1999 in the demonstrations in Seattle at the World Trade Organization meeting, and in the protests in Quebec against the Free Trade Areas of the Americas.

Cultural studies theorists must revitalize a cultural politics that links political economy and the economy of representations, desires, and bodies to scholarly work, public conversations, and everyday life. Moreover, such work can be addressed as part of a broader attempt to reclaim the culture of politics, to rethink and expand the possibilities for social agency as part of an ongoing effort to reverse the evisceration of public goods, and to prevent the increasing commodification and privatization of public spaces, especially the public schools and higher education. Similarly, cultural studies must directly engage the question of how to imagine and build political alliances and social movements. This suggests producing, whenever possible, the theoretical tools, political strategies, and pedagogical practices necessary to wage multiple struggles in a variety of sites against those institutions and cultural formations that provide social guarantees only to the privileged and provide suffering, uncertainty, and insecurity to everybody else. Cultural studies theorists should continue their efforts to raise questions about and rethink not only diverse articulations of culture and power, but also how such relations work both to close down and open up democratic relations, spaces, and transformations, and what the latter mean theoretically and strategically for how we think of the meaning and purpose of politics. As admittedly difficult as such a task might appear, it offers the opportunity for cultural studies advocates to rethink their role as oppositional public intellectuals within a global context, and provides incentives for mastering new technologies of communication, exchange, and distribution.

In opposition to the alleged guardians of "authentic" radicalism who believe that cultural politics undermines "real" struggles, cultural studies theorists must demonstrate that cultural questions are central to understanding struggles over resources and power as well as organizing a politics that enables people to have a voice and an investment in shaping and transforming the conditions through which they live their everyday lives. Such a collective voice and investment requires that people experience themselves as critical social agents along multiple axis of identification, investment, and struggle. Only then can we provide the basis for opening up the space of resistance, for imagining different futures, for drawing boundaries and making connections, and for offering a language of critique and possibility that makes visible the urgency of politics and the promise of a vibrant and radical democracy.

2

YOUTH, DOMESTIC MILITARIZATION, AND THE POLITICS OF ZERO TOLERANCE

There is growing evidence in American life that citizenship is being further emptied of any critical social and political content. Of course, citizenship itself is a problematic and contested concept. Even in its best moments historically, when it was strongly aligned with concerns for human rights, equality, justice, and freedom as social provisions, citizenship never completely escaped from the exclusionary legacies of class, gender, and racial inequality.[1] Yet, in spite of such drawbacks, social citizenship contained, even within the watered-down version characteristic of liberal democracy, the *possibility* for both reflecting critically upon its own limitations and implementing the promises of radical democracy. Accentuating the importance of public issues, social citizenship provided a referent, however limited, for individuals to think of themselves as active citizens and not merely as taxpayers and homeowners. Moreover, as the site of many diverse struggles, citizenship often brought to the fore models of political agency in which people were encouraged to address public issues that would benefit the larger collective good. Substantive citizenship also recognized that, for democracy to work, individuals must feel a connection with each other that transcends the selfishness, competitiveness, and brutal self-interests unleashed by an ever-expanding market economy.

In this context, the state was forced at times to offer a modicum of social services and forums designed to meet basic social needs. State-supported social provisions paralleled modest efforts to affirm public goods such as schools and to provide public spaces in which diverse individuals had the opportunity to debate, deliberate, and acquire the know-how to be critical and effective citizens. This is not meant to suggest that, before neoliberalism's current onslaught on all things public, liberal, democratic culture encouraged widespread critical thinking and inclusive debate. On the contrary, liberal democracy offered little more than the swindle of formalistic, ritualized democracy, but, at least, it contained a referent for addressing the deep gap between the promise of a radical democracy and the existing reality. With the rise of neoliberalism, referents for imagining even a weak democracy, or for that matter understanding the tensions between capitalism and democracy, which animated political discourse for the first half of the twentieth century, appear to be overwhelmed by market discourses, identities, and practices. Democracy has now been reduced to a metaphor for the alleged "free" market. It is not that a genuine democratic public space once existed in some ideal form and has now been corrupted by the values of the market, but that these democratic public spheres, even in limited forms, seem no longer to be animating concepts for making visible the contradiction and tension between what Jacques Derrida refers to as the reality of existing democracy and "the promise of a democracy to come."[2]

With the advent of neoliberalism, corporate culture has made efforts to privatize all things social, stripping citizenship of its emancipatory possibilities. As a result, the state has been hollowed out as its police functions increasingly overpower and mediate its diminishing social functions. Consequently, government at all levels is largely abandoning its support for child protection, health care for the poor, and basic social services for the aged.[3] The government is now discounted as a means of addressing basic, economic, educational, environmental, and social problems. Market-based initiatives are touted as the only avenue for resolving issues such as unemployment, education, housing, and poverty. Public goods are now disparaged in the name of privatization, and those public forums in which association and debate thrive are being replaced by what Paul Gilroy calls an "info-tainment telesector" industry driven by dictates of the marketplace.[4]

Consumerism increasingly drives the meaning of citizenship as the principles of self-preservation and self-interest sabotage political agency, if not public life itself. As the public sector is remade in the image of the market, commercial values replace social values, and the spectacle of politics gives way to the politics of the spectacle. For example, in the summer of 2000, the prime time entertainment hit, *Survivor,* drew an audience of over 50 million viewers for its final show, twice the number of viewers who tuned in on the best night to watch either the Republican or Democratic national party conventions. New "reality"-based TV spectacles, with their aggressive celebration of individualism, competitiveness, and social Darwinism, do more than mimic the market and put into place notions of agency that assist the transformation of the political citizen into a consumer. They also signify the death of those public forums where private troubles can be translated into public concerns by gradually displacing those noncommodified spaces that offer resources and possibilities for resisting the dissolution of civic culture, democratic politics, and social citizenship itself. This is not to suggest that neoliberalism's celebration of commercial values and hyperindividualism simply turns everybody into a customer or merely expresses itself in the rise of a sensation-seeking public searching for relief from its alienation and boredom in mass-produced spectacles. But it does create, on the whole, a depoliticized citizenry by drastically limiting not only the access to but also the capacity for imagining those public spheres and democratic cultures that might offer the skills, knowledge, and values necessary to engage human suffering, define responsible public action as an enabling quality, and provide public forums, spaces, and events "where the occupants of different residential areas [can] meet face-to-face, engage in casual encounters, accost and challenge one another, talk, quarrel, argue or agree, lifting their private problems to the level of public issues and make public issues into matters of private concerns."[5]

In what follows, I examine the social and political costs that neoliberal and neoconservative policies are exacting on a generation of youth who, increasingly, are being framed as a generation of suspects. In addressing the interface between youth and public policy, especially the rapid growth of zero tolerance policies within public schools, I consider some broader questions about how the growing popular perception of youth as a threat to public life is connected to the collapse of public discourse, the increasing militarization of public space, and the rise of a state apparatus bent on substituting policing functions for social services. I then examine the implications these shifts in public discourse have for rethinking the relationship between pedagogy, political agency, and the imperatives of an energized and vibrant culture and radical democracy.

PRIVATIZING AND COMMODIFYING YOUTH

In the summer of 2000, the *New York Times Magazine* ran two major stories on youth within a three-week period between the latter part of July and the beginning of August. The stories are important, because they signify not only how youth fare in the politics of representation but also what identifications are made available for them to locate themselves in public discourse. The first article to appear, "The Backlash Against Children," by Lisa Belkin, is a feature story represented on the magazine's cover by a visually disturbing, albeit familiar, close-up of a young boy's face. The boy's mouth is wide open in a distorted manner, and he appears to be in the throes of a tantrum. The image goes right to that subliminal place that conjures up the ambiguities adults feel in the presence of screaming children, especially when they appear in public places, such as R-rated movies or upscale restaurants, where their presence is seen as an intrusion on adult life. The other full-page image that follows the opening text is even more grotesque, portraying a young boy dressed in a jacket and tie with chocolate cake smeared all over his face. His hands, covered with the gooey confection, reach out toward the viewer, capturing the child's mischievous attempt to grab some hapless adult by the lapels and add a bit of culinary dash to his or her wardrobe. The images match the text.

According to Belkin, a new movement is on the rise in American culture, one founded by individuals who don't have children, militantly describing themselves as "child free," and who view the presence of young people as an intrusion on adults' private space and rights. Belkin charts this growing phenomenon with the precision of an obsessed accountant. She commences with an ethnographic account of thirty-one-year-old Jason Gill, a software computer consultant from California, who is looking for a new place to live because the couple who have moved in next door have a new baby, and he can hear "every wail and whimper." Even more calamitous for the yuppie consultant, the fence he replaced to prevent another neighbor's children from peering through at him is now used by the kids as a soccer goal, "often while Gill is trying to read a book or have a quiet glass of wine."[6] But Belkin doesn't limit her analysis to such anecdotal evidence; she also points to the emergence of national movements, such as No Kidding! an organization that sets up social events only for those who remain childless. She reports that No Kidding! had only two chapters in 1995 but had forty-seven by the end of the century. In addition, she comments on the countless number of online "child free" sites with names such as "Brats!" and a growing number of hotels that do not allow children under eighteen unless they are paying guests.[7]

Of course, many parents and nonparents alike desire, at least for a short time, a reprieve from the often chaotic space of children, but Belkin takes such ambivalences to new heights. To be sure, her real ambition has very little to do with providing a space for adult catharsis. Rather, it is to give public voice to a political and financial agenda captured by Elinor Burkett's *The Baby Boon: How Family-Friendly America Cheats the Childless*—an agenda designed to expose and rewrite governmental policies that relegate "the childless to second-class citizens."[8] Included in Burkett's laundry list of targets are: the federal tax code and its dependent deductions, dependent care credits, and child tax credits among "dozens of bills designed to lighten the tax burden of parents" and, "most absurd of all," an executive order prohibiting discrimination against parents in all areas of federal employment. Her position is straightforward enough: to end "fancy" benefits (for example, on-site child-care and health insurance for dependents) that privilege parents *at the expense of the childless* and to bar discrimination on the basis of family status. "Why not make it illegal to presuppose that a nonparent is free to work the night shift or presuppose that nonparents are more able to work on Christmas than parents?" Burkett demands.[9] Indeed, in an era marked by zero tolerance policies, why should the government provide any safety nets for the nation's children at all? Why should whole communities be taxed to pay for the education and health of other people's children? In the face of such irresponsible claims, it seems all too obvious to suggest that society nurture children because they will be our future leaders and workers and parents—because they are the nation's future workers, who will, in turn, support a generation of elderly (parents and "child-free" alike) and pay taxes for Medicare, social security, and those other "fancy perks" provided to senior citizens. Ironically, Burkett's arguments are as childish and thoughtless as the worst offenders in the group she attempts to mobilize public sentiment against.

Belkin modifies her somewhat sympathetic encounter with the child-free worldview by interviewing Sylvia Ann Hewlett, a Harvard-educated economist, who is a nationally known spokesperson for protecting the rights of parents and the founder of the National Parenting Association. Hewlett argues that parents have become yet another victimized group and are being portrayed by the media as the enemy. She translates her concerns into a call for parents to organize in order to wield more economic and political power. As important as Hewlett's comments are, they occupy a minor place in an article where the voices of those individuals and groups who view children and young people as a burden—a personal irritant, rather than a social good—are overwhelmingly featured.

The notion that children should be understood as a crucial social resource who present for any healthy society important ethical and political considerations about the quality of public life, the allocation of social provisions, and the role of the state as a guardian of public interests appears to be lost in Belkin's article. Indeed, Belkin ignores the social gravity and implications of these issues and focuses on youth exclusively as a private consideration rather than as part of a broader public discourse about democracy and social justice. In addition, she participates in an assault on youth, buttressed by two decades of a Reagan-Bush New Right neoconservativism and a more recent period of neoliberalism and hypercapitalism during which the language of democracy, solidarity, and the social are subordinated to the ethos of self-interest and self-preservation in the relentless pursuit of private satisfactions and pleasures. In this sense, the backlash against children that Belkin attempts to chronicle are symptomatic of an attack on public life itself, on the very legitimacy of those noncommercial values that are critical to defending a just and substantive democratic society.

I have spent some time on Belkin's article because it highlights, though uncritically, how market pressures work in society to undermine social structures and public spaces, which are capable of raising questions about how particular groups, such as youth, are being abstracted from the language of justice, reciprocity, and compassion; and how the institutional and collective structures that once protected such groups are also being privatized, displaced, and defined almost entirely through the logic of the market. As the language of the public is emptied of its social considerations, private troubles and personal pathologies occupy center stage, and matters of resistance and struggle are displaced by the spectacle of a competitive war-against-all ethos that may offer fodder for prime time television but proves disastrous for children, the poor, the aged, and those groups consigned to the margins of society.

The second article to appear in the *Times Magazine* is titled "Among the Mooks," and is by R. J. Smith.[10] According to the author, there is an emerging group of poor white males, called "mooks," whose cultural style is fashioned out of an interest in fusing the transgressive languages, sensibilities, and styles that cut across and connect the worlds of rap and heavy metal music, ultraviolent sports, such as professional wrestling, and the misogyny rampant in the subculture of pornography. For Smith, the kids who inhabit this cultural landscape are losers from broken families, working-class fatalities whose anger and unexamined bitterness translates into bad manners, antisocial music, and uncensored rage.

Smith appears uninterested in contextualizing the larger forces and conditions that give rise to this matrix of cultural phenomena—deindustrialization, economic restructuring, domestic militarization, poverty, joblessness.[11] The youth portrayed in Smith's account live in a historical, political, and economic vacuum. The ideological, cultural, and institutional forces that work on and through these teens simply disappear. Moreover, the teens represented by Smith have little recourse to adults who try to understand and help them navigate a complex and rapidly changing cultural landscape in which they must attempt to locate and define themselves. Along with the absence of adult protection and guidance, there is a lack of serious critique and social vision in dealing with the limits of youth culture. No questions are raised about the relationship between the popular forums that teens inhabit and the ongoing commercialization and commodification of youth culture, or what the relationship might be between the subject positions young people invest in and those mainstream, commercially saturated dreamscapes of affect and representation that increasingly eat up social space and displace noncommodified public spheres. There is no understanding in Smith's analysis of how market-driven politics and established forms of power increasingly eliminate noncommodified social domains through which young people might learn an oppositional language for challenging those adult ideologies and institutional forces that both demonize them and limit their sense of dignity and capacity for political agency.

Of course, vulgarity, pathology, and violence are not limited to the spaces inhabited by the hypermasculine worlds of gangsta rap, porn, extreme sports, and professional wrestling. But Smith ignores all of this because he is much too interested in depicting today's teens, and popular culture in general, as the embodiment of moral decay and bad cultural values, an assessment that mimics the retrograde neoconservative ideological attacks on youth that have taken place since the 1980s.[12] Smith suggests that poor white kids are nothing more than semi-Nazis with a lot of pent-up rage. There are no victims among youth in his analysis, as social disorder is reduced to individualized pathology, and any appeal to injustice is viewed as mere whining. He is too intent on reinforcing images of demonization and ignorance that resonate comfortably with right-wing moral panics about youth culture. He succeeds, in part, by focusing on the icons of this movement in terms that move between caricature and scapegoating. For instance, The Insane Clown Posse is singled out for appearing on cable-access porn shows; the group Limp Bizkit is accused of using their music to precipitate a gang rape at a late '90s Woodstock melee; and the performer Kid Rock is defined in racially coded terms as a "vanilla version of a blackploitation pimp," whose concerts inspire fans to commit vandalism and prompt teenage girls to "pull off their tops as the boys whoop."[13] It gets worse.

At one level, "mooks" are portrayed as poor, working-class, white kids who have seized upon the most crude aspects of popular culture in order to provide an outlet for their rage. But for Smith, the distinctive form this culture takes, with its appropriation of the transgressive symbolism of rap music, porn, and wrestling, does not entirely explain its descent into pathology and bad taste. Rather, he charges that black youth culture is largely responsible for the self-destructive, angst-ridden journey that poor white male youth are

making through the cultural landmines of hypermasculinity, unbridled violence, "ghetto" discourse, erotic fantasy, and drugs. He points an accusing
finger at the black "underclass" and the recent explosion of hip-hop, which
allegedly offers poor white kids both an imaginary alternative to their trailer
park boredom and a vast array of transgressive resources that they proceed to
fashion through their own lived experiences and interests. Relying on all too
common racist assumptions about black urban life, Smith argues that black
youth culture offers white youth

> a wide-screen movie of ghetto life, relishing the details, relating the intricacy of
> topics like drug dealing, brawling, pimping and black-on-black crime. Rap
> makes these things seem sexy, and makes life on the street seem as thrilling as a
> Playstation game. Pimping and gangbanging equal rebellion, especially for
> white kids who aren't going to get pulled over for driving, while black, let alone,
> die in a hail of bullets (as Tupac and B.I.G. both did).[14]

Trading substantive analysis for right-wing clichés, he is indifferent to both
the complexity of rap as well as the "wide array of complex cultural forms"
that characterize black urban culture.[15] He alleges that, if poor white youth
are in trouble, it is not because of regressive government policies, the growing
militarization of urban space, the attack on basic social provisions for the
poor and young, the disinvestment in such public goods as public schools, or
the growing criminalization of social policy.[16] On the contrary, the problem
of white youth is rooted in the seductive lure of a black youth, marked by
criminality, violent hypermasculinity, welfare fraud, drug abuse, and un-
checked misogyny. Smith unapologetically relies on this analysis of black
youth culture to portray poor white youth as dangerous and hip-hop culture
as the source of that danger. Within this discourse, the representation of
youth moves from caricature to that poisonous terrain Toni Morrison calls
race talk: "The explicit insertion into everyday life of racial signs and symbols
that have no meaning other than pressing African Americans to the lowest
level of the racial hierarchy . . . the rhetorical [and representational] experience renders blacks as noncitizens, already discredited outlaws."[17]

Whatever his intentions, Smith's analysis contributes to the growing assumption in the popular imagination that young people are, at best, a social
nuisance and, at worse, a danger to social order. Clearly, his analysis of working-class and black youth bespeaks an ideological and political irresponsibility
rooted in an overidentification with the recklessness of the young. As such,
these representations contribute not only to the ongoing demonization of
youth, especially youth of color, but further legitimate the emergence of a

state that is radically moving from a politics of social investment to a politics of containment and militarization.[18]

These articles reflect and perpetuate in dramatically different ways not only the ongoing demonization of young people but also the growing refusal within the larger society to understand the problems of youth (and especially youth of color) as symptomatic of the crisis of democratic politics itself. Under the rule of neoconservative and neoliberal ideology, American society increasingly finds it difficult to invest in those ethical and political values that support public spaces in an earnest, if not fully realized, manner in which norms are made explicit and debated, institutions are maintained that promote democratic notions of the collective good, and support is given to forms of civic education that provide the foundation for nurturing and sustaining individual and collective agency. As the state is stripped of its power to mediate between capital and human needs, thus losing its capacity to offer social guarantees to youth and other marginalized groups, public life becomes barren, vacuous, and stripped of substance.[19] Of course, the crisis over public schools has been escalating for at least a decade, as forms of civic education that promote individual agency, social responsibility, and noncommercial values have been abandoned for job-training and accountability schemes.

As the state is divested of its capacity to regulate social services and limit the power of capital, those public spheres that traditionally served to empower individuals and groups to strike a balance between "the individual's liberty from interference and the citizen's right to interfere"[20] are dismantled. At the same time, it becomes more difficult for citizens to put limits on the power of neoliberalism to shape daily life—particularly as corporate economic power is feverishly consolidated on a transnational level. Nor can they prevent the assault on the state as it is being forced to abandon its already limited social role as the guardian of public interests. The result is a state increasingly reduced to its policing functions, and a public sector reduced to a replica of the market. As neoliberalism increases its grip over all aspects of cultural and economic life, the relative autonomy once afforded to the worlds of cinema, publishing, and media production begins to erode. Public schools are increasingly defined as a source of profit rather than a public good. And, as Pierre Bourdieu points out, neoliberalism emerges throughout the social order as a "new kind of moral Darwinism which, with the cult of the 'winner,' establishes the struggle of all against all and cynicism as the norm of all practices."[21] Through talk shows, film, music, and cable television, for example, the media promote a growing political apathy and cynicism by providing a steady stream of daily representations and spectacles in which abuse becomes the primary vehicle for registering human interaction. At the same time, dominant media such as the *New York Times* condemn the current cultural landscape—represented in their account through reality-based television, professional wrestling, gross-out blockbuster films, and the beat-driven boasts and retorts of hip-hop—as aggressively evoking a vision of humanity marked by a "pure Darwinism," in which "the messages of popular culture are becoming more brutally competitive."[22]

Unfortunately, for mainstream media commentators in general, the emergence of such representations and values is about the lack of civility and has little to do with considerations of youth bashing, racism, corporate power, and politics. In this sense, witness to degradation now becomes the governing feature of community and social life. Most importantly, what critics take up as a "youth problem" is really a problem about the corruption of politics, the shriveling up of public spaces and resources for young people, the depoliticization of large segments of the population, and the emergence of a corporate and media culture that is defined through an unadulterated "authoritarian form of kinship that is masculinist, intolerant and militaristic."[23] At issue here is how we understand the ways youth produce and engage popular culture at a time in history when deprivation is read as depravity. How do we comprehend the choices young people are making under circumstances in which they have become the object of policies that signal a shift from investing in their future to assuming they have no future? Certainly not a future in which they can depend on adult society for either compassion or support.

ZERO TOLERANCE AND THE POLITICS/COLOR OF PUNISHMENT

In what follows, I will address the social costs and implications of removing youth from the inventory of ethical and political concerns through policies that replace social compassion with containment while increasingly abandoning young people, especially youth of color, to the dictates of a repressive penal state in which government, at all levels, addresses social problems through the police, courts, and prison system. More specifically, by examining, in particular, the emergence of zero tolerance policies in the public schools, I will address how the policing function of the state bears down on young people. While my focus is on the relationship between education and zero tolerance policies, the context for my analysis points to a broader set of repressive conditions that not only target young people across a wider variety of public spheres but also undermine the guarantee of rights and institutional structures that a realized democracy represents. I begin with a definition of domestic militarization taken from critical educator and activist Ruth Wilson Gilmore, in order to provide the larger political, social, and cultural context for understanding the growing attacks on youth through the emergence of zero tolerance policies.[24] According to Gilmore, expressions of domestic militarization can be found in the deadly violence waged against people of color such as Amadou Diallo, an unarmed black man shot forty-one times by New York City policemen, and Tyisha Miller, shot a dozen times by California police while she was sitting in her car. Such violence can also be found in the countless acts of humiliation, harassment, and punishment handed out to the poor and people of color everyday in the United States by the forces of the repressive state.[25] In this regard, the brutal attacks by police on Rodney King and Abner Louima stand out. Evidence of domestic militarization can also be seen in the rise of the prison-industrial complex, the passing of retrograde legislation that targets immigrants, the appearance of gated communities, the widespread use of racial profiling by the police, and the ongoing attacks on the welfare state. Of course, state repression is not new, but contemporary political culture is unique in that:

> [t]he new State is shedding social welfare in favor of domestic militarization. Programs that provide for people's welfare, protect the environment, or regulate corporate behavior have been delegitimized and jettisoned. There is a new consensus among the powers that be that focuses the domestic State on defense against enemies, both foreign and U.S.-born. What's new is the scale of militarism being directed at people inside the U.S., and the scope for what comes into the crosshairs of the prison industrial complex rather than some helping agency.[26]

Critics such as Gilmore and Christian Parenti rightfully argue that as the War on Poverty ran out of steam with the social and economic crises that emerged in the 1970s, it has been replaced with an emphasis on domestic warfare, and that the policies of social investment, at all levels of government, have given way to an emphasis on repression, surveillance, and control.[27] Starting with Reagan's war on drugs[28] and the privatization of the prison industry in the 1980s, and escalating to the war on immigrants in the early 1990s, and the rise of the prison-industrial complex by the close of the decade, the criminalization of social policy has now become a part of everyday culture and provides a common reference point that extends from governing prisons and regulating urban culture to running schools. Hence, it comes as no surprise when New York City Mayor Rudi Giuliani, "over the opposition of most parents and the schools chancellor, formally assigns the oversight of discipline in the public schools to the police department."[29] Once it was clear that Giuliani would receive high marks in the press for lowering the crime rate due to zero tolerance policies adopted by the city's police force, it seemed reasonable to him to use the same policies in the public schools. What the popular press ignored, until the killing of Diallo at the hands of New York City's police, was that zero tolerance policing strategies exacted a heavy price on the poor and people of color and resulted in more people being stopped and searched as well as larger settlements being paid out to those victimized by the police to quell charges of abuse.[30] What was also ignored by the public and popular press nationally was that, as the call for more police, prisons, and "get tough" laws reached fever pitch among politicians and legislators, the investment in domestic militarization began to exceed more than $100 billion a year.[31]

Domestic militarization as a central feature of American life is evident in the ongoing criminalization of social policy and is probably most visible in the emergence of zero tolerance laws that have swept the nation since the 1980s and gained full legislative strength with the passage of the Violent Crime Control and Law Enforcement Act of 1994. Following the mandatory sentencing legislation and "get tough" policies associated with the "war on drugs" declared by the Reagan and Bush administrations, this bill calls for a "three strikes and you're out" policy, which puts repeat offenders, including nonviolent offenders, in jail for life, regardless of the seriousness of the crime. The general idea behind the bill is "to increase the prison sentence for a second offense and require life in custody without parole for a third offense."[32] It also provides sixty new offenses punishable by death, while at the same time limiting the civil rights and appeal process for those inmates sentenced to die. In addition, the largest single allocation in the bill is for prison construction.[33] Since the crime bill was passed in 1994, the prison industry has become big business, with many states spending "more on prison construction than on university construction."[34] Yet, even as the crime rate plummets dramatically, more people, especially people of color, are being arrested, harassed, punished, and put in jail.[35] At the millennium, the United States was the biggest jailer in the world. Between 1985 and 2000, the prison population grew from 744,206 to 2.0 million (approaching the combined populations of Idaho, Wyoming, and Montana), and prison budgets jumped from $7 billion in 1980 to $40 billion in 2000.[36] Manning Marable points out that the United States is "spending $35,000 a year to maintain a single prisoner, one prisoner, in a minimum security cell. It costs nearly $80,000 a year to confine a prisoner in a maximum security cell. We are building over a hundred new prison cells a day"[37]

The explosion in the prison population has also resulted in a big increase in the move toward privatizing prisons.[38] As Robin D. G. Kelley points out, by the close of 1997, at least 102 for-profit private prisons existed in the United States, "each receiving some form of federal subsidy with limited federal protection of prisoners' rights or prison conditions."[39] Prisoners, especially the widely disproportionate pool of African American inmates, which has tripled since 1980, provide big business not only "with a new source of consumers but a reservoir of cheap labor."[40] The Report of the National Criminal Justice Commission noted in 1996 that, as "spending on crime fighting has risen three times faster than defense spending," the biggest beneficiary appears to be "private businesses [that] reap enormous profits from the fear of crime and the expansion of the criminal justice system."[41] Moreover, as many critics of the private prison system have correctly pointed out, it "is particularly disturbing that corporations should be making a profit from policies that are not in the public interest—such as excessive prison sentences and the incarceration of nonviolent offenders."[42] At a time when over 550,000 black males are interned in jails in the United States, "the concept of private companies profiting from prisoners evokes the convict leasing system of the Old South."[43]

As the "prison-industrial complex" becomes a dominant force in the economy of states such as California, competing with land developers, service industries, and unions, it does more than rake in huge profits for corporations; it also contributes to what Mike Davis calls a "permanent prison class."[44] One measure of the power of the prison-industrial complex as a high-powered growth industry can be gauged by the increasing power of prison guard unions to shape legislative policy in many states. For instance, the California Correctional Peace Officers Union has grown in one decade from 4,000 to over 29,000 members. During the 1998 political campaign, the prison guard union was the state's number one "donor to legislative races, setting a record by spending $1.9 million."[45] Yet, the prison-industrial complex does more than fuel profits and shape legislative policies for those eager to invest in high-growth industries; it also legitimates a culture of punishment and incarceration, aimed most decisively at "African American males who make up less than 7 percent of the U.S. population, yet they comprise almost half of the prison and jail population."[46] The racist significance of this figure can be measured by a wide range of statistics, but the shameful fact is that the number of African Americans in prison far exceeds the number of African American males who commit crime. For instance, law professor, David Cole, in his unsparing analysis of the racial disparities that fuel the government's drug war, points out that while "76 percent of illicit drug users were white, 14 percent black, and 8 percent Hispanic—figures which roughly match each group's share of the general population," African Americans constitute "35 percent of all drug arrests, 55 percent of all drug convictions, and 74 percent of all sentences for drug offences."[47] A Justice Department report points out and that, on any give day in this country, "more than a third of the young African American men aged 18–34 in some of our major cities are either in prison or under some form of criminal justice supervision."[48] The same department reported in April 2000 that "black youth are forty-eight times more likely than whites to be sentenced to juvenile prison for drug offenses."[49]

Domestic militarization in this instance functions not only to contain "surplus populations" and provide new sources of revenue, it also actively promotes and legitimates retrograde social policies. For example, an increasing number of states, including California and New York, are spending more on prison construction than on higher education and are hiring more prison guards than teachers. A recent study by the Correctional Association of New York and the Washington, D.C.-based Justice Policy Institute claims that millions of dollars are being diverted from the public university budget in New York and invested in prison construction. The reports point out that "between fiscal year 1988 and fiscal year 1998, New York's public universities saw their operating budgets plummet by 29 percent while funding for prisons rose 76 percent. In actual dollars, there has been nearly a one-to-one trade-off, with the Department of Corrections in New York State receiving a $761 million increase during that ten-year period, while state funding for New York City and state university systems, declined by $615 million."[50] In California, the average prison guard now earns $10,000 more than the average public school teacher and, increasingly, more than many professors working in the state university system.[51] This is more than a travesty of justice; it is a stern lesson for many students of color and working-class white youth— viewed as a generation of suspects by the dominant society—that it is easier for them to go to jail than it is to get a decent education. For the wider public, the lesson to be learned is that there is a greater payoff when society invests more in prisons than in those public institutions that educate young people to become public servants in crucial spheres such as education. In this instance, the culture of punishment and its policies of containment and brutalization become more valued by the dominant social order than any consideration of what it means for a society to expand and strengthen the mechanisms and freedoms central to sustaining a substantive democracy.[52]

Rather than viewing "three strike" policies and mandatory sentencing as part of a racist-inspired expression of domestic militarization and a source of massive injustice, corporate America and conservative politicians embrace it as both a new venue for profit and a legitimate expression of the market-driven policies of neoliberalism. Within this discourse, social costs and racial injustice, when compared to corporate profit, are rendered irrelevant.[53] How else to explain a *New York Times* article by Guy Trebay, which focuses on "jailhouse chic" as the latest in youth fashion.[54] Surrendering any attempt at socially responsible analysis, Trebay reports that the reason so many teens are turning prison garb into a fashion statement is that an unprecedented number of youth are incarcerated in the United States. When they get released, "they take part of that culture with them." The retail market for prison-style work clothes is so strong, Trebay points out, that prisons, such as those managed by the Oregon Corrections Department, are gaining a foothold in the fashion market by producing their own prison blues clothing lines (which can be found on their web site: www.prisonblues.com). The market trumps social justice in this account as incarcerated youth are praised for being fashion trendsetters, prisons are celebrated for their market savvy, and cheap prison labor is affirmed for its contribution to cutting-edge street culture.

Zero tolerance policies, as one manifestation of domestic militarization, have been especially cruel in the treatment of juvenile offenders.[55] Rather than attempting to work with youth and making an investment in their psychological, economic, and social well-being, a growing number of cities are passing sweep laws—curfews and bans against loitering and cruising—designed not only to keep youth off the streets but to make it easier to criminalize their behavior. For example, within the last decade, "45 states . . . have passed or amended legislation making it easier to prosecute juveniles as adults" and in some states "prosecutors can bump a juvenile case into adult court at their own discretion."[56] A particularly harsh example of these Draconian measures can be seen in the recent passing of Proposition 21 in California. The law makes it easier for prosecutors to try teens fourteen and older, who are charged with felonies, in adult court. These youth would automatically be put in adult prisons and given lengthy mandated sentences if convicted. As Louise Cooper points out, "It also . . . increases the discretionary powers for routine police surveillance, random searches, and arrest of young people."[57] The overall consequence of the law is to largely eliminate intervention programs, increase the number of youth in prisons, especially minority youth, and keep them there for longer periods of time. Moreover, the law is at odds with a number of studies that indicate that putting youth in jail with adults both increases recidivism and poses a grave danger to young offenders who, as a recent Columbia University study suggested, are "five times as likely to be raped, twice as likely to be beaten, and eight times as likely to commit suicide than adults in the adult prison system."[58]

Paradoxically, the moral panic against crime that increasingly feeds the calls for punishment rather than rehabilitation programs for young people exists in conjunction with the disturbing facts that the United States is currently one of only seven countries (Congo, Iran, Nigeria, Pakistan, Saudi Arabia, and Yemen) in the world that permit the death penalty for juveniles and that, in the last decade, it has executed more juvenile offenders than all other countries combined that allow such executions.[59] Given the assumption among neoliberal hardliners that market values are more important than values that involve trust, compassion, and solidarity, it is not surprising that Wall Street, which emphasizes profits, views the growth in the prison industry and the growing incarceration of young people as good news. For instance, even though "crime has dropped precipitously," stock analyst Bob Hirschfield notes that "males 15–17 years old are three times as likely to be arrested than the population at large, and the proportion of 15–17 year olds is expanding at twice the overall population." Rather than being alarmed, if not morally repulsed, by these figures, Hirschfield concludes that it is a "great time to purchase shares" in the new prison growth industry.[60]

While the social costs for such policies are cause for grave alarm, they are all the more disturbing since the burden they inflict upon society appears to be far greater for young people of color than for any other group. The National Criminal Justice Commission Report claims that while "get tough" policies are likely to be more severe when dealing with children, they are particularly repressive when applied to youth of color, especially as a result of the war on drugs and the more recent eruption of school shootings. Numerous studies have documented that, unlike middle-class white youth, minority youth are "more likely to be arrested, referred to court, and placed outside the home when awaiting disposition of their cases. . . . [Moreover] all things being equal, minority youths face criminal charges more often than white youths for the same offenses. Also, African American youths are charged more often than whites with a felony when the offense could be considered a misdemeanor. . . . Minority youth are also more likely to be waived to adult court, where they will face longer sentences and fewer opportunities for rehabilitative programs."[61] Fed by widespread stereotypical images of black youth as superpredators and black culture as the culture of criminality, minority youth face not only a criminal justice system that harasses and humiliates them but also a larger society that increasingly undercuts their chances for a living wage, quality jobs, essential social services, and decent schools.[62] Within such a context, the possibilities for treating young people of color with respect, dignity, and support vanishes and, with it, the hope of overcoming a racial abyss that makes a mockery out of justice and a travesty of democracy.

The growing influence of zero tolerance laws in the United States can be seen in the application of such laws in areas as different as airport security, the criminal justice system, immigration policy, and drug testing programs for athletes. The widespread use of these policies has received a substantial amount of critical analysis within the last decade. Unfortunately, these analyses rarely make connections between what is going on in the criminal justice system and the public schools.[63] While schools share some proximity to prisons in that they are both about disciplining the body, though for allegedly different purposes, little has been written about how zero tolerance policies in schools resonate powerfully with prison practices that signify a shift away from treating the body as a social investment (i.e., rehabilitation) to viewing it as a threat to security, demanding control, surveillance, and punishment.[64] Also, little has been written on how such practices have exceeded the boundaries of the prison-industrial complex, providing models and perpetuating a shift in the very nature of educational leadership and pedagogy. Of course, there are exceptions, such as Lewis Lapham's lament that schools do more than teach students to take their place within a highly iniquitous class-based society. In many larger cities, according to Lapham, high schools now "possess many of the same attributes as minimum-security prisons—metal detectors in the corridors, zero tolerance for rowdy behavior, the principal as a warden and the faculty familiar with the syllabus of concealed weapons." According to Lapham, schools resemble prisons in that they both warehouse students to prevent flooding the labor market while simultaneously "instilling the attitudes of passivity and apprehension, which in turn induce the fear of authority and the habits of obedience."[65] Another notable and insightful exception is Manning Marable who argues that "[o]ne of the central battlegrounds for democracy in the U.S. in the twenty-first century will be the effort to halt the dismantling of public education and public institutions in general for the expansion of [the] prison-industrial complex."[66]

As schooling is defined largely as a disciplinary institution that prepares students for the workplace, the discourse of leadership has been superseded by a pragmatics of classroom management. Similarly, pedagogy often ignores the specificity of contexts that informs students' lives and substitutes issues of accountability (measured through test scores) for a qualitative interest in producing critical citizens. Moreover, such pedagogies of transmission are particularly intolerant of notions of difference, critical questioning, or resistance. Pedagogy in this model of control relies heavily on those forms of standardization and values that are consistent with the norms and relations that drive the market economy. Teachers teach for the tests as students' behaviors are consistently monitored, and knowledge is increasingly quantified.

Made over in the image of corporate culture, schools are no longer valued as a public good but as a private interest; hence, the appeal of such schools is less in their capacity to educate students according to the demands of critical citizenship than in enabling students to master the requirements of a market-driven economy. Under these circumstances, many students increasingly find themselves in schools that lack any language for relating the self to public life, social responsibility, or the imperatives of democratic life. In this instance, democratic education, with its emphasis on respect for others, critical inquiry, civic courage, and concern for the collective good, is suppressed and replaced by an excessive emphasis on the language of privatization, individualism, self-interest, and brutal competitiveness. Lost in this discourse of schooling is any notion of democratic community or models of leadership capable of raising questions about what public schools should accomplish in a democracy and why, under certain circumstances, they fail.

The growth and popularity of zero tolerance policies within public schools have to be understood as part of a broader educational reform movement in which the market is now seen as the master design for all pedagogical encounters. At the same time, the corporatizing of public schooling cannot be disassociated from the assault on those public spheres within the larger society that provide the conditions for greater democratic participation in shaping society. As the state is downsized and support services dry up, containment policies become the principal means to discipline youth and restrict dissent. Within this context, zero tolerance legislation within the schools simply extends to young people elements of harsh control and administration implemented in other public spheres where inequalities breed the conditions for dissent and resistance. Schools increasingly resemble other enervated public spheres as they cut back on trained psychologists, school nurses, and programs such as music, art, athletics, and valuable after-school activities. Jesse Jackson argues that, under such circumstances, schools do more than fail to provide students with a well-rounded education; they often "bring in the police, [and] the school gets turned into a feeder system for the penal system."[67] In addition, the growing movement to define schools as private interests rather than as public assets not only reinforces the trend to administer them in ways that resemble how prisons are governed but also points to a disturbing tendency on the part of adult society to direct a great deal of anger and resentment toward youth. In what follows, I analyze zero tolerance policies in schools and address the implications these policies have for a society in signaling a dramatic shift away from civic education—the task and responsibility of which is to prepare students for shaping and actively participating in democratic public life—to models of training and regulation whose purpose opens the door to ultraconservative forms of political culture and authoritarian modes of social regulation.

SCHOOLING AND THE PEDAGOGY OF ZERO TOLERANCE

Across the nation, school districts are lining up to embrace zero tolerance policies. Emulating state and federal laws passed in the 1990s, such as the federal Gun-Free Act of 1994, that were based on mandatory sentencing and "three strikes and you're out" policies, many educators first invoked zero tolerance rules against those kids who brought guns to schools. But over time, the policy was broadened and now includes a range of behavioral infractions that includes everything from possessing drugs to harboring a weapon to *threatening* other students—all broadly conceived. For instance, "in many districts, school administrators won't tolerate even one instance of weapon possession, drug use, or harassment."[68] One of the most publicized cases illustrating the harshness of zero tolerance policies took place recently in Decatur, Illinois, when seven African American students, who participated in a fight that lasted seventeen seconds at a football game and was marked by the absence of any weapons, were expelled for two years. Two of the young men were seniors who were about to graduate. At their hearing, none of the boys was allowed counsel or the right to face his accusers; nor were their parents allowed any degree of involvement in the case. When Jesse Jackson brought national attention to the incident, the Decatur school board reduced the expulsions to one year.

Fueled by moral panics about the war on drugs and images of urban youth of color as ultraviolent, drug pushing gangbangers, a national mood of fear provided legitimacy for zero tolerance policies in the schools as both an ideology of disdain and a policy of punishment. Unfortunately, any sense of perspective seems lost, as school systems across the country clamor for metal detectors, armed guards, see-through knapsacks, and, in some cases, armed teachers. Some school systems are investing in new software in order to "profile" students who might exhibit criminal behavior.[69] Overzealous laws relieve educators of exercising deliberation and critical judgment as more and more young people are either suspended or expelled from school—often for ludicrous reasons. For example, two Virginia fifth-graders who allegedly put soap in their teacher's drinking water were charged with a felony.[70] Officials at Rangeview High School in Colorado, after trying unsuccessfully to expel a student because they found three baseball bats on the floor of his car, ended up suspending him.[71] In a similar litany of absurdities, *USA Today* reported on two Illinois 7-year-olds who were "suspended for having nail clippers with knifelike attachments."[72] Jesse Jackson offers the example of a student who was suspended on a weapons charge because school officials discovered a little rubber hammer as part of his Halloween costume. He provides another equally absurd example of a student accused with a drug charge because he gave another youth two lemon cough drops.[73]

As *Boston Globe* columnist Ellen Goodman points out, zero tolerance does more than offer a simple solution to a complex problem; it has become a code word for a "quick and dirty way of kicking kids out" of school.[74] This becomes clear as states such as Colorado, in their eagerness to appropriate and enforce zero tolerance policies in their districts, do less to create a safe environment for students than they do to simply kick more kids out of the public school system. For example, the *Denver Rocky Mountain News* reported in June of 1999 that "partly as a result of such rigor in enforcing Colorado's zero tolerance law, the number of kids kicked out of public schools has skyrocketed since 1993—from 437 before the law to nearly 2,000 in the 1996–1997 school year."[75] In Chicago, the widespread adoption of zero tolerance policies in 1994 resulted in a 51 percent increase in student suspensions for the next four years, and a 3000 percent increase in expulsions, jumping "from 21 in 1994–95 to 668 in 1997–98."[76] Within such a climate of disdain and intolerance, expelling students does more than pose a threat to innocent kids; it also suggests that local school boards are refusing to do the hard work of exercising judgment, trying to understand what the conditions are that undermine school safety, and providing reasonable services for all students and viable alternatives for troubled ones. But there is more at stake than merely bad judgment behind the use of zero tolerance laws in American public schools. As the criminalization of young people finds its way into the classroom, it becomes easier to punish students rather than listen to them.[77] Even though such policies clog up the courts and put additional pressure on an already overburdened juvenile justice system, educators appear to have few qualms about implementing them. And the results are far from inconsequential for the students themselves.

Zero tolerance laws make it easier to expel students than for school administrators to work with parents, community justice programs, religious organizations, and social service agencies. Moreover, automatic expulsion policies do little to either produce a safer school or society, since, as Clare Kittredge points out, "we already know that lack of attachment to the school is one of the prime predictors of delinquency."[78] Most insidiously, zero tolerance laws, while a threat to all youth and any viable notion of democratic public education, reinforce in the public imagination the image of students of color as a source of public fear and a threat to public school safety. Zero tolerance policies and laws appear to be well-tailored to mobilizing racialized codes and race-based moral panics that portray black and brown urban youth as a new and frighteningly violent threat to the safety of "decent" Americans. Not only do most of the high-profile zero tolerance cases, such as the Decatur school incident, often involve African American students, but such policies also reinforce the racial inequities that plague school systems throughout the United States. For example, Tamar Lewin, a writer for the *New York Times,* has reported on a number of studies illustrating "that black students in public schools across the country are far more likely than whites to be suspended or expelled, and far less likely to be in gifted or advanced placement classes."[79] Even in a city such as San Francisco, considered a bastion of liberalism, African American students pay a far greater price for zero tolerance policies. Libero Della Piana reports that "[a]ccording to data collected by Justice Matters, a San Francisco agency advocating equity in education, African Americans make up 52 percent of all suspended students in the district—far in excess of the 16 percent of the general population."[80] Marilyn Elias reports in a recent issue of *USA Today* that, "[i]n 1998, the first year national expulsion figures were gathered, 31 percent of kids expelled were black, but blacks made up only 17 percent of the students in public schools."[81] The tragedy underlying such disparities in treating black and white students appears to be completely lost on those educators defending zero tolerance policies. For instance, Gerald Tirozzi, executive director of the National Association of Secondary School Principals, argues, without irony, that such policies "make everything very clear" and "promote fair, equitable treatment in school discipline."[82]

As compassion and understanding give way to rigidity and intolerance, schools increasingly become more militarized and function as a conduit to the penal system. The measure of such a transformation is not limited to the increasing fortress quality of American schools—which are marked by the foreboding presence of hired armed guards in the corridors, patrolled cafeterias, locked doors, video surveillance cameras, electronic badges, police dogs, and routine drug searches. It is also present in the racist culture of fear that exhibits a deep distrust in, if not hostility and revulsion, toward young people, especially youth of color.[83] For instance, in Louisiana, board member Ray St. Pierre proposed that any student in junior high or high school who is caught fighting "would be handcuffed inside the school by sheriff's deputies and taken to a juvenile facility where he would be charged with disturbing the peace."[84] In case parents miss the point, they would have to pay a cash bond for their child's release. As a result of St. Pierre's notion of getting tough on misbehavior, the school provides an opportunity for students not only to leave with a diploma but also with a police record. The image of kids being handcuffed, pulled out of a school, and dragged away in the back of a police van or patrol car has become so commonplace in the United States that the psychological, political, and social consequences of such brutal practices barely lift an eyebrow and are more routinely met with public approval. In some instances, the zero tolerance policies are not just affecting students in schools. In an attempt to root out pedophiles in the public school system in the state of Maine, the F.B.I. is demanding that teachers submit to finger-printing and criminal history checks. Many teachers have refused to comply and may lose their certification and jobs.[85] Within the current climate of domestic militarization, it may be just a matter of time before the surveillance cameras, profiling technologies, and other tools of the penal state become a routine part of the climate of teaching in America's schools. Stanley Aronow-itz is right in arguing that as the "state's police functions tend to overpower and mediate its diminishing social functions," one consequence is that "[p]olice now routinely patrol urban public high schools and universities as if they were identical with the mean streets of the central cities or, more to the point, tantamount to day-prisons."[86]

To be sure, zero tolerance policies turn schools into an adjunct of the criminal justice system, but they also further rationalize misplaced legislative priorities. And that has profound social costs. Instead of investing in early childhood programs, repairing deteriorating school buildings, or hiring more qualified teachers, schools now spend millions of dollars to upgrade security. Moral panic and fear reproduce a fortress mentality in which the logic of domestic militarization produces an authoritarian irrationalism, as in Fremont High School in Oakland, California, where school administrators decided to build a security fence costing $500,000, "while the heating remained out of commission."[87] Another instance of such irrationality can be found, as I mentioned earlier, in the fact that many states now spend "more on prisons than on university construction."[88] Young people are quickly realizing that schools have more in common with military boot camps and prisons than they do with other institutions in American society. In addition, as schools abandon their role as democratic public spheres and are literally "fenced off" from the communities that surround them, they lose their ability to become anything other than spaces of containment and control. As schools become militarized, they lose their ability to provide students with the skills to cope with human differences, uncertainty, and the various symbolic and institutional forces that undermine political agency and democratic public life itself. In this context, discipline and training replace education for all but the privileged, as schools increasingly take on an uncanny resemblance to oversized police precincts, tragically disconnected both from the students who inhabit them and the communities that give meaning to their historical experiences and daily lives. Coupled with the corporate emphasis on privatizing schools, the motif of punishment and withdrawal—civic and interpersonal—governs this new form of school regulation and administration.

Zero tolerance policies in schools have been criticized roundly by a number of social and educational critics. William Ayers and Bernardine Dohrn rightly argue that zero tolerance policies do not teach but punish, and that students need not less but more tolerance.[89] Goodman echoes this view by claiming that schools which implement such laws are not paying attention to children's lives, because, as she nicely puts it, it is "harder to talk with troubled teens than to profile them."[90] Daniel Perlstein has argued that zero tolerance programs not only fail to ensure school safety; they also deflect educators from addressing crucial considerations that structure racial, class, and social divisions in schools.[91] Of course, as all of these critics point out, zero tolerance laws do more than turn schools into policing institutions that ignore the problems of tracking, racism, and the exclusionary and hierarchical nature of school culture; they also further reproduce such problems. These critiques are important, and I have addressed them elsewhere.[92] But these criticisms do not go far enough. It is also necessary for educators to place school-based zero tolerance policies within a broader context that makes it possible to see them as part of the ideology of neoconservatism, neoliberalism, and domestic militarization that is ravaging conditions for critical political agency, destroying the deployment of even minimal ethical principles, and undermining the conditions necessary within schools and other public spheres to produce the symbolic and material resources necessary to engage in the struggle for critical citizenship, freedom, democracy, and justice.

SCHOOLING AND THE CRISIS OF PUBLIC LIFE

Zero tolerance policies in both the schools and other domestic spheres cannot be understood outside of a range of broader considerations that constitute a crisis in the very nature of civic agency, ethics, politics, and democracy. As the state disengages from its role as a mediator between capital and human

needs, and as market forces bear heavily on redefining the meaning of education as a private enterprise, it becomes all the more difficult to imagine public
schools as important contested sites in the struggle for civic education and
authentic democracy. If neoconservatism provides the ideological ammuni-
tion to turn a generation of youth into suspects, neoliberalism works both
to produce a deregulated consumer culture and to limit the possibilities for
noncommodified social domains where young and old alike can experience
dissent and difference as part of a multicultural democracy, locate metaphors
of hope, respond to those who carry on the legacies of moral witnessing, and
imagine relationships outside of the dictates of the market and the authoritarian rule of penal control. Educators and others need to rethink what it would
mean both to interrogate and break away from the dangerous and destructive
representations and practices of zero tolerance policies as they work to reinforce modes of authoritarian control and social amnesia in a vast and related
number of powerful institutional spheres. This suggests a struggle for public
space and a public dialogue about how to imagine reappropriating a notion
of politics that is linked to the regime of authentic democracy while simultaneously articulating a new discourse, a set of theoretical tools, and social possibilities for re-visioning civic education as the basis for political agency and
social transformation in ways that go beyond its historical limitations. Zero
tolerance is not *the* problem as much as it is symptomatic of a much broader
set of issues centered around the gulf between the *regime of the political*—
everything that concerns modes of power—and the *realm of politics*—the
multiple ways in which human beings question established power, transform
institutions, and reject "all authority that would fail to render an account and
provide reasons . . . for the validity of its pronouncements."[93] Neoliberalism
offers no intellectual tools or political vocabulary for addressing this gap, because it has no stake in defining political culture outside of the interest of the
market. Nor does it have any interest in supporting forms of civic education
designed to question, challenge, and transform power as part of a political
and ethical response to the demise of democratic public life. Neoliberalism
has thrown into question the very feasibility of politics and democracy, and,
in part, has been successful in doing so because it defines citizenship through
the narrow logic of consumerism, and politics as having no foundation in
agency as a form of self-determination and critical strategic action. Hence,
there is no room in this discourse for providing the knowledge, skills, and
values necessary for young people and adults to define anew civic education
as an "essential step towards agency, self-representation, and an effective democracy."[94]

Against the social and economic policies of neoliberalism, educators, youth, parents, and various cultural workers need to rethink the meaning of democracy, ethics, and political agency in an increasingly globalized world in which power is being separated from traditional political forms such as the nation-state. But the war against youth must be understood as an attempt to contain, warehouse, control, and even eliminate all those groups and social formations that the market finds expendable (in other words, unable to further the interests of the bottom line or the logic of cost effectiveness). For progressives, this suggests a decisive and important struggle over a notion of politics that refuses the ongoing attempts on the part of huge corporations, conservatives, and other "masters of the private economy"[95] to make public life irrelevant, if not dangerous, by replacing an ethic of reciprocity and mutual responsibility with a market-driven ethic of individualism in which "competitiveness is the only human ethic, one that promotes a war against all."[96]

There is more at stake here than recognizing the limits and social costs of a neoliberal philosophy that reduces all relationships to the exchange of goods and money; there is also the responsibility on the part of critical intellectuals and other activists to rethink the nature of the public. Challenging neoliberalism also demands new forms of social citizenship and civic education that have a purchase on people's everyday lives and struggles, expressed through a wide range of institutions. Central here is the need to rethink a notion of cultural politics that makes politics more pedagogical and the pedagogical a permanent feature of politics in a wide variety of sites, including schools. In this instance, politics is inextricably connected to pedagogies that effectively mobilize the beliefs, desires, and forms of persuasion that organize and give meaning to particular strategies of social engagement and policy transformation.[97] Education as a form of persuasion, power, and intervention is constitutive of those ongoing struggles that shape the social. Challenging neoliberal hegemony as a form of domination is crucial to reclaiming an alternative notion of the political and rearticulating the relationship between political agency and substantive democracy.

Intellectuals and other cultural workers bear an enormous responsibility in opposing neoliberalism not only by reviving the rhetoric of democratic political culture but also by expanding its social consequences in ways that democratic societies have yet to realize. Part of this challenge suggests creating new locations of struggle, vocabularies, and subject positions that allow people in a wide variety of public spheres to become more than they are now, to question what it is they have become within existing institutional and social formations, and "to give some thought to their experiences so that they can transform their relations of subordination and oppression."[98] Cornelius Castoriadis insightfully argues that, for any regime of democracy to be vital, it needs to create citizens who are critical thinkers, capable of calling existing institutions into question, asserting individual rights, and assuming public responsibility. In this instance, critical pedagogy as an alternative form of civic education and literacy provides oppositional knowledges, skills, and theoretical tools for highlighting the workings of power and reclaiming the possibility of intervening in its operations and effects. But Castoriadis also suggests that civic education must be linked to the task of creating new locations of struggle that offer critical opportunities for experiencing political agency within social domains that provide the concrete conditions in which people can exercise their capacities and skills "as part of the very process of governing."[99] In this context, culture becomes a space for hope, and pedagogy becomes a valuable tool in reclaiming the promise of democracy and reabsorbing the political back into a viable notion of politics.

Zero tolerance has become a metaphor for hollowing out the state and expanding the forces of domestic militarization, for reducing democracy to the rule of capital, and for replacing an ethic of mutual aid with an appeal to excessive individualism and social indifference.[100] Within this logic, the notion of the political increasingly equates power with domination and politics with consumerism and passivity. Under this insufferable climate of manufactured indifference, increased repression, and unabated exploitation, young people become the new casualties in an ongoing war against justice, freedom, social citizenship, and democracy. As despairing as these conditions appear at the present moment, they increasingly have become the basis for a surge of political resistance on the part of many youth, intellectuals, labor unions, educators, and other activists and social movements.[101] Under such circumstances, it is time to remind ourselves that collective problems deserve collective solutions and that what is at risk is not only a generation of young people now considered to be a generation of suspects but the very promise of democracy itself. The issue is no longer whether it is possible to invest in the idea of the political and politics but what the consequences are of not doing so.

3

PRIVATE SATISFACTIONS AND PUBLIC DISORDERS

Fight Club, Patriarchy, and the Politics
of Masculine Violence

*The "public" has been emptied of its own separate contents; it
has been left with no agenda of its own—it is now but an
agglomeration of private troubles, worries and problems.*

—Zygmunt Bauman, *In Search of Politics*

In the epigraph above, Zygmunt Bauman gives voice to a troubling feature
of American society. Amidst the growing privatization of everyday life, the
greatest danger to human freedom and democracy no longer appears to come
from the power of the overzealous state eager to stamp out individual freedom and critical inquiry in the interest of loyalty and patriotism. Authoritarianism no longer breeds a contempt for the virtues of individualism, all things
private, and the dynamics of self-interest. On the contrary, totalitarianism
now resides in a thorough dislike for all things social, public, and collective.
Under the growing influence of the politics, ideology, and culture of neoliberalism, "the individual has been set free to construe her or his own fears, to
baptize them with privately chosen names and to come with them on her or
his own."[1] Agency has now been privatized and personal liberty atomized and
removed from broader considerations about the ethical and political responsibilities of citizens to defend those vital institutions that expand the rights and
services central to a meaningful democracy. Stripped of its political possibili-

ties and social underpinnings, freedom finds few opportunities for translating private worries into public concerns or individual discontent into collective struggle. Utopia is now conjured up as the privatized space of the shopping mall, intellectual effort is reduced to an instrument of the entrepreneurial self, and social visions are dismissed as hopelessly out of date. Public space is portrayed exclusively as an investment opportunity, and the public good increasingly becomes a metaphor for public disorder. As the public sphere is consistently removed from social consideration and notions of the public good are replaced by an utterly privatized model of citizenship and the good life, the collapse of public imagination and a vibrant political culture is *celebrated* by neoliberal warriors rather than perceived as a dangerous state of affairs that Americans should be both contemptuous of and ashamed to support.[2]

Within the discourse of neoliberalism—which construes profit making as the essence of democracy and provides a rationale for a handful of private interests to control as much of social life as possible in order to maximize their personal profit—issues regarding persistent poverty, inadequate health care, racial apartheid in the inner cities, and the growing inequalities between the rich and the poor have been either removed from the inventory of public discourse and social policy or factored into talk-show spectacles. The latter highlight private woes bearing little relationship either to public life or to potential remedies that demand collective action. Within this growing marketization and privatization of everyday life, democratic principles are either scorned as holdovers of an outmoded sixties radicalism or equated entirely with the imperatives of capitalism.[3]

As Robert W. McChesney points out, Milton Friedman, the reigning guru of neoliberalism, perfectly captures and legitimates this sentiment in *Capitalism and Freedom,* arguing unabashedly that "because profit making is the essence of democracy, any government that pursues antimarket policies is being antidemocratic, no matter how much informed popular support they might enjoy. Therefore, it is best to restrict governments to the job of protecting private property and enforcing contracts, and to limit political debate to minor issues."[4] Within neoliberal discourse, freedom is negatively reduced to freedom from government restraint, and the rights of citizenship translate into the freedom to consume as one chooses. The state, in this instance, becomes a threat to freedom, particularly the freedom of the market, as its role as guardian of the public interests is actively disassembled, though its powers are still invoked by dominant interests to ensure their own privileges, such as free trade agreements, government subsidies for business, and strike "negotiations." But, as Pierre Bourdieu points out, while neoliberals highlight the threat the state poses to the freedom of the market, the real threat comes from a state, which, under the control of neoliberal ideology, is increasingly transformed into a repressive apparatus aimed at those individuals and groups who get caught in its ever-expanding policing interventions. Bourdieu is worth quoting at length on this issue:

> In the United States, the state is splitting into two, with on the one hand a state which provides social guarantees, but only for the privileged, who are sufficiently well-off to provide themselves with insurance, with guarantees, and a repressive, policing state, for the populace. In California, one of the richest states of the United States . . . and also one of the most conservative, and which has perhaps the most prestigious university in the world, since 1994 the prison budget has been greater than the budget of all the universities together. The blacks in the Chicago ghetto only know the state through the police officer, the judge, the prison warder and the parole officer. We see there a kind of realization of the dream of the dominant class, a state which, as Loic Wacquant has shown, is increasingly reduced to its policing functions.[5]

As the laws of the market take precedence over the laws of the state as guardians of the public good, the state increasingly offers little help in mediating the interface between the advance of capital and its rapacious commercial interests, on the one hand, and those noncommodified interests and nonmarket spheres that create the political, economic, and social conditions vital for critical citizenship and democratic public life on the other. As the state is forced to abandon its social functions, its dominant concerns support the exercise of police power concerned primarily with surveillance, containment, repression, and control as it increasingly criminalizes social antagonisms.[6] Humanitarian concerns are largely impotent against the driving interests of capital and its voracious search for new markets and greater profits. As the welfare state is dismantled, social agencies aimed at providing crucial social provisions and a safety net for society's most vulnerable are replaced by institutions designed to train rather than educate, punish rather than nurture, and contain rather than serve the public interest. Rationalized self-interest goes hand-in-hand with growing incidents of racial injustice, class injustice, economic downsizing, and the growth of a criminal justice system that incarcerates youth of color at a rate that exceeds the formerly racially apartheid regime of South Africa. As the public good gets eaten up by private gain, public services, such as health care, social housing, schools, hospitals, and transportation, are transformed from social investments into profit options for the powerful and wealthy. As the novelist Walter Mosely reminds us, "Capitalism has no humanity. All that exists in the capitalist bible is the margin of profit, the market share, and those quirks of individualism that must be dealt with in much the same manner as a mechanic must deal with a faulty element: removal and replacement."[7]

The ascendancy of neoliberalism and corporate culture into every aspect of American life not only consolidates economic power in the hands of the few, it also aggressively attempts to break the power of unions, decouple income from productivity, subordinate the needs of society to the market, and deem public services and amenities an unconscionable luxury. But it does more. It thrives on a culture of cynicism, boredom, and despair. Americans are now convinced that they have little to hope for—and gain from—the government, nonprofit public spheres, democratic associations, or other nongovernmental social forces. With few exceptions, the project of democratic transformation has fallen into disrepute in the popular imagination as the logic of the market undermines the most basic social solidarities.[8] The consequences include not only a weakened state, but a growing sense of insecurity, cynicism, and political retreat on the part of the general public. The call for self-reliance betrays an enfeebled state that neither provides adequate safety nets for its populace, especially those who are young, poor, or marginalized, nor gives any indication that it either needs or is willing to care for its citizens. In this scenario, private interests trump social needs, and profit becomes more important than social justice. As Bauman's argues

> The more legless is the state, the more its spokesmen spell out the need for, the duty of, its self-reliance, of counting on one's own resources alone, of making one's own balances of gains and losses– in short, of standing of one's own individual legs. [The result is] the brutal tearing up of social solidarities . . . [as] individuals have been left to lick their wounds and exorcize their fears in solitude and seclusion.[9]

The "brutal tearing up of social solidarities" is mediated through the force of corporate structural power and commercial values that both dominates and weakens those competing public spheres and values systems that are critical to a just society and to democracy itself. The liberal democratic vocabulary of rights, entitlements, social provisions, community, social responsibility, living wage, job security, equality, and justice seems oddly out of place in a country in which the promise of democracy has been replaced by the lure of the lottery and the Dow-Jones Industrial Average, reinforced by a pervasive fear and insecurity about the present, and a deep-seated skepticism in the public mind that the future holds nothing beyond a watered-down version of the present. Within the prevailing discourse of neoliberalism that has taken hold of the public imagination, there is no vocabulary for political or social transformation, no collective vision, no social agency to challenge the ruthless downsizing of jobs, resist the ongoing liquidation of job security, or spaces from which to struggle against the elimination of benefits for people now hired on a strictly part-time basis. Moreover, against the reality of low-wage jobs, the erosion of social provisions for a growing number of people, and the expanding war against young people of color, the market-driven consumer juggernaut continues to mobilize desires in the interest of producing market identities and market relationships that ultimately appear as, as Theodor Adorno once put it, nothing less than "a prohibition on thinking itself."[10]

It is against this ongoing assault on the public, and the growing preponderance of a free market economy and corporate culture that turns everything it touches into an object of consumption that David Fincher's film, *Fight Club*, must be critically engaged. Ostensibly, *Fight Club* appears to offer a critique of late-capitalist society and the misfortunes it generates out of its obsessive concern with profits, consumption, and the commercial values that underline its market-driven ethos. But *Fight Club* is less interested in attacking the broader material relations of power and strategies of domination and exploitation associated with neoliberal capitalism than it is in rebelling against a consumerist culture that dissolves the bonds of male sociality and puts into place an enervating notion of male identity and agency. Contrary to the onslaught of reviews accompanying the film's premier that celebrated it as a daring social critique[11]—the filmic equivalent of magazines like the *Baffler* or *Adbusters,* or even of political protests in Seattle, Washington, D.C., Windsor (Ontario), Geneva, and Prague against international agents of capitalism like the World Bank, the World Trade Organization, and the International Monetary Fund. But the truth is that *Fight Club* has nothing to say about the structural violence of unemployment, job insecurity, cuts in public spending, and the destruction of institutions capable of defending social provisions and the public good. On the contrary, *Fight Club* defines the violence of capitalism almost exclusively in terms of an attack on traditional, not to say regressive, notions of masculinity, and, in doing so, reinscribes white heterosexuality within a dominant logic of stylized brutality and male bonding that appears predicated on the need to denigrate and wage war against all that is feminine. In this instance, the crisis of capitalism is reduced to the crisis of masculinity, and the nature of the crisis lies less in the economic, political, and social conditions of capitalism itself than in the rise of a culture of consumption in which men are allegedly domesticated, rendered passive, soft, and emasculated.

Fight Club, along with films such as *Pulp Fiction, Rogue Trader, American*

Psycho, Boiler Room, and *Croupier,* inaugurates a new subgenre of cult-film that combines a fascination with the spectacle of violence, enlivened through tired narratives about the crisis of masculinity, along with a superficial gesture toward social critique designed to offer the tease of a serious independent/art film.[12] While appearing to address important social issues, these films end up reproducing the very problems they attempt to address. Rather than turning a critical light on crucial social problems, such films often trivialize them within a stylized aesthetics that revels in irony, cynicism, and excessive violence. Violence in these films is reduced to acts of senseless brutality, pathology, and an indifference to human suffering. Reproducing such hackneyed representations of violence ("senseless," "random"), they conclude where engaged political commentary should begin. Yet, I am less interested in moralizing about the politics of Fincher's film than I am in reading it as a form of public pedagogy that offers an opportunity to engage and understand its politics of representation as part of broader commentary on the intersection of consumerism, masculinity, violence, politics, and gender relations. Moreover, *Fight Club* signifies the role that Hollywood films play as teaching machines. A far cry from simple entertainment, such films function as public pedagogies by articulating knowledge to effects, purposely attempting to influence how and what knowledge and identities can be produced within a limited range of social relations. At the same time, I recognize that such texts "are radically indeterminate with respect to their meaning, [and] any reading of a text must be determined by factors not prescribed by the text itself."[13]

As public pedagogies, texts such as *Fight Club* attempt to bridge the gap between private and the public discourses, while simultaneously putting into play particular ideologies and values that resonate with broader public conversations regarding how a society views itself and the world of power, events, and politics. Reading a film such as *Fight Club,* in more specific terms, suggests engaging how it offers up particular notions of agency in which white working-class and middle-class men are allowed to see themselves as oppressed and lacking because their masculinity has been compromised by and subordinated to those social and economic spheres and needs that constitute the realm of the feminine.

In taking up these issues, I first analyze the narrative structure of the film, addressing its simultaneous critique of consumerism and its celebration of masculinity. In doing so, I address critically the representational politics that structure *Fight Club*—especially its deeply conventional views of violence, gender relations, and masculinity—and how such representations work in conjunction with a deeply entrenched culture of cynicism. Finally, I argue that such cynicism—far from being innocent—works in tandem with broader public discourses to undermine the faith of individuals and groups in the potential of a politics designed to struggle against the rising tide of antidemocratic forces and movements that threaten the already weakened fabric of democracy. Obviously, I am not arguing that Hollywood films such as *Fight Club* are a cause of these problems, but they are symptomatic of a wider symbolic and institutional culture of cynicism and senseless violence that exerts a powerful pedagogical influence on shaping the public imagination. In treating *Fight Club* as a pedagogical and political text, my aim is to reveal its socially constructed premises, demystify its contradictions, and challenge its reactionary views. In part, I want to ask questions about *Fight Club* that have not been generally asked in the popular press and engage in a discussion of how dominant public pedagogies prevent us from asking such questions in the first place. In addition, I take up the role that *Fight Club* and other cultural texts might provide as public pedagogies that can be read against themselves; that is, how such texts can be deconstructed and reworked theoretically within a wider set of associations and meanings that can be both challenged and rearticulated in order to strengthen rather than weaken a public politics, while furthering the promise of democratic transformation.

FIGHT CLUB AND THE CRISIS OF EVERYDAY LIFE

> In [commercial cinema's] seeming transformation of violence into entertainment, choreography, and macho ebullience, one could say that the reality of violence has been infantilized. One cannot take it too seriously, and yet, one is compelled to ask if any idiom of violence can be regarded as 'innocent', distanced from reality through its apparent autonomy of signs.[14]

White, heterosexual men in America have not fared well in the nineties. Not only have they been attacked by feminists, gays, lesbians, and various subaltern groups for a variety of ideological and material offenses, they have also had to endure a rewriting of the very meaning of masculinity.[15] As Homi Bhabha has stated, the manifest destiny of masculinity, with its hardboiled, tough image of manliness has been disturbed, and its blocked reflexivity has been harshly unsettled.[16] Moreover, the shift from a manufacturing-based to an information-based economy, from the production of goods to the production of knowledge, has offered men, at least according to Susan Faludi, fewer and fewer meaningful occupations.[17] Consequently, the male body has been transformed from an agent of production to a receptacle for consumption. A rampant culture of consumption, coupled with a loss of manufacturing and middle-management jobs presents white males with an identity crisis of unparalleled proportions. The male hero of the modern day workforce is no longer defined in the image of the tightly hewn worker using his body and labor to create the necessities for everyday life. The new workforce hero is now modeled on the image of the young, computer-whiz yuppie who defines his life and goals around hot, start-up, e-commerce companies, day trading, and other "get rich before I'm twenty-one" schemes as well as by his conspicuous consumption of expensive products. Moreover, as white, heterosexual, working-class and middle-class men face a life of increasing uncertainty and insecurity, they no longer have easy access to those communities in which they can inhabit a form of masculinity that defines itself in opposition to femininity. In simple terms, the new millennium offers white, heterosexual men nothing less than a life in which ennui and domestication define their everyday existence.

David Fincher's 1999 film, *Fight Club,* based on a novel by Chuck Palahniuk, attempts to critically engage the boredom, shallowness, and emptiness of a stifling consumer culture, redefine what it might mean for men to resist compromising their masculinity for the sofa or cappuccino-maker that "speaks to them," and explore the possibilities for creating a sense of community in which men can reclaim their virility and power. The film opens with an inside shot of the brain of Jack (Edward Norton), tracking a surge of adrenaline that quickly finds an opening in Jack's mouth and then exits up the barrel of a gun. Jack then proceeds to lead the audience into the nature of his predicament and, in doing so, narrates his journey out of corporate America and his evolving relationship with Tyler Durden (Brad Pitt), who functions as Jack's alter ego and significant other. The first section of the film functions primarily as a critique of contemporary consumerism and how corporate culture positions men in jobs and lifestyles that are both an affront to their manhood and male sociality, leaving them to seek refuge in communities of self help/support—portrayed as the dreaded cult of victimhood—which only accentuates the contemporary crisis of masculinity. As the film unfolds, Jack is portrayed as a neoliberal Everyman—an emasculated, repressed corporate drone whose life is simply an extension of a reified and commodified culture.

As a recall coordinator, Jack travels around the country, investigating accidents for a major auto company in order to decide whether it's cheaper for the corporation to assign recalls or payment to a likely number of lawsuits. Alienated from his job, utterly lacking any sense of drive or future, Jack's principal relief comes from an insatiable urge for flipping through and shopping from consumer catalogues. A slave to the "IKEA nesting instinct," Jack self-consciously offers up rhetorical questions like "What kind of dining set defines me as a person?" But Jack's IKEA-designed apartment appears to offer him no respite from the emptiness in his life, and his consumerist urges only seem to reinforce his lack of enthusiasm for packaging himself as a corporate puppet and presenting himself as a Tom Peters up-and-coming "brand name."[18] Tormented by the emptiness of his daily life and suffering from near terminal insomnia, Jack visits his doctor, claiming he is in real pain. His thirty-something doctor refuses to give him drugs and tells him that, if he really wants to see pain, he should visit a local testicular cancer survivor group. Jack not only attends the self-help meeting but discovers that the group offers him a sense of comfort and community, and, in an ironic twist, he becomes a support group junkie. At his first meeting of the Remaining Men Together survival group, Jack meets Bob (Meat Loaf Aday), a former weightlifter who has enormous breasts (described as "bitch tits") as a result of hormonal treatments. The group allows Jack to participate in a form of male bonding that offers him an opportunity to release his pent-up emotions and provides a cure for his insomnia. Bob becomes a not-too-subtle symbol in the film, personifying how masculinity is both degraded (he has breasts like a woman) and used in a culture that relies upon the "feminine" qualities of support and empathy rather than "masculine" attributes of strength and virility to bring men together. When Bob hugs Jack and tells him, "You can cry now," *Fight Club* does more than mock New Age therapy for men; it also satirizes and condemns the "weepy" process of feminization that such therapies sanction and put into place.

Jack eventually meets Marla (Helena Bonham Carter), a disheveled, chain-smoking, slinky, street urchin, who is slumming in the same group therapy sessions as Jack. Jack views Marla as a tourist—addicted only to the spectacle of the meetings. Marla reminds him of his own phoniness, and she so upsets him that his insomnia returns and his asylum is shattered. Jack can't find emotional release with another phony in the same session. In the voice-over, Jack claims that "if I had a tumor, I would name it Marla." Once again, repressed white masculinity is thrown into a crisis by the eruption of an ultra-conservative version of post-'60s femininity that signifies both the antithesis of domestic security, comfort, and sexual passivity—offering only neurosis and blame in their place. We now begin to understand Jack's comment in the beginning of the film, after the gun is pulled from his mouth, that "Marla is at the root of it."

On the heels of this loss, Jack meets Tyler Durden (Brad Pitt) on an airplane. Tyler is the antithesis of Jack—a bruising, cocky, brash, soap salesman, part-time waiter, and movie projectionist, with a whiff of anarchism shoring up his speech, dress, and body language. If Tyler is a model of packaged conformity and yuppie depthlessness, Tyler is a no-holds-barred charismatic rebel who, when working as a projectionist, offers his own attack on family values by splicing frames of pornography into kiddie films, or, when working as a banquet waiter in a luxurious hotel, urinates into the soup to be served to high-paying yuppie customers. Tyler also creatively affirms his disgust for women by making high-priced soaps from liposuctioned human fat and proudly telling Jack that he is "selling rich ladies their own fat asses back to them at $20.00 a bar." Jack is immediately taken with Tyler, who taunts him with the appellation "IKEA boy," and offers himself as his personal guide to the pitfalls of consumer culture. Mesmerized by Tyler's high octane talk and sense of subversion, Jack exchanges phone numbers with him.

When Jack returns home, he finds that his apartment has been mysteriously blown to bits. He calls Tyler, who meets him at a local bar and tells him that things could be worse: "A woman could cut off your penis while you are sleeping and toss it out the window of a moving car." Tyler then launches into a five-minute cliché-ridden tirade against the pitfalls of bourgeois life, mixing critique with elements of his own philosophical ramblings about the fall of masculinity. He tells Jack that issues such as crime and poverty don't trouble him. According to Tyler, the real problems that men like him confront are "celebrity magazines, television with five hundred channels, some guy's name on my underwear, Rogaine, Viagra, Olestra." And, as for the IKEA consumer hype of an idyllic domesticated existence, Tyler indignantly tells Jack: "Things you own end up owning you. . . . Fuck Martha Stewart. . . . Fuck off with your sofa units . . . stop being perfect. Let's evolve." And evolve they do. As they leave the bar, Tyler offers Jack the opportunity to move in with him in what turns out to be a dilapidated, abandoned house near a toxic dump.

Then the magic happens. Before they go back to Tyler's place, Tyler asks Jack to hit him—which Jack does—and then Tyler returns the favor. Pain leads to exhilaration, and they sit exhausted, bloodied, and blissful after their brute encounter. Soon Tyler and Jack start fighting repeatedly in a bar parking lot, eventually drawing a crowd of men who want to participate in brutally pummeling each other. Hence, Fight Club, a new religion and secret society open only to males, is born. Groups of men soon afterwards start meeting in the cellar of a local nightclub in order to beat each other's heads into a bloody mess so as to reclaim their instincts as hunters within a society that has turned them into repressed losers and empty consumers. While Tyler enumerates several rules for the members of Fight Club ("The first rule of

Fight Club is that you don't talk about Fight Club"), the one that actually captures the driving sentiment of his philosophy is the exhortation that "Self-improvement is masturbation . . . self-destruction is the answer." For Tyler, physical violence becomes the necessary foundation for masculinity and collective terrorism, the basis for politics itself. In other words, the only way Tyler's followers can become agents in a society that has deadened them is to get in touch with the primal instincts for competition and violence, and the only way their masculine identity can be reclaimed is through the literal destruction of their present selves—beating each other senseless—and their only recourse to community is to collectively engage in acts of militia-inspired terrorism aimed at corporate strongholds.

Eventually, when Tyler's narcissism and bravado mutate into an unbridled megalomania that appears more psychotic than anarchistic, Jack has second thoughts about his homoerotic attraction to his friend. Before long Tyler is spending more and more time with Marla, who appears, to Jack's chagrin, to be screwing him on an almost hourly basis. And Tyler ups the stakes of Fight Club by turning it into Project Mayhem, a nationwide organization of terrorist graduates of the Fight Clubs, whose aim is to wage war against the rich and powerful. The acts of "resistance" carried out by Operation Mayhem range from what has been described as "culture jamming" (transforming advertising billboards into political slogans, replacing airline safety cards with ones whose images depict the real outcome of a plane crash) to various forms of petty vandalism (demagnetizing an entire store's worth of video rentals, encouraging pigeons to shit all over a BMW dealership) to outright anarchic violence against what Tyler sees as the central symbols of domesticated masculinity: computers, the chief agents behind the end of industrialization; yuppie coffee bars, taken as symptomatic of the feminization of a drink once associated with labor; and credit card companies, whose products lie at the very center of contemporary consumer culture.[19] Eventually, the line between giving pain and risking death as part of the redeeming power of "masculine recovery" and the performance of barbaric fantasies worthy of the most ruthless right-wing militia movements becomes blurred. Before long, one of Operation Mayhem's terrorist forays is botched, and one of the members is killed by the police. The victim is Bob, the oversized testicular cancer survivor who has recently reaffirmed his own manliness by joining Fight Club. Jack is shocked by the killing; this, in turn, enables him to recognize that Tyler has become a demagogue and that the Fight Club has evolved into a fascist paramilitary group more dangerous than the social order it has set out to destroy.

In a psychic meltdown that is long overdue, Jack realizes that he and Tyler are the same person, signaling a shift in the drama from the realm of the sociological to the psychological. Jack discovers that Tyler has planned a series of bombings around an unmentioned city, and so he goes to the police to turn himself in. But the cops are members of Project Mayhem and attempt to cut off his testicles because of his betrayal. Once more, Jack rescues his manhood by escaping and eventually confronting Tyler in a building that has been targeted for demolition by Project Mayhem. Jack fares badly in his fight with Tyler and ends up at the top of the building with a gun in his mouth. Jack finally realizes that he has the power to take control of the gun and that he has to shoot himself in order to kill Tyler. He puts the gun in his mouth and pulls the trigger. Tyler dies on the spot and Jack mysteriously survives. Marla is brought to the scene by some Project Mayhem members. Jack orders them to leave, and he and Marla hold hands and watch as office buildings explode all around them. In an apparent repudiation of all that he/Tyler has been about, Jack turns to Marla and tells her not to worry: "You met me at a weird time in my life," suggesting that life will get better for the both of them in the future.

CONSUMERISM, CYNICISM, AND HOLLYWOOD RESISTANCE

> Consumerism . . . is less of an ideological falsification of well-being than a mark that no benefit exterior to the system can be imagined.[20]

As I have attempted to demonstrate, central to *Fight Club* is the interrelated critique of late capitalism and the politics of masculinity. The central protagonists, Jack and Tyler, represent two opposing registers that link consumerism and masculinity. Jack is representative of a generation of men condemned to corporate peonage whose emotional lives and investments are mediated through the allure of commodities and goods. No longer a producer of goods, Jack exemplifies a form of domesticated masculinity—passive, alienated, and without ambition. On the other hand, Tyler exemplifies an embodied masculinity that refuses the seductions of consumerism, while fetishizing forms of production—from soaps to explosives—the ultimate negative expression of which is chaos and destruction. Tyler represents the magnetism of the isolated, dauntless antihero, whose public appeal is based on the attractions of the cult-personality rather than on the strengths of an articulated, democratic notion of political reform. Politics for Tyler is about doing, not thinking. As the embodiment of aggressive masculinity and hyperindividualism, Tyler cannot imagine a politics that connects to democratic movements, and he is less a symbol of vision and leadership for the next millennium than a hold-over of early–twentieth-century fascist ideologies that envisioned themselves as an alternative to the decadence and decay of the established order of things. Tyler, played by superstar Brad Pitt (a contradiction that cannot be over-looked), seems appropriate as the founding father of Operation Mayhem—a vanguardist political movement, hierarchically organized through rigid social relations and led by a charismatic cult leader as the only enabling force to contest the very capitalism of which it is an outgrowth.[21] If Jack represents the crisis of capitalism repackaged as the crisis of a domesticated masculinity, Tyler represents the redemption of masculinity repackaged as the promise of violence in the interests of social and political anarchy.

While *Fight Club* registers a form of resistance to the rampant commodifi-cation and alienation of contemporary neoliberal society, it ultimately has little to say about those diverse and related aspects of consumer culture and contemporary capitalism structured in iniquitous power relations, material wealth, or hierarchical social formations. *Fight Club* largely ignores issues sur-rounding the breakup of labor unions; the slashing of the U.S. workforce; the extensive plant closings, downsizing, and outsourcing; the elimination of the welfare state; the attack on people of color; and the growing disparities be-tween the rich and the poor. All of these issues get factored out of *Fight Club*'s analysis of consumerism and corporate alienation. Hence, it comes as no sur-prise that class as a critical category is nonexistent in this film. When work-ing-class people do appear, they are represented primarily as brown shirts, part of the nonthinking herd, looking for an opportunity to release their ten-sions and repressed masculine rage through forms of terrorist violence and self-abuse. Or, they appear as people who willingly take up jobs that are de-humanizing, unskilled, and alienating. There is one particularly revealing scene in *Fight Club* that brings this message home while simultaneously sig-naling a crucial element of the film's politics. At one point in the story, Tyler takes Jack into a convenience store. He pulls out a gun and forces the young Korean clerk to get on his knees. Putting the gun to the clerk's head, Tyler tells him he is going to die. As a kind of parting gesture, he then asks Ray-mond, the clerk, what he really wanted to be in life. A veterinarian, Raymond replies, but he had to drop out of school for lack of money. Tyler tells him that, if he isn't on his way to becoming a veterinarian in six weeks, he is going to come back and kill him. He then lets Raymond go and tells Jack that tomorrow morning will be the most important day in Raymond's life because he will have to address what it means to do something about his future. Choice for Tyler appears to be an exclusively individual act, a simple matter of personal will that functions outside of existing relations of power, resources, and social formations. As Homi Bhabha points out, this notion of agency "suggests that 'free choice' is inherent in the individual [and]. . . is based on an unquestioned 'egalitarianism' and a utopian notion of individualism that bears no relation to the history of the marginalized, the minoritized, the oppressed."[22]

This privatized version of agency and politics is central to understanding Tyler's character as emblematic of the very market forces he denounces. For Tyler, success is simply a matter of getting off one's back and forging ahead; individual initiative and the sheer force of will magically cancel out institutional constraints, and critiques of the gravity of dominant relations of oppression are dismissed as either an act of bad faith or the unacceptable whine of victimization. Tyler hates consumerism, but he values a "Just Do It" ideology appropriated from the marketing strategists of the Nike Corporation and the ideology of the Reagan era. It is not surprising that, in linking freedom to the dynamics of individual choice, *Fight Club* offers up a notion of politics in which oppression breeds contempt rather than compassion, and social change is fueled by totalitarian visions rather than democratic struggles. By defining agency through such a limited (and curiously Republican) notion of choice, *Fight Club* reinscribes freedom as an individual desire rather than the "testing of boundaries and limits as part of a communal, collective process." In the end, *Fight Club* removes choice as a "public demand and duty"[23] and, in doing so, restricts the public spaces people are allowed to inhabit as well as the range of subject positions they are allowed to take up. Those spaces of debate, dialogue, and resistance, such as union halls, democratic social movements, clubs, and other educational/political sites, simply disappear in this film. Hence, it is no wonder that *Fight Club* is marked by an absence of working men and women who embody a sense of agency and empowerment, focusing, instead, on largely middle-class, heterosexual, white men who are suffering from blocked hypermasculinity.

Consumerism in *Fight Club* is criticized primarily as an ideological force and an existential experience that weakens and domesticates men, robbing them of their primary role as producers whose bodies affirm and legitimate their sense of agency and control. The importance of agency is not lost on director David Fincher, but it is restricted to a narrowly defined notion of masculinity that is as self-absorbed as it is patriarchal.[24] Fincher is less interested in fighting oppressive forms of power than he is in exploring how men yield to it. Freedom in *Fight Club* is not simply preoccupied within the depoliticized self; it also lacks a language for translating private troubles into public rage, and, as such, succumbs to the cult of immediate sensations in which freedom degenerates into collective impotence. Given Fincher's suggestion that men have no enduring qualities outside of their physicality, resistance and affirmation are primarily taken up as part of a politics of embodiment that has little concern for critical consciousness, social critique, or democratic social relations of resistance. In *Fight Club*, the body is no longer the privileged space of social citizenship or political agency, but becomes "the location of violence, crime, and [aggression]."[25] What changes in *Fight Club* is the context enabling men to assault each other, but the outside world remains the same, unaffected by the celebration of a hypermasculinity and violence that provides the only basis for solidarity.[26]

Fight Club's critique of consumerism suffers from a number of absences that need to be addressed. First, the film depicts capitalism and the ideology of consumerism as nearly sutured, impenetrable, and totalizing, offering few, if any, possibilities for resistance or struggle, except by the heroic few. There is no sense of how people critically mediate the power of capitalism and the logic of consumerism, turn it against itself, and, in doing so, offer up daily possibilities for resistance, survival, and democratic struggles.[27] No space exists within *Fight Club* for appropriations that might offer critical engagements, political understanding, and enlightened forms of social change. Moreover, consumerism, for Fincher, can only function with the libidinal economy of repression, particularly as it rearticulates the male body away from the visceral experiences of pain, coercion, and violence to the more "feminized" notions of empathy, compassion, and trust. Hence, masculinity is defined in opposition to both femininity and consumerism, while simultaneously refusing to take up either in a dialectical and critical way.

Second, *Fight Club* functions less as a critique of capitalism than as a defense of a highly stereotypical and limited sense of masculinity that is seen as wedded to the immediacy of pleasure sustained through violence and abuse. Once again, *Fight Club* becomes complicitous with the very system of commodification it denounces since both rely upon a notion of agency largely constructed within the immediacy of pleasure, the cult of hypercompetitiveness, and the market-driven desire of winning and exercising power over others. Third, *Fight Club* resurrects a notion of freedom tied to a Hobbesian world in which cynicism replaces hope, and the ideology of the "survival of the fittest" becomes literalized in the form of a clarion call for the legitimization of dehumanizing forms of violence as a source of pleasure and sociality. Pleasure in this context has less to do with justice, equality, and freedom than with hypermodes of competition mediated through the fantasy of violence. More specifically, this particular rendering of pleasure is predicated on legitimating the relationship between oppression and misogyny, and masculinity gains its force through a celebration of both brutality and the denigration of the feminine. Hence, *Fight Club* appears to have no understanding of its own articulation with the very forces of capitalism it appears to be attacking, and this is most evident in its linking of violence, masculinity, and gender. In other words, *Fight Club*'s vision of liberation and politics relies on gendered and sexist hierarchies that flow directly from the consumer culture it claims to be criticizing.

VIOLENCE AND THE POLITICS OF MASCULINITY

Unlike a number of Hollywood films in which violence is largely formulaic and superficially visceral, designed primarily to shock, titillate, and celebrate the sensational, *Fight Club* uses violence as both a form of voyeuristic identification and as a pedagogical tool. Although *Fight Club* offers up a gruesome and relentless spectacle of bare-knuckled brutality and bloodcurdling and stylistic gore, violence becomes more than ritualistic kitsch. It also provides audiences with an ideologically loaded context and mode of articulation for legitimating a particular understanding of masculinity and its relationship to important issues regarding moral and civic agency, gender, and politics. Violence in *Fight Club* is treated as a sport, a crucial component that lets men connect with each other through the overcoming of fear, pain, and fatigue, while reveling in the illusions of a paramilitary culture. For example, in one vivid scene, Tyler initiates Jack into the higher reaches of homoerotically charged sadism by pouring corrosive lye on his hand, watching as the skin bubbles and curls. Violence in this instance signals its crucial function in both affirming the natural "fierceness" of men and in providing them with a concrete experience that allows them to connect at some primal level. As grotesque as this act appears, Fincher does not engage it—or similar representations in the film—as expressions of pathology.[28] On the contrary, such senseless brutality becomes crucial to a form of male bonding, glorified for its cathartic and cleansing properties.[29] By maximizing the pleasures of bodies, pain, and violence, *Fight Club* comes dangerously close to giving violence a glamorous and fascist edge.[30] In many respects, *Fight Club* mimics fascism's militarization and masculinization of the public sphere with its exultation of violence "as a space in which men can know themselves better and love one another legitimately in the absence of the feminine."[31] As a packaged representation of masculine crisis, *Fight Club* reduces the body to a receptacle for pain parading as pleasure, and, in doing so, fails to understand how the very society it attempts to critique uses an affirmative notion of the body and its pleasures to create consuming subjects. Terry Eagleton captures this sentiment:

> Sensation in such conditions becomes a matter of commodified shock-value regardless of content: everything can now become pleasure, just as the desensitized morphine addict will grab indiscriminately at any drug. To posit the body and its pleasures as an unquestionably affirmative category is a dangerous illusion in a social order which reifies and regulates corporeal pleasure for its own ends just as relentlessly as it colonizes the mind.[32]

But the violence portrayed in *Fight Club* is not only reductionistic in its affirmation of physical aggression as a crucial element of male bonding, it also fails to make problematic those forms of violence that individuals, dissidents, and various marginalized groups experience as sheer acts of oppression deployed by the state, racist and homophobic individuals, and a multitude of other oppressive social forces. What are the limits of romanticizing violence in the face of those ongoing instances of abuse and violence that people involuntarily experience everyday because of their sexual orientation, the color of their skin, their gender, or their class status?[33] There is no sense in *Fight Club* of the complex connections between the operations of power, agency, and violence, or how some forms of violence function to oppress, infantalize, and demean human life.[34] Nor is there any incentive—given the way violence is sutured to primal masculinity—to consider how violence can be resisted, alleviated, and challenged through alternative institutional forms and social practices. It is this lack of discrimination among diverse forms of violence and the conditions for their emergence, use, and consequences, coupled with a moral indifference to how violence produces human suffering that positions *Fight Club* as a morally bankrupt and politically reactionary film.[35] Representations of violence, masculinity, and gender in *Fight Club* seem all too willing to mirror the pathology of individual and institutional violence that informs the American landscape, extending from all manner of hate crimes to the far right's celebration of paramilitary and protofascist subcultures.

Fight Club does not rupture conventional ways of thinking about violence in a world in which casual violence and hip nihilism increasingly pose a threat to human life and democracy itself. Violence in this film functions largely through a politics of denial, insulation, and disinterest and is unable to criticize with any self-consciousness the very violence that it gleefully represents and celebrates. *Fight Club* portrays a society in which public space collapses and is filled by middle-class white men—disoriented in the pandemonium of conflicting social forces—who end up with a lot of opportunities for violence and little, perhaps none at all, for argument and social engagement.[36] Macho ebullience in *Fight Club* is directly linked to a foreclosure of dialogue and critical analysis and moves all too quickly into an absolutist rhetoric that easily lends itself to a geography of violence in which there are no ethical discriminations that matter and no collective forces to engage or stop the numbing brutality and rising tide of aggression. While Jack renounces Tyler's militia-like terrorism at the end of *Fight Club,* it appears as a meaningless gesture of resistance, as all he can do is stand by and watch as various buildings explode all around him. The message here is entirely consistent with the cynical politics that inform the film—violence is the ultimate language, referent, and state of affairs through which to understand all human events, and there is no way of stopping it. This ideology becomes even more disheartening, given the film's attempt to homogenize violence under the mutually determining forces of pleasure and masculine identity formation, as it strategically restricts not only our understanding of the complexity of violence but also, as Susan Sontag has suggested in another context, "dissolves politics into pathology."[37]

The pathology at issue, and one which is central to *Fight Club,* is its intensely misogynist representation of women, and its intimation that violence is the only means through which men can be cleansed of the dire affect women have on the shaping of their identities. From the first scene of *Fight Club* to the last, women are cast as the binary opposite of masculinity. Women are both the other and a form of pathology. Jack begins his narrative by claiming that Marla is the cause of all of his problems. Tyler consistently tells Jack that men have lost their manhood because they have been feminized; they are a generation raised by women. And the critical commentary on consumerism presented throughout the film is really not a serious critique of capitalism as much as it is a criticism of the feminization and domestication of men in a society driven by relations of buying and selling. Consumerism is criticized because it is womanish stuff. Moreover, the only primary female character, Marla, appears to exist to make men unhappy and simultaneously to service their sexual needs. Marla has no identity outside of the needs of the warrior mentality, the chest-beating impulses of men who revel in patriarchy and enact all of the violence associated with such traditional, hypermasculine stereotypes.[38] But representations of masculinity in *Fight Club* do more than reinscribe forms of male identity within a warrior mentality and space of patriarchical relations. They also work to legitimate unequal relations of power and oppression, while condoning a view of masculinity predicated on the need to wage violence against all that is feminine both within and outside of their lives.[39] Masculinity in this film is directly linked to male violence against women by virtue of the way in which it ignores, and thus sanctions, hierarchical, gendered divisions and a masculinist psychic economy. By constructing masculinity on an imaginary terrain in which women are seen as the other, the flight from the feminine becomes synonymous with sanctioning violence against women as it works simultaneously to eliminate different and opposing definitions of masculinity. Male violence offers men a performative basis on which to construct masculine identity, and it provides the basis for abusing and battering an increasing number of women. According to the National Center for Victims of Crime, an estimated six million women are assaulted by a male partner each year in the United States and, of these, 1.8 million are severely assaulted.[40] Affirming stereotypical notions of male violence while remaining silent about how such violence works to serve male power in subordinating and abusing women both legitimates and creates the pedagogical conditions for such violence to occur. *Fight Club* provides no understanding of how gendered hierarchies, mediated by a misogynist psychic economy, encourages male violence against women. In short, male violence in this film appears directly linked to fostering those ideological conditions that justify abuse toward women by linking masculinity exclusively to expressions of violence and defining male identity against everything that is feminine.

FIGHT CLUB AS PUBLIC PEDAGOGY

There is a link between epistemology and morality: between how we get to know what we know (through various, including electronic media) and the moral life we aspire to lead. . . . Terrible things, by continuing to be shown, begin to appear matter-of-fact, a natural rather than man-made catastrophe. Zygmunt Bauman has labeled this the "production of moral indifference."[41]

While *Fight Club* generated a number of critical commentaries, few reviewers addressed the misogynistic nature of the film or the warrior mythology of the 1980s that it so closely resembled ideologically and politically.[42] In some cases, high-profile critics, such as Janet Maslin, writing in the *New York Times,* not only defended the film as a serious attempt to examine the "lure of violence" in a "dangerously regimented, dehumanized culture," she also condemned as mindless those critics who might view the film as a nihilistic "all-out assault on society."[43] Oddly enough, 20th Century Fox, the studio that produced *Fight Club,* viewed such criticism as dangerous, rather than simply mindless, and proceeded to withdraw all of its movie advertising in the trade paper *The Hollywood Reporter* because it had published two critical reviews of the film. But while such politics are not new to Hollywood, the overt attempts by a major studio to censor the voices of dissent—because some critical reviews spoke to the willing use of political power by corporate institutions in the cultural sphere to close down democratic relationships, denigrate women, and celebrate mindless violence—should nevertheless elicit public outrage. Certainly, 20th Century Fox has little to fear from "progressive" critics who largely praised the film. For example, Amy Taubin, writing for *Sight and Sound,* extolled the film for "screwing around with your biorhythms" and for expressing some "right-on-the-*zeitgeist* ideas about masculinity."[44] Taubin, it seems, was also bowled over with Brad Pitt's new-found masculinity, and claimed that "Pitt has never been as exquisite as he is with a broken nose and blood streaming down his cut body."[45] Susan Faludi made the remarkable statement in *Newsweek* that *Fight Club* is a *feminist film* (my emphasis).[46] It seems that the connection between *Fight Club*'s underlying misogynist premises and its similarity to a number of recent Hollywood films that offer denigrating images of women has been lost on critics such as Maslin, Taubin, and feminist backlash expert Faludi. It gets worse. Online journal, *Slate,* argued that veteran rock video director Fincher, had transformed cinema with his hip digital editing style and that the most "thrilling thing about *Fight Club* isn't *what it says* but how . . . Fincher pulls you into its narrator's head and simulates his adrenaline rushes" (my emphasis).[47] Gary Crowdus, reviewing the video release of *Fight Club,* praises it as a "pitch-black comedy, an over-the-top, consciously outrageous social satire, characterized by excess and satire."[48] The violence in this film for Crowdus is merely an expression of comic fun and for those critics who missed it, each scene of violence "simply provided a comic or dramatic context for every fight, with each bout functioning in terms of character development or to signal a key turning point in the plot."[49] Largely formalist in nature, Crowdus's praise of the film completely ignores how it might be taken up as a form of public pedagogy or public transcript. There is no sense of how *Fight Club* resonates and functions through its refusal to rupture dominant codes within a much larger discursive arena in which violence, masculinity, and sexism are being presented by the right-wing and dominant media. Crowdus makes the mistake of treating this text as if it were merely hermetic and, in doing so, he appears unable to engage it through a language of articulation that addresses *Fight Club* in the context of contemporary representations and politics, particularly around the interrelationship among gender, violence, and masculinity.

Fight Club's overall success with a large number of critics was also buoyed by an ongoing series of interviews with its stars Edward Norton, Brad Pitt, and Helena Bonham Carter, as well as a number of well-placed interviews with the film's director David Fincher.[50] Norton, for example, argues that the film is about young men having a problem defining their manhood and that it has little to do with fighting: "The fight club is not about fighting; it is a manifestation of a desire to strip away everything and rediscover yourself."[51] Norton goes so far as to claim that *Fight Club* is really a comedy, similar to the classic coming-of-age film, *The Graduate*.

One of the more incredible, if not entirely inane, comments comes from Helena Bonham Carter who defends the film by claiming that Fincher is a feminist. In describing why she took on the role of Marla, she claims "The script was awfully dark, and in bad hands it could have been immature or possibly even irresponsible. But after meeting him, I could tell that it wasn't going to be a concern. He's not just an all-out testost package. He's got a healthy feminist streak."[52]

Fincher appeared at times to be caught on the defensive in having to provide some theoretical explanation and ethical justification for the film. Claiming that *Fight Club* was a film "that's downloaded in front of you. It doesn't wait for you," he seemed to suggest that many critics were tripping over themselves trying to understand the film. He has also argued that, while the film is a coming-of-age narrative, he doesn't "purport for a second to know what a film should be, what entertainment should be, how much it should teach, how much it should titillate. I am just trying to make a good, funny movie."[53] And, of course, the implication is that neither should his audience know. Fincher's comments are more than disingenuous; they represent, at the very least, an apologetic discourse for the increasing merger of over-the-top violence, hypermasculinity, and sexist inscriptions of women in Hollywood films.[54]

All of these comments exhibit a cavalier indifference to the ways in which films operate as public pedagogies within a broader set of articulations. That is, they ignore how such films function as public discourses that address or at least resonate with broader issues in the historical and sociopolitical context in which they are situated. There is no sense of how *Fight Club*—or films in general—bridge the gap between public and private discourses, playing an important role in placing particular ideologies and values into public conversation while offering a pedagogical space for addressing specific views of how everyday lives are intertwined with politics, social relations, and existing institutional formations. For instance, Fincher seems completely unaware of how his portrayal of violence and hypermasculinity resonates with the reactionary mythology of warrior culture that reached its heyday during Ronald Reagan's presidency and found its cultural embodiment in figures such as John Wayne, Oliver North, and a host of Hollywood movies celebrating rogue warriors such as *Lethal Weapon, Missing in Action, Robocop,* and *Rambo.*[55]

Given the enormous violence, misogyny, aggression, and political indifference that permeate contemporary daily life, it is crucial to understand how representations of male violence, scorn for everything that is feminine, and a protofascist politics in a film such as *Fight Club* resonate with a broader assemblage of historical and contemporary forces to reproduce rather than challenge some of the more oppressive forces in American society. Clearly, many critics of *Fight Club,* as well as Fincher, and the film's stars, appear completely indifferent to the kind of ideological work *Fight Club* performs in linking masculinity, violence, and politics at a historical moment when public politics is collapsing into privatized discourses and pleasures, and the crisis of masculinity is widely perceived as the most important manifestation of changing economic conditions. While it would be easy to dismiss the comments by Fincher, Norton, and Bonham Carter as nothing more than self-serving publicity—or simply idiotic in light of the representational politics of the film—such comments exemplify a period in which, as Hannah Arendt has pointed out in another context, violence might best be understood less by connecting it to people who are "cold-blooded enough to 'think the unthinkable,' [than to the fact] that they do not think."[56] Against the emergence of films such as *Fight Club* and the refusal on the part of critics and others to link the violence in the film to the violence directed against women, public life, and democracy itself, progressives and others need to question not only the conditions for the production of such films but also how they work to construct particular definitions of agency. Such questions are crucial if progressives are going to critically explore what tools are needed to resist such romanticized notions of violence and masculinity.

Equally important is the need to understand *Fight Club* within both the heritage and the growing reemergence of fascist cultural formations.[57] Paul Gilroy argues convincingly that contemporary formations are organized around "the special investment that fascist movements have made in the ideal of fraternity. The comprehensive masculinization of the public sphere and the militaristic style with which this has been accomplished in many different settings . . . [as well as] the strongly masculinist character derived principally from the exultation of war . . ."[58] *Fight Club* emulates elements of what Gilroy calls a generic fascism, partially rehabilitating certain fascist ideas and principles that debase civic culture, and it does so by allowing an "armed and militarized political subject . . . to know itself"[59] through the aestheticization of politics in which libidinal pleasure, paramilitary rituals, and authoritarian rule intersect to authenticate "proto-fascistic, fascistic, and pseudo-fascistic forms of political culture."[60] Homegrown fascism may be easy to spot in the growing presence and violence of neo-Nazi organizations and other hate groups, such as the National Association for the Advancement of White People, but it is less obvious in those popular modes of representations and image making—including films such as *Fight Club*—that feature excessive doses of paramilitary spectacle, appeal to the logic-defying patterns of conspiracy theory, and mobilize forms of identification around the temptations of fascist investments in militarized forms of male bonding and solidarity. Gilroy rightly argues that militarization was and remains the center of fascist style and aesthetic values and increasingly finds its most persuasive expressions in the pedagogical space that links entertainment with politics. Fincher's film reminds us that "[t]he heritage of fascist rule survives inside democracy as well as outside it."[61]

In opposition to films such as *Fight Club,* progressives need to consider developing pedagogies of disruption that unsettle the commonsensical assumptions and ways of thinking that inform films and other cultural texts, particularly those that construct and legitimate certain subject positions, identities, values, and social relations that both celebrate pathologizing violence and render hypermasculinity as a space in which to reinscribe the hierarchies of gender, race, sexuality, and politics. James Snead is right in arguing that

[m]ass culture in America today consists of an entirely new set of artifacts— mass visual productions. These new artifacts require new ways of seeing and new ways of thinking about what we are seeing. . . . We have to be ready, as filmgoers, not only to see films, but also to see through them; we have to be willing to figure out what the film is claiming to portray, and also to scrutinize what the film is actually showing. Finally, we need to ask from whose social vantage point any film becomes credible or comforting, and ask why?[62]

But this should not suggest that educators, progressives, and others simply need to teach students and others the skills of critical literacy in order to demythologize representations of violence, or to engage gendered representations, for instance, in radically new ways. This is an important, but inadequate, strategy. We need to go beyond questions of literacy and textual critique to issues of politics, power, and social transformation.

At the very least, the emergence of films such as *Fight Club* suggests that progressives need a new civic language and vocabulary to address the contemporary relevance of culture, politics, and pedagogy. A new vocabulary is necessary to understand not just how to read texts critically. It is also crucial in order to comprehend how knowledge circulates through various circuits of power and promotes images, experiences, representations, and discourses that objectify others and create the ideological conditions for individuals to become indifferent to how violence in its diverse expressions results in human suffering. This suggests developing forms of public pedagogy that critically engage how language, images, sounds, codes, and representations work to structure basic assumptions about freedom, citizenship, public memory, and history. It also means creating public pedagogies that are attentive to how the material relations of power that produce and circulate forms of common sense can be challenged and transformed on both a national and transnational level. In this instance, public pedagogy links knowledge to power in an effort to understand how to effect social change. At stake here is both recognizing and developing a new vision of what we want the future to be and struggling to acknowledge that the fundamental nature of cultural politics and knowledge production has not only changed dramatically in the last fifty years but that the culture industries and visual culture have become the primary pedagogical/political forces/spaces in shaping consciousness and legitimating dominating social practices. This is not meant to suggest that culture exists in opposition to what some have called a material politics as much as it points to the necessity of recognizing the pedagogical nature of any attempt both to unlearn and to relearn what it might mean to challenge those commonsense assumptions and institutional forms that shape oppressive relations, regardless of how and where they manifest themselves.

Films such as *Fight Club* become important as public pedagogies because they play a powerful role in mobilizing meaning, pleasures, and identifications. They produce and reflect important considerations of how human beings should live, engage with others, define themselves, and address how a society should take up questions fundamental to its survival. At the same time, if we are to read films such as *Fight Club* as social and political allegories, articulating deeply rooted fears, desires, and visions, they have to be understood within a broader network of cultural spheres and institutional formations rather than as isolated texts. The pedagogical and political character of such films resides in the ways in which they align with broader social, sexual, economic, class, and institutional configurations.

Needless to say, *Fight Club,* as well as any other cultural text, can be read differently by different audiences, and this suggests the necessity of taking up such texts in the specificity of the contexts in which they are received. But, at the same time, educators, social critics, and others can shed critical light on how such texts work pedagogically to legitimate some meanings, invite particular desires, and exclude others. Acknowledging the educational role of such films requires that educators and others find ways to make the political more pedagogical. One approach would be to develop a pedagogy of disruption that would attempt to make students and others more attentive to visual and popular culture as an important site of political and pedagogical struggle. Such a pedagogy would raise questions regarding how certain meanings under particular historical conditions become more legitimate as representations of the real than others or how certain meanings take on the force of commonsense assumptions and go relatively unchallenged in shaping a broader set of discourses and social configurations. Such a pedagogy would raise questions about how *Fight Club,* for instance, resonates with the ongoing social locations and conditions of fear, uncertainty, sexism, and political despair, through which many people now live their lives. More specifically, a pedagogy of disruption would engage a film's attempts to shift the discourse of politics away from issues of justice and equality to a focus on violence and individual freedom as part of a broader neoliberal backlash against equity, social citizenship, and human rights. Such an approach would not only critically engage the dominant ideologies of masculinity, violence, and sexism that give *Fight Club* so much power in the public imagination but also work to expose the ideological contradictions and political absences that characterize the film by challenging it as symptomatic of the growing reaction against feminism, the right-wing assault on the welfare state, and the increasing use of violence to keep in check marginalized groups, such as young black males, who are now viewed as a threat to order and stability.

Any attempt to critically address *Fight Club* and the implications its presence suggests for the changing nature of representational politics must also acknowledge that power is never totalizing and that, even within an increasingly corporatized social landscape, there are always cracks, openings, and spaces for resistance. *Fight Club* reminds us of the need to reclaim the discourses of ethics, politics, and critical agency as important categories in the struggle against the rising tide of violence, human suffering, and the specter of fascism that threatens all vestiges of democratic public life. Precisely because of its ideological implications, *Fight Club* posits an important challenge to anyone concerned about the promise of democracy and what it might mean for critical intellectuals and others to take a stand against the dominant media, while providing opportunities to develop what Paul Gilroy calls in another context, "minimal ethical principles."[63] At the heart of such an engagement is the need to accentuate the tension between the growing threat to public life and the promise of a democracy that both remembers the history of human suffering and works to prevent its reoccurrence. The political limits of *Fight Club*'s attack on capitalism and consumerism should point to the need for a more sustained and systematic critique of the dire conditions of contemporary social life, especially as such conditions render a critique of neoliberalism that does not confuse it with fascism but at the same time points to those elements within global capitalism that remind us of what makes fascism possible.

4

PEDAGOGY OF THE DEPRESSED

The trouble with our civilization is that it has stopped questioning itself. No society which forgets the art of asking questions or allows this art to fall into disuse can count on finding answers to the problems that beset it—certainly not before it is too late and the answers, however correct, have become irrelevant.

—Cornelius Castoriadis, cited in Zygmunt Bauman,
In Search of Politics

POLITICS, PEDAGOGY, AND THE CULTURE OF CYNICISM

At the present moment in American history, there appears to be a developing hostility, if not cynicism, toward addressing the basic problems of society.[1] The absence of a widespread public debate or even substantive resistance over issues such as racial injustice, the dismantling of social welfare programs, the alarming incarceration rates among youth of color in the inner cities, the full-scale attack on the public schools, the widening gap between the rich and the poor, along with the refusal on the part of many individuals, especially young people, to participate meaningfully in political elections indicate a far-reaching public cynicism and indifference to the world of public politics. As freedom is defined increasingly through the logic of consumerism, the dynamics of self-interest, an e-commerce investment culture, and all things private, there seems to be a growing disinterest on the part of the general population in such noncommercial values as empathy, compassion, love, and solidarity that bridge the private and the public and give substance to the meaning of citizenship, democracy, and public life.[2] *New York Times* columnist Frank Rich captured the mood of such cynicism in his claim that "more Americans care about who is going to be voted off the island on *Survivor* or will succeed Kathie Lee Gifford on the Regis morning ticket than who will be the next vice president."[3] As the obligations of citizenship are narrowly defined through the imperatives of consumption and the dynamics of the market place, commercial space replaces noncommodified public spheres, and the first casualty is a language of social responsibility capable of defending those vital public spheres that provide education, health care, housing, and other services crucial to a healthy democracy.[4] Instead of celebrating the historical struggle to advance public life, the media now largely celebrate financial markets. Models of leadership are no longer drawn from the ranks of those heroic individuals who, in connection with social movements, have struggled to expand civil rights, individual liberties, and relations of democracy. On the contrary, political leadership has now given way to celebrity, representatives of whom are drawn from Hollywood film studios and the ranks of corporate culture. Narcissistic behavior now generates media attention as never before, while admiration for private success turns people like Bill Gates into cultural icons. Collapsing intellectual ambition and social vision are matched by a mounting disdain toward matters of equality, justice, and politics.

The upshot is a rising indifference toward those aspects of education that foster critical consciousness, engender a respect for public goods, and affirm the need to energize democratic public life and reinvigorate the imperatives of social citizenship. Evidence of the privatization of public life and the pervasive culture of cynicism are most obvious in the debates over educational reform and the speed at which public schools and colleges have become training grounds for corporate agendas. Ties between universities and corporations are now hailed in the popular and academic media as legitimate models of change. Typically, the *Chronicle of Higher Education,* reporting on a deal between the University of Oxford and the investment bank Beeson Gregory, in which the latter pays for one-third of a newly proposed state-of-the-art chemistry building in return for a share of the profits from any spin-off companies, treated the story as a matter of educational reform and barely offered a critical commentary, except to note that the "deal at Oxford has not drawn any opposition."[5] As Jeffrey Williams rightly argues, "universities have become licensed storefront[s] for name brand corporations . . . reconfigured according to corporate management, labor, and consumer models and delivering a name brand product. . . . The traditional idea of the university as a not-for-profit institution that offers a liberal education and enfranchises citizens of the republic, not to mention the more radical view that the university should foster a socially critical, if not revolutionary, class, has been evacuated without much of a fight."[6]

In what follows, I want to analyze various ways in which the institution of education and the discourse of pedagogy have been largely eliminated from discussions of politics, power, and democratic transformation. In so doing, I will provide examples that extend from high-profile conservatives and progressives to those with radical views on critical pedagogy. All of these ideologies share a willingness either to depoliticize pedagogy or to render its critical attributes a reinscription of particular forms of oppression. In many respects, there is a cynical refusal on the part of all of these ideologies to engage schools as critical sites of cultural and political struggle and pedagogy as a crucial element in waging such battles. All of these discourses abstract forms of personal and social development from any association with power, struggle, and social transformation, and, in so doing, they both confirm and legitimate the retreat from pedagogical and political engagement. Politics in these views is considered either a corrupting force or is relegated to other spheres and practices largely removed from public and higher education. In an effort to highlight the tension between the possibilities of schooling and the promise of democracy itself, I want to explore and challenge such criticisms as they emerge across the ideological spectrum and conclude with a brief commentary on the importance of situating pedagogy as a *political and ethical* practice grounded in a notion of hope. Throughout this chapter, I use pedagogy as a referent for analyzing how knowledge, values, desire, and social relations are constructed, taken up, and implicated in relations of power in the interaction among cultural texts, institutional forms, authorities, and audiences. At stake here is acknowledging the productive, political, and ethical character of pedagogy as a deliberate attempt to influence how and what knowledge, experiences, and identities are produced within particular social formations and relations. By viewing critical pedagogy as a performative practice that must be understood, in part, as the outcome of numerous struggles, I attempt to provide an alternative commentary that redefines the implications of a critical pedagogy as part of a broader ethical and political project wedded to furthering social and economic justice and making multicultural democracy operational.

DISAVOWING PEDAGOGY AS A POLITICAL PRACTICE

Individuals cannot be free unless they are free to institute a society which promotes and guards their freedom; unless they institute together an agency capable of achieving just that. . . . This is not going to be an easy job, considering the present [perilous] state of the private/public sphere. . . . To make the *agora* [public space] fit for autonomous individuals and autonomous society, one needs to arrest, simultaneously, its privatization and depoliticization. One needs to reestablish the translation of the private into the public. One needs to restart (in the *agora*, not just in philosophy seminars) the interrupted discourse of the common good—which renders individual autonomy both feasible and worth struggling for.[7]

In the above quotation, Zygmunt Bauman highlights one of the growing dangers faced by democratic societies in an age dominated increasingly by the forces of neoliberalism, thus commenting implicitly on an important challenge that educators must address as engaged intellectuals. For Bauman, democratic life is now under siege by those commercial and market-driven pressures that exalt an utterly privatized notion of citizenship that undermines not only a commitment to valuing and investing in public goods but also devalues forms of critical citizenship that encourage people to organize collectively to engage and resolve pressing social issues. As the forces of domestic militarization overpower and diminish the states' social functions, those social agencies aimed at providing opportunities for debate, deliberation, and solidarity are eliminated, and there is less and less room within the dominant society to develop forms of education based on a respect for both individual rights and public goods.[8] Moreover, as market-driven policies eliminate crucial public spaces, critical inquiry fashioned in the spirit of social justice, the common good, and the promise of democracy appear either irrelevant or threatening to the cultural and political managers of neoliberalism. For Bauman, one of the central obligations of education in the current era is to provide forms of pedagogy that foster a respect for public life and provide the conditions for translating private issues into public considerations. Additionally, Bauman rightly argues that critique and dissent are central to any viable notion of democracy but are increasingly under siege as a growing number of public spheres are commodified, making it all the more difficult for educators and others to provide the conditions for students to learn how to be critical agents willing to take risks, think oppositionally, and participate in shaping the larger social order.

Central to the rise of a depoliticized citizenry, marked by apathy and cynicism, is the emergence of a view of education in which schools are defined as a private rather than a public good. This emergent view of education is clearly complicitous with the mounting vocationalization of public and higher education. In addition, it makes a strong claim for pedagogical practices that venerate political disinterestedness while fostering modes of aesthetic analysis that celebrate a retreat into private experience at the expense of critical inquiry and an active social engagement with public life. Perhaps unsurprising in a climate of mounting cynicism, the move toward a depoliticized pedagogy that strips students of any sense of critical and social agency cuts across the ideological spectrum. Before focusing on those progressive and radical theorists who align themselves with this view of pedagogy, I want to address briefly how high-profile conservatives such as Harold Bloom legitimate such a position.

In *How to Read and Why,* Bloom argues that the function of reading is neither self- nor social improvement but to alleviate loneliness. The pleasures of reading are, in short, "selfish rather than social."[9] Bloom wants to separate reading as an act of pleasure from reading as a form of self-production that connects the reader to a wider public conversation and involvement in society. He argues that good reading demands clearing one's mind of "academic cant" in order to reject the assumption that reading might have a social function, particularly improving "your neighborhood by what or how you read."[10] According to Bloom, "self-improvement is a large enough project for your mind and spirit: There are no ethics of reading. The mind should be kept at home until its primal ignorance has been purged; premature excursions into activism have their charm, but are time-consuming, and for reading there will never be enough time."[11] Clearly, for Bloom, time is predominantly a burden when it infringes on reading; as such, it appears to be an important precondition *only* for the act of privatized reading and *problematic* only if it takes the reader outside of "home."[12] Bloom's elitist attitude toward temporality, his reduction of reading to an act of pleasure, and his exclusively bourgeois focus on the unproblematic comforts of "home" collapse reading as a public pedagogy into the aesthetics of privatized pleasure. Moreover, Bloom depoliticizes pedagogy by defining it solely as an instrument of self-improvement and a form of high-minded diversion, thereby eliminating it as a practice for critical engagement and social transformation. There is no sense in Bloom's notion of reading that the act of pedagogy is dependent upon a number of political circumstances and conditions. For instance, teaching always takes place within an arena of diverse political and social relations organized around particular relations of power. As Paul Smith points out, the "universities, colleges, and schools we inhabit are crucial for the production and reproduction of social relations of power," but "in all cases, the production and transmission of what we call (in shorthand) 'knowledge' always comports a relation to the *polis* and to the *oikos*—in our contexts, a relation to the political economy of an apparently ever-expanding capitalist entity, to which our knowledge is always related, in which it is always implicated, and which defines and is defined by it."[13] Bloom is indifferent to the cultural capital that both defines his notion of authority and the pedagogical categories he uses to give meaning to his definition of correct reading, legitimate knowledge, culturally sanctioned texts, acceptable values, and the admissible uses of literature by his students within the broader industrial circuits of neoliberal society. To teach students how to read, to teach in general under these conditions, is already to engage in a irrefutable political act.[14]

Politics in Bloom's view is an unwarranted, if not barbaric, intrusion into the sphere of higher education—a degrading affirmation of forms of dissent and inquiry that emerged out of the upheavals of the 1960s—that are antithetical to the world of contemplation and civility. According to this logic, critical pedagogy and critical learning as preconditions for social change have no place in the university and simply represent "speech overflowing with pious platitudes, the peculiar vocabulary of a sect or coven."[15] And, Bloom adds, in case the sexist implication is missed, that "[a] university culture where the appreciation of Victorian women's underwear now replaces the appreciation of Charles Dickens and Robert Browning sounds like the outrageousness of a new Nathaniel West, but is merely the norm."[16] For Bloom, the covens not only gather together in haunted domiciles but have now gone public on university campuses, empowered through struggles waged in the name of multiculturalism, gender, and sexuality, all of which he abruptly dismisses as "a mask for mediocrity for the thought-control academic police, the Gestapo of our campuses."[17] Bloom wants to situate knowledge, literacy, and pedagogy strictly within the sphere of aesthetic transcendence, unhampered and uncorrupted by theoretical considerations, the struggle over public goods, or what it might mean for students to become social agents capable of influencing those political, economic, and cultural conditions that shape their lives.[18] Politics for Bloom is a form of pathology, but it is exclusively a left-wing disease. Though a facile attack, even in terms of his own standards, it allows him to ignore the corporate assault on public and higher education and the tearing apart of all forms of solidarities that do not mirror the logic of the market. For Bloom, those pedagogical practices that prompt critical engagement—that provide students with the conditions necessary for them to reconceptualize themselves as active citizens capable of altering the terms of debate and structures of power that bear down on their lives—represent one aspect of the excesses of democracy and should be avoided by educators at all costs. Bloom believes that the political irrelevance of the intellectual is a mark of distinction rather than an embarrassment and consequently he becomes an apologist for the status quo. In the end, Bloom showers contempt on those academics who would bridge the world of higher education and public life. More importantly, Bloom represents a new breed of public relations intellectual, what Pierre Bourdieu calls "fast thinkers-specialists in throw-away thinking,"[19] whose willingness to heap contempt on any individual or group that critically engages public life ensures them high-visibility coverage in all of the dominant media outlets.

ERASING THE POLITICS OF PEDAGOGY

It ultimately comes down to *individuals;* the students, the parents, and the teachers. Students don't care about their own futures let alone about anyone else's (as the "kids having babies" phenomenon shows), and the teachers don't want to give a real education. It's much easier, after all, to "affirm students' personal lives and experiences" than to write a rigorous lecture on *A Portrait of the Artist as a Young Man.*[20]

Traditional theories of education generally begin with the premise that knowledge is the fulfillment of (Western) tradition, and pedagogy is a technical practice primarily concerned with the process of transmission. Although it seems reasonable to assume that there is a relationship between what we know and how we act, it does not follow (although it often does in conservative educational discourse and theory) that what we learn and how we learn can be measured solely by the content of an established discipline. This is a fatally flawed argument with respect to its refusal to engage the particular discursive and institutional conditions under which learning takes place. And yet, against the onslaught of an educational reform movement that emphasizes standards and excellence while ignoring issues of equity, this position is increasingly being taken up by a number of progressives who seem unaware of the longstanding criticisms it has received among many critical educators over the last thirty years.[21]

Many liberal and leftist educators emulate their conservative counterparts by either refusing to engage pedagogy as an immanently political and ethical practice or by simply dismissing critical pedagogy as an authoritarian, if not oppressive, practice. Missing from much of this work is a concern with the role that schools play in either extending or closing down the possibilities for students to participate within a wider democratic culture. Nor is there interest in exploring how power works through particular texts, social practices, and institutional structures to produce differences organized around complex forms of subordination and empowerment. Given these omissions, it is not surprising that little is said about how the dominant culture of schooling legitimates as well as excludes, under vastly different conditions of learning, different forms of cultural capital, or what ideological and institutional conditions are necessary to provide teachers with the opportunities they need to function as critical public intellectuals. Among both groups, there is little sense of what it means to "turn pedagogy into an exploration of its own limits."[22] While progressives make a claim to the discourse of educational reform, they simultaneously undermine such possibilities by generally ignoring the discourses of power and politics. While clearly sensitive to the politics of education, many radical educators can only theorize politics within notions of domination that reify the complexities of power, authority, and teacher resistance. Distancing themselves from the discourse of social change, a number of these critics appear utterly cynical, if not paralyzed, in exploring the connection between pedagogy and the possibilities of moral and civic agency. As such, they have little to say about the ways in which educators might develop strategies to unsettle and disrupt ongoing attempts by right-wing ideologues and other conservative forces to deskill teachers, corporatize higher education, and dismantle public education as part of a broader attack on democratic public life. The most egregious of such criticisms deal largely in polemical diatribes against other progressives, while the less cynical attempt to address some of the problems facing public and higher education but do so in ways that abstract such issues from broader political considerations.[23]

In both discourses, there is a theoretical indifference to what it might mean to seize upon the paradox of appropriating authority vested in dominant institutions in order to push against the grain and subvert the very ideological and institutional foundations on which such authority rests. At the very least, turning authority against itself might suggest making visible and challenging how dominant intellectuals and institutions function to incapacitate the intersection of critical thought, political agency, and collective struggle. Taking seriously the relationship among power, politics, agency, and pedagogy might also enable critical educators to connect meaning and pleasure with commitment and passion. Refusing to treat pedagogy as a moral and political practice does more than undermine the opportunity for educators to explore its transformative possibilities; it also means that they often have no language for recognizing the abuses often exercised under the rubric of teaching. For instance, how would an educator who defines pedagogy as either irrelevant or as simply a mechanism for transmitting knowledge as a technical function unpack the pedagogical terrorism implicit in the following pronouncement by a conservative educator:

It's not fashionable to blame the students for anything, but there are plenty of fools among them too. What is most shocking is the fact that many of them seem not to have even a clue as to what's good for them. When we were studying Saint Anselm's proof for the existence of God, one girl was noticeably impatient; finally, I called on her. She wanted to know why she needed to learn "this stuff," of what use it would be to her. My answer was short: "Because it is better to be smart than stupid. Because there is dignity in being educated and cultivated." Her face was a mask of utter puzzlement. . . . And so she simply stopped coming to class.[24]

The above scenario is reflective of the ideologically driven assumptions at work in dominant notions of knowledge as fixed and indisputable; it also points to the ways in which pedagogy can be used to silence and humiliate students. Within this approach to pedagogy, the ideological nature of knowledge production, legitimation, and circulation is often subsumed by appeals for excellence and standards. At the same time, the productive character of pedagogy as a moral and political practice is routinely dismissed as the imposition of bias, derided as a utopian fantasy, renounced as an obstacle to learning, or relegated to a grab bag of depoliticized methods that define pedagogy largely in technical and instrumental terms. The latter two positions (obstacle and depoliticization) are not limited to conservative educators and politicians such as Diane Ravitch[25] and Florida Governor, Jeb Bush. They can be found in the work of Leon Botstein, the outspoken president of Bard College, and in the recent foray with pedagogy undertaken by Elaine Showalter, the former president of the Modern Language Association.[26] While it might be argued that neither of these individuals provides a sustained scholarly argument, I focus on them because they not only command a large popular following as well known public intellectuals but also because their positions—unlike those of many academics such as E. D. Hirsch, Jr., and Nat Gage who develop these views in much greater detail[27]—get enormous public exposure through extensive distribution in the mainstream media. Though occupying seemingly divergent positions on the role of education and the value of pedagogy, both theorists represent examples of so-called progressive educational reforms that deny the political nature of education and the transformative possibilities of pedagogy itself.

In an editorial in the *New York Times,* Botstein suggests that the failure of education in the United States is largely due to the inadequate preparation of teachers. Taking aim at education programs in universities nationally, Botstein argues that prospective teachers are taught pedagogy at the expense of formal training in subject matter and, consequently, are inadequately prepared to teach students even the fundamentals of the basic subject disciplines, contributing both to the lowering of academic standards and the failure of students to learn.[28] The solution, according to Botstein, is to "disband the education schools and integrate teacher education into the core of the university."[29] In short, Botstein argues that schools of education do prospective teachers a great disservice by focusing on the social, historical, and philosophical trajectories of education's own disciplinary traditions at the expense of learning subject matter taught by professionals in the liberal arts.

For Botstein, the key to educational reform lies in raising academic standards, particularly through the mastering of discipline-based subject matter. Missing from Botstein's short-sighted and simplistic appeal is any attempt to engage broader questions of what public schools or higher education should accomplish in a substantive democracy, and why they sometimes fail.[30] His appeal to academic content cannot engage the relationship between schools and democracy because it has been depoliticized within the discourse of disciplinary purity. Botstein does not have anything to say about how knowledge is related to the power of self-definition and self-determination. Rather, pedagogy is generally assumed to be about processing received knowledge rather than actually transforming it in the interest of the public good. Botstein is utterly indifferent to questions regarding the purpose and meaning of schooling, which actually set the context for understanding the relationship between knowledge and power, as well as to the fact that the real crisis in schools is not simply about whether students are learning subject matter but whether students are capable of meeting traditional educational goals—learning to think critically about the knowledge they gain, engaging larger social issues, and developing a sense of social responsibility and political agency. Botstein's appeal to standards ignores what it means to educate prospective teachers about the roles they might play as critical intellectuals informed about how power works both within and outside of the classroom. What the role of education should be in a democratic society, how the conditions of teaching affect how students learn, and what it might mean to educate students to discern between academic norms and critical intellectual work or to use knowledge critically in the service of shaping democratic identities and institutional arrangements are questions left unanswered in Botstein's analysis. Knowledge for Botstein is an end in itself as opposed to an ongoing process of struggle and negotiation, and the conditions of its production or the limits it embodies in its institutionalized and disciplinary forms appear irrelevant to him.

Botstein's inclusive emphasis on teaching disciplinary knowledge in opposition to any serious engagement with pedagogical issues reveals a fundamental incapacity to address what it might mean to create the conditions necessary to make knowledge meaningful in order to become either critical or transformative. Botstein aside, knowledge doesn't speak for itself. Unless the pedagogical conditions exist to connect forms of knowledge to the lived experiences, histories, and cultures of the students we engage, such knowledge is reified, or "deposited" in the Freirian sense, through transmission models that ignore the context in which knowledge is produced and simultaneously function to silence as much as deaden student interest. Moreover, the emphasis on teaching as knowledge production has little to say about teaching as self-production. In this discourse, it becomes almost impossible to use pedagogy as a way of making teachers attentive to their own biases, values, and ideologies as they work through and shape what and how they teach. In other words, Botstein's exclusive emphasis on disciplinary knowledge offers no theoretical language for helping prospective educators register and interrogate their own personal and social complicities in what, how, and why they teach and learn within particular institutional and cultural formations. This may explain why educators such as Botstein, while opposed to standardized testing, decline to address the plight of students in rundown urban schools whose performance is largely framed within a vicious cycle of poverty, inadequate school resources, and endless turnover of poorly trained teachers.[31] Nor do such educators offer any concrete challenge to the ways in which such standardized tests function to deskill teachers, remove knowledge from the context and experience in which students negotiate everyday life, or address the pedagogical implications of state-mandated forms of testing—for example, how the latter do not just standardize knowledge but make a mockery of educating students to be critical citizens.[32] At most, Botstein can only suggest new ways to redesign testing procedures while having nothing to say about the necessity to change the very conditions for the production of knowledge, the distribution of power in schools, or the dissemination of resources. Lost here is the possibility of addressing educational reforms that deny the centrality of providing teachers with more control over their academic labor, the necessity of linking equity and excellence by closing the resource gap between rich and poor schools, and the primacy of developing pedagogical practices that both respect students' differences and empower them as critical and active citizens.

Botstein's emphasis on the virtues of disciplinary knowledge as a way of discrediting both pedagogy and colleges of education ignores the crucial importance of pedagogy for raising a number of serious questions. Moreover, it denies the obvious fact that education has its own disciplinary body of knowledge worthy of investigation, ironically reinforcing the necessity of schools of education. There is a long tradition, for instance, of educational knowledge, extending from Thomas Jefferson and John Dewey to Lawrence Cremin and Maxine Greene, that examines the relationships between democracy and schooling, theory and practice, formal and hidden curricula, as well as analyzing the ethical, social, political, and historical foundations of schooling. Such knowledge is crucial both for contextualizing and engaging the ways in which academic knowledge has been mobilized to define the race, gender, and class-specific purposes of public and higher education. Similarly, the history of education provides a rich and expansive literature for analyzing pedagogy as a moral and political practice through which knowledge, values, and social relations are deployed within unequal relations of power in order to produce particular forms of citizenship and national identity. Botstein depoliticizes knowledge and pedagogy in his analysis and, in doing so, renders mute the need to understand how they mutually inform each other and what their complicated interaction suggests for addressing both the teaching of prospective educators and teaching itself as a deeply ethical and political issue. For Botstein, education is about the management of knowledge, divorced from questions of power, place, ideology, self-management, and politics. In this context, Botstein provides a model of education that is unaware of its own pedagogical assumptions and deeply indebted to a theory of learning that is indifferent to either how power works in education or how teachers and students alike might employ education in the service of democratic struggles.

In contrast to Botstein, Elaine Showalter, in a commentary in the *Chronicle of Higher Education,* recognizes the importance of sound pedagogical practice, particularly the responsibility of faculty in preparing their graduate students to teach undergraduate courses. Showalter rejects the popular attitude among her professional colleagues that any "interest in pedagogy [be seen] as the last refuge of a scoundrel."[33] For Showalter, such derision is unfounded and simply perpetuates the general complaint that teaching assistants don't know how to teach and that faculty are unwilling to do anything about it. Born out of a general impatience with the lack of will and effort in addressing the problem of pedagogy, Showalter brought together in 1998 a number of graduate students in a noncredit course on teaching in order to take up the problem. The first challenge for Showalter was to locate materials on teaching in order to "find out what other people are doing behind their closed classroom doors."[34] Conducting an intensive search on the Internet, Showalter surprised herself and her students by how many books she was able to find on teaching. For Showalter, texts on university education fall into four general categories: personal memoirs, spiritual and ethical reflections, practical guidebooks, and reports on education research. Unfortunately, Showalter's search left her and her students unaware of a long tradition of critical theoretical work on pedagogy, schooling, and society. The result is that both she and her graduate students came away with a conception of teaching as simply a matter of methods, exclusively and reductively concerned with practical and technical issues. Hence, their enthusiasm for books that "provide lots of pointers on subjects as varied as choosing textbooks and getting feedback from students and colleagues" or books that help "instructors make the most effective use of the lecture/discussion mode."[35] Even those books that Showalter claims deal with ethical and spiritual issues become significant to the degree that they "can offer both inspiration and some surprisingly concrete advice."[36] In the end, Showalter recommends a number of books, such as Wilbert J. McKeachie's *McKeachie's Teaching Tips* and Joseph Lowman's *Mastering the Techniques of Teaching,* because they "offer practical, concrete advice about learning to ask students good questions and encouraging them to participate."[37]

The upshot is that Showalter and her students ignore an entire generation of scholarship in critical pedagogy that addresses, once again, teaching as a moral and political practice, as a deliberate attempt to influence how and what knowledge and identities are produced within very particular contexts and relations of power.[38] In her zest for "concreteness," she abstracts pedagogical practices from the ethico-political visions that inform them and has little to say about how pedagogy relates the self to public life, social responsibility, or the demands of critical citizenship. Showalter has no pedagogical language for dealing with student voices and experiences, nor with the social, racial, and class inequalities that animate them. Nor does she offer her students guidance on matters of justice, equality, liberty, and fairness that should be at the core of pedagogical practices designed to enable students to recognize social problems and injustices in a society founded on deep inequalities. Even basic pedagogical issues regarding how teacher authority can manifest itself without being inimical to the practice of freedom are ignored in Showalter's discourse. By defining pedagogy as an a priori discourse that simply needs to be uncovered and deployed, Showalter has nothing to say about pedagogy as the outcome of specific struggles between diverse groups to name history, experience, knowledge, and the meaning of everyday life in one's own terms. Unfortunately, Showalter offers up a depoliticized pedagogy of "tips" that is effectively silent on matters of how knowledge, values, desire, and social relations are always implicated in power and broader institutional practices. Showalter's stripped-down version of pedagogy is not surprising given her conservative views on the increasing corporatization of the university and the ongoing proletarianization of faculty as adjunct workers.[39] What is surprising is her silence on the role that her own version of pedagogy plays in preparing students in the "new corporate university" for forms of citizenship that define them exclusively as consumers and forms of knowledge whose only value appears to be in helping them put together attractive job resumes. What Showalter conveniently refused to engage is the role pedagogy might play in educating students to take risks, engage in learning how to exercise power, and extend the boundaries of economic and social justice.

If Botstein depoliticizes and instrumentalizes questions concerning the production of knowledge and reduces pedagogy to the logic of transmission, Showalter similarly reifies pedagogy by stripping it of its political and ethical referents and transforming it into a grab bag of practical methods and techniques. Neither scholar can theorize the productive character of pedagogy as a political and moral discourse. Hence, both are silent about the institutional conditions that bear down on the ability of teachers to link conception with execution and what it means to develop a better understanding of pedagogy as a struggle over the shaping of particular identities. Nor can they raise questions about education as a form of political intervention that cannot elude its role in creating potentially empowering or disempowering spaces for students, critically interrogate the role of teacher authority, or engage the limits of established academic subjects in sustaining critical dialogues about educational aims and practices. These questions barely scratch the surface of issues that are often excluded when education is linked solely to the teaching of content, and pedagogy is instrumentalized to the point of irrelevance.

A number of radical educational and cultural theorists have also argued against the relevance and importance of critical pedagogy. Advocates of this position include Ian Hunter, Elizabeth Ellsworth, and Tony Bennett.[40] All of these theorists dismiss critical pedagogy by claiming it is simply another instrument for reconciling the self with the dominant social order; moreover, they reject the importance of pedagogical practices that call critical attention to the ways in which authority might be used to challenge the ideologies and practices that characterize much of public and higher education: tracking, cutbacks in student loans, aggressive advertising in schools, corporate-friendly curricula, "zero tolerance" policies aimed mostly at minorities of race and color, use of noncertified teachers, and downsizing of full-time faculty by increasing adjunct positions.

Reducing critical pedagogy to the imposition of dominant authority, Hunter, for instance, can only imagine teacher authority working in the interest of moral regulation and social control. Self-reflexive dialogue drops out of his argument, as does the possibility of teachers and students to become critical of the very institutional forms, academic relations, and disciplinary knowledges and regulations that constitute the complex and varied spaces of schooling. Within this narrow understanding of the relationship between culture and politics, there is no possibility for imagining schools as a place to resist hegemonic authority, unsettle strategies of domination, or reelaborate institutional authority from a position of engaged self-criticism and as a critical object of classroom analysis. That the legacy of such cultural and moral regulation can be challenged, pedagogically turned in on itself, or used as a resource to refigure the basis of teaching as a deliberative practice in the service of a progressive cultural politics seems impossible within this discourse.[41]

Critical pedagogy in this approach is not only reduced to a form of oppression; it is also commodified and turned into an inert theory to be enacted irrespective of the historical realities and material circumstances that shape the context in which it is produced. Treated merely as a commodity, if not a caricature, critical pedagogy is transformed into a fixed body of knowledge and reified as a taken-for-granted and totalizing theory. Under such circumstances, critical pedagogy is no longer shaped, in part, by the contexts it attempts to address. Nor are its aims mediated and modified with respect to the questions posed by different circumstances, enabling it to be used differently by educators as a resource to produce new social relations, spaces of opposition, or forms of critical agency. Lost here is the important recognition that critical pedagogy is not an a priori discourse that imposes itself on teachers and students alike with the arrogance of theoretical certainty. On the contrary, any viable notion of critical pedagogy has to recognize its own indeterminate and partial character, particularly since it is constantly being shaped by the particular contexts in which it is taken up. Given that its usefulness rests on its ability to respond to the problems posed within particular contexts, marked by changing configurations of students, cultural resources, community histories, and relations of power, critical pedagogy can neither be defined as a static theory nor can it be required to provide theoretical and political guarantees.

In an article that has been and continues to be cited as a seminal argument against critical pedagogy,[42] Elizabeth Ellsworth contends that, when she attempted to put into practice the basic principles of critical pedagogy in a class she taught at the University of Wisconsin-Madison in 1988, "the results were not only unhelpful, but actually exacerbated the very conditions we were trying to work against, including Eurocentrism, racism, sexism, classism, and 'banking education.'"[43] According to Ellsworth, the failure of critical pedagogy lies in its claims of enforcing the "rules of reason in the classroom"[44] which reproduce violence against all those "others" traditionally excluded within its purview. Additionally, it prevents those critical pedagogues who make a claim to authority in the service of a political project from making their own ideologies and practices problematic. Authority and reason in this context are always on the side of domination, and any attempts to forge a connection between critical learning and social change are doomed to reproduce an oppressive master narrative and an elitist pedagogical posture. Theorists such as Ellsworth ignore the radically contextual nature of critical pedagogy and, not surprisingly, condemn it for being dogmatic and oppressive rather than open, contextually strategic, and potentially liberatory. Commenting on how pedagogy becomes commodified in Ellsworth's work, particularly as it relates to a course she taught, Bruce Horner rightly critiques her propensity to treat power, authority, and domination as if they were identical. Horner also argues that the failure of Ellsworth's class was inevitable, given the way in which she reduces critical pedagogy to a commodity isolated from the material circumstances in which it was enacted. Rather than recognizing that it was *her* reification of critical pedagogy that guaranteed its failure, Ellsworth blames critical pedagogy for functioning as a commodity unable to address the particular issues and problems that emerged within the context specific conditions of her own teaching. Horner is worth quoting at length on this issue:

> That she expected critical pedagogy to operate as a commodity is apparent in the ways in which she was asked by her students what she meant by "critical" in her syllabi descriptions of critical pedagogy. She simply "referred them to answers provided in the literature," as if such a pedagogy were monolithic and fixed in meaning and effect. . . . [Ellsworth] was shocked to discover that the actual historical realities of the students, herself as professor, and C&I607 failed to match the ideal to which critical pedagogy aims. But rather than concluding with a recognition of the need for both students and teacher to rework the meaning and substance of critical pedagogy anew in each historical instance of its practice, as one might expect, Ellsworth uses the inevitable gap between the aims of critical pedagogy and the lived experience of the C7I607 course to condemn the pedagogy for its failure, by itself, to close that gap. Like an angry consumer, she rejects critical pedagogy as repressive rather than liberatory, as a commodity that does not "work" as advertised.[45]

Under such circumstances, power is almost exclusively associated with domination, and teacher authority simply becomes another register of authoritarianism. This is not to suggest that critical educators should overlook either the kind of pedagogical abuses that can take place in the name of authority that makes a claim to critical pedagogy or ignore the long history in which pedagogy has been complicitous with constructing the state's version of citizenship and national identity. Nor should critical educators be indifferent to the fact that institutional practices forged within dominant economic, cultural, and political conditions exercise an enormous influence in shaping the very conditions under which pedagogy takes place. But to acknowledge the latter, as Alan O'Shea has recently pointed out, does not legitimate the presupposition that power is entirely on the side of domination within schools or that teachers and students can only be complicitous with hegemonic power, however they challenge its structures, ideologies, and practices.[46] Such criticism rests on more than passé functionalist accounts of society and its social forms; it also legitimates a totalizing model of power and authority that marks a retreat from making the political more pedagogical as it simultaneously celebrates the marginalized role of the detached, objective educator. This notion of power and education rooted in a Foucauldian notion of governmentality signals a form of theoretical paralysis (not simply anti-utopianism) that undermines the more crucial problem of how schooling as a terrain of struggle functions to shape the possibilities of political agency and critical engagement against dominant cultural and institutional formations. Missing in this approach is any understanding of the importance of teachers and students analyzing how authority is used in public and higher education to give particular forms of knowledge, culture, and social relations political and ethical valence. Nor is there any attempt to construct and analyze pedagogical authority as a tool for social critique. Instead, authority and the rule of reason come to symbolize a form of violence, offset by the wonders of indeterminancy and endless excursions into auto-critique. Social critique tends to drop out of this formulation, while politics is reduced to the level of formalistic critique. Under such circumstances, authority itself becomes antithetical to transformative politics, and any determinate form of political engagement exercised in its name becomes synonymous with all that is dogmatic. This is a politics that seems made for the academy because it threatens no one since it is against nothing that would challenge material relations of power.

Such versions of authority, pedagogy, and politics preclude engaging pedagogy as the outgrowth of specific struggles that take place within varied contexts marked by unequal relations of power, differentiated opportunities, and varied resources for social change. In some cases, theorists such as Tony Bennett actually replicate older models of social and cultural reproduction that were prevalent among radical educational theorists in the United States in the 1970s and early 1980s.[47] According to Bennett, radical classroom interventions are caught within the paralyzing grip of governmental institutions that normalize all pedagogical practices. Similarly, Bennett argues that radical educators overemphasize agency at the expense of institutional pressures, embracing what he calls "all agency and no structure."[48] This criticism, however, does little to explore or highlight the complicated, contradictory, and determining ways in which the institutional pressures of schools and the social capacities of educators are mediated within unequal relations of power. Instead, Bennett simply reverses the formula and buttresses his own notion of governmentality as a theory of structures without agents. Ultimately, Bennett's pessimism collapses into something worse than the liberalism he accuses radical educators of emulating.

BEYOND PEDAGOGIES OF DESPAIR AND THE POLITICS OF CYNICISM

> The irreducible distance, the always [irresolvable tension] between the "idea of democracy" and that which presents itself in its name remains forever ambiguous. That idea is not altogether a "Kantian idea," at the same time regulating and infinitely expanded. It commands the most concrete urgency, here and now. If I keep its old name of "democracy" nevertheless, and often speak of a "democracy to come," it is because that is the only name for a political regime which declares its historicity and its perfectibility, in that it carries in its concept the dimension of inadequation and of that which is to come. Democracy allows us in all liberty to invoke these two openings publicly in order to criticize the current state of all so-called democracy.[49]

In opposition to these increasingly dominant views of education and cultural politics, I want to argue for a transformative pedagogy—rooted in the project of resurgent democracy—that relentlessly questions the kinds of labor, practices, and forms of production that are enacted in public and higher education. Such an analysis should be both relational and contextual, as well as self-reflective and theoretically rigorous. By relational, I mean that the current crisis of schooling must be understood in relation to the broader assault that is being waged against all aspects of democratic public life. Jeffrey Williams underscores this point in arguing that "the current restructuring of higher education is only one facet of the restructuring of civic life in the U.S. whereby previously assured public entitlements such as healthcare, welfare, and social security have evaporated or been 'privatized,' so no solution can be separated from a larger vision of what it means to enfranchise citizens or our republic."[50] But as important as such articulations are in understanding the challenges that public and higher education face in the current historical conjuncture, they do not go far enough. Any critical comprehension of those wider forces that shape public and higher education must also be supplemented by an attentiveness to the conditional nature of pedagogy itself. This suggests that pedagogy can never be treated as a fixed set of principles and practices that can be applied indiscriminately across a variety of pedagogical sites. Pedagogy must always be contextually defined, allowing it to respond specifically to the conditions, formations, and problems that arise in various sites in which education takes place. Rather than treating pedagogy as commodity, progressive educators need to engage their teaching as a theoretical resource that is both shaped by and responds to the very problems that arise in the in-between space/places/contexts that connect classrooms with the experiences of everyday life. Under such circumstances, educators can both address the meaning and purpose that schools might play in their relationship to the demands of the broader society while simultaneously being sensitive to the distinctive nature of the issues educators address within the shifting contexts in which they interact with a diverse body of students, texts, and institutional formations.

Critical pedagogy locates discursive practices in a broader set of interrelations, but it analyzes and gives meaning to such relations by defining them within particular contexts constructed through the operations of power as articulated through the interaction among texts, teachers, and students. Questions of articulation and contexts need to be highlighted as matters of ethics and politics. Ethically, critical pedagogy requires an ongoing indictment "of those forms of truth-seeking which imagined themselves to be eternally and placelessly valid." [51] Simply put, educators need to cast a critical eye on those forms of knowledge and social relations that define themselves through a conceptual purity and political innocence that clouds not only how they come into being but also ignores the reality that the alleged neutrality on which they stand is already grounded in ethico-political choices. Thomas Keenan rightly argues that ethics on the pedagogical front demands an openness to the other, a willingness to engage a "politics of possibility" through a continual critical engagement with texts, images, events, and other registers of meaning as they are transformed into public pedagogies.[52] One consequence of linking pedagogy to the specificity of place is that it extends the possibility of making the pedagogical more political. Not only does it foreground the need for educators to rethink the cultural and political baggage they bring to each educational encounter, it highlights the necessity of making educators ethically and politically accountable for the stories they produce, the claims they make upon public memory, and the images of the future they deem legitimate. Pedagogy is never innocent, and if it is to be understood and made problematic as a form of academic labor, educators must not only critically question and register their own subjective involvement in how and what they teach, they must also resist all calls to depoliticize pedagogy through appeals to either scientific objectivity or ideological dogmatism. Far from being disinterested or ideologically frozen, critical pedagogy is concerned about the articulation of knowledge to social effects and succeeds to the degree in which educators encourage critical reflection and moral and civic agency rather than simply mold it. Crucial to the latter position is the necessity for critical educators to be attentive to the ethical dimensions of their own practice.

But as an act of intervention, critical pedagogy needs to be grounded in a project that not only problematizes its own location, mechanisms of transmission, and effects, but also functions as part of a larger project to contest various forms of domination and to help students think more critically about how existing social, political, and economic arrangements might be better suited to address the promise of a radical democracy as an anticipatory rather than messianic goal. Jacques Derrida has suggested that the social function of intellectuals, as well as any viable notion of education, should be grounded in a vibrant politics that makes the promise of democracy a matter of concrete urgency. For Derrida, making visible a "democracy" that is to come, as opposed to that which presents itself in its name, provides a referent for both criticizing everywhere what parades as democracy—"the current state of all so-called democracy"—and for critically assessing the conditions and possibilities for democratic transformation.[53] Derrida sees the promise of democracy as the proper articulation of a political ethics and, by implication, suggests that when higher education is engaged and articulated through the project of democratic social transformation, it can function as a vital public sphere for critical learning, ethical deliberation, and civic engagement. Moreover, the utopian dimension of pedagogy articulated through the project of radical democracy offers the possibility of resistance to the increasing depoliticization of the citizenry, provides a language to challenge the politics of accommodation that connects education to the logic of privatization, refuses to define the citizen as simply a consuming subject, and actively opposes the view of teaching as market-driven practice and learning as a form of training. Utopian, in this sense, is not an antidote to politics, a nostalgic yearning for a better time or for some "inconceivably alternative future." But, by contrast, it is an "attempt to find a bridge between the present and future in those forces within the present which are potentially able to transform it."[54]

In opposition to dominant forms of education and pedagogy that simply reinvent the future in the interest of a present in which ethical principles are scorned and the essence of democracy is reduced to the imperatives of the bottom line, critical pedagogy must address the challenge of providing students with the competencies they need to cultivate the capacity for critical judgment, thoughtfully connect politics to social responsibility, and expand their own sense of agency in order curb the excesses of dominant power, revitalize a sense of public commitment, and expand democratic relations. Animated by a spirit of critique and possibility, critical pedagogy at its best attempts to provoke students to deliberate, resist, and cultivate a range of capacities that enable them to move beyond the world they already know without insisting on a fixed set of meanings.

Against the current onslaught to privatize public schools and vocationalize higher education, progressives need to defend public and higher education as a resource vital to the democratic and civic life of the nation. Central to such a task is the challenge to academics, cultural workers, and labor organizers to find ways to join together in broad-based social movements and oppose the transformation of the public schools and higher education into commercial spheres, to resist what Bill Readings has called a consumer-oriented corporation, more concerned about accounting than accountability.[55] The crisis of public schooling and higher education—while having different registers—needs to be analyzed in terms of wider configurations of economic, political, and social forces that exacerbate tensions between those who value such institutions as public goods and those advocates of neoliberalism who see market culture as a master design for all human affairs. The threat corporate power poses can be seen in the ongoing attempts by neoliberals and other hypercapitalists to subject all forms of public life, including public and higher education, to the dictates of the market while simultaneously working to empty democracy itself of any vestige of ethical, political, and social considerations. What progressives must challenge is the attempt on the part of neoliberals to either define democracy exclusively as a liability or to enervate its substantive ideals by reducing it to the imperatives and freedoms of the marketplace. This requires that educators consider the political and pedagogical importance of struggling over the meaning and definition of democracy and situate such a debate within an expansive notion of human rights, social provisions, civil liberties, equity, and economic justice. What must be challenged at all costs is the increasingly dominant view propagated by neoliberal gurus such as Milton Friedman that profit making is the essence of democracy and accumulating material goods the essence of the good life.

Defending public and higher education as vital democratic spheres is necessary to develop and nourish the proper balance between public values and commercial power, between identities founded on democratic principles and identities steeped in forms of competitive, self-interested individualism that celebrate selfishness, profit making, and greed. Progressives also must reconsider the critical roles educators might take up within public and higher education so as to enable them to oppose those approaches to schooling that corporatize and bureaucratize the teaching process. A critical pedagogy should, in part, be premised on the assumption that educators vigorously resist any attempt on the part of liberals and conservatives to reduce their role in schools to either that of technicians or corporate pawns. Instead, progressive educators might redefine their roles as engaged public intellectuals capable of teaching students the language of informed judgment and possibility as a precondition for social agency. Such a redefinition of purpose, meaning, and politics suggests that educators critically interrogate the fundamental link between knowledge and power, pedagogical practices and social consequences, and authority and civic responsibility.

By redefining the purpose and meaning of schooling as part of a broader attempt to struggle for a radical democratic social order, progressive educators can begin to vigorously challenge a number of dominant assumptions and policies currently structuring public and higher education, including, but not limited to, ongoing attempts by corporate culture to define educators as multinational operatives; escalating efforts by colleges and universities to deny students the loans, resources, and public support they need in order to have access to a quality education; the mounting influence of corporate interests in pressuring universities to reward forms of scholarship that generate corporate profits; increasing attempts to deny women and students of color access to higher education through the reversal of affirmative action policies; and a growing emphasis on the production of knowledge and modes of teaching designed to create marketable products and active consumers.

Increasingly, the corporatization of education functions so as to cancel out the democratic values, impulses, and practices of a civil society by either devaluing or absorbing them within the logic of the market. Educators need a critical language to address these challenges to public and higher education. But they also need to join with other groups outside of the spheres of public and higher education in order to create a national movement that links the defense of noncommodified education with a broader struggle to deepen the imperatives of democratic public life. The quality of educational reform can, in part, be gauged by the caliber of public discourse concerning the role that education plays in furthering not the market driven agenda of corporate interests but the imperatives of critical agency, social justice, and an operational democracy. In this capacity, educators need to develop a language of possibility for raising critical questions about the aim of schooling and for the purpose and meaning of what and how educators teach. In so doing, pedagogy draws attention to engaging classroom practice as moral and political consideration animated by a fierce sense of commitment to expanding the range of individual capacities that enable students to become critical agents, capable of linking knowledge, responsibility, and democratic social transformation.

Approaching pedagogy as a critical and political practice suggests that educators refuse all attempts to reduce classroom teaching exclusively to matters of technique and method. In opposition to such approaches, progressives can highlight the performative character of education as an act of intervention in the world—focusing on pedagogy as a calculated attempt to legitimize and structure the knowledge, values, and social relations that give meaning to everyday classroom life. Within this perspective, critical pedagogy emphasizes the diverse conditions under which authority, knowledge, values, and subject positions are produced and interact within unequal relations of power; it also questions the ideologically laden and often contradictory roles and social functions that educators assume within the classroom. Pedagogy in this view can also be reclaimed as a form of academic labor that bridges the gap between individual considerations and public concerns, affirms bonds of sociality and reciprocity, and interrogates the relationship between individual freedom and privatized notions of the good life and the social obligations and collective structures necessary to support a vibrant democracy.

The question of what educators teach is inseparable from what it means to locate oneself in public discourses and invest in public commitments. Implicit in this argument is the assumption that the responsibility of critical educators cannot be separated from the consequences of the subject positions they have been assigned, the knowledge they produce, the social relations they legitimate, and the ideologies they disseminate to students. Educational work at its best represents a response to questions and issues posed by the tensions and contradictions of the broader society; it is an attempt to understand and intervene in specific problems that emanate from those sites that people concretely inhabit and actually live out their lives and everyday existence. Teaching in this sense becomes performative and contextual, and it highlights considerations of power, politics, and ethics fundamental to any form of teacher-student-text interaction. As I mentioned previously, this suggests the importance of addressing education in political and ethical terms. By drawing attention to pedagogy's productive character, critical educators can highlight pedagogy as the outcome of specific deliberations and struggles that need to be addressed in terms of the "material and historical specificities of (its) enactments"[56] and, in doing so, reject the conservative notion that pedagogy can be theorized as either an a priori set of prescriptions or as a commodity to be applied in any context.

It is crucial to reiterate that any pedagogy that is alive to its own democratic implications is always cautious of its need for closure; it self-consciously resists rigid certainties and a priori answers. Refusing the pull of dogmatism and imperious authority, progressive educators must, at the same time, grasp the complexity and contradictions that inform the conditions under which they produce and disseminate knowledge. Recognizing that pedagogy is the outgrowth of struggles that are historically specific, as are the problems that govern the questions and issues that guide what and how we teach, should not suggest that educators renounce their authority. On the contrary, it is precisely by recognizing that teaching is always an act of intervention inextricably mediated through particular forms of authority that teachers *can* offer students—for whatever use they wish to make of them—a variety of analytic tools, diverse historical traditions, and a wide ranging knowledge of dominant and subaltern cultures and how they influence each other. This is a far cry from suggesting that critical pedagogy define itself either within the grip of a self-righteous mode of authority or completely remove itself from any sense of commitment whatsoever. On the contrary, at stake here is the need to insist on modes of authority that are directive but not imperious, linking knowledge to power in the service of self-production, and encouraging students to go beyond the world they already know to expand their range of human possibilities. Robert Miklitsch rightly argues that teacher authority and institutional positioning are pivotal considerations for analyzing the politics of teaching and the ethical responsibilities that define both the project and the articulation of pedagogy to particular effects. He writes:

> I want to argue . . . that teachers must begin from the pedagogic subject-position to which they have been assigned. If the latter position is not necessarily one of mastery (in either sense of the word), it nonetheless remains one of authority. In other words, to attempt absolutely to renounce the pedagogic subject-position—from whatever motivation, liberal or otherwise—is not only to accede to a "bad" egalitarian logic, it is to evade our responsibility as teachers. And that responsibility—which needless to say, is an implicitly political one—involves recognizing those structures (social, cultural, economic, and so forth) that both enable and constrain our activities.[57]

Academics must deliberate, make decisions, take positions, and, in so doing, recognize that authority "is the very condition for intellectual work" and pedagogical interventions.[58] Miklitsch suggests here that teacher authority cannot be merely renounced as an act of domination, but should be addressed dialectically and deployed strategically so as to enable students to become witnesses to the material and cultural relations of power that often prevent them and others from speaking and acting in particular ways. Authority in this perspective is not simply on the side of oppression but is used to intervene and shape the space of teaching and learning to provide students with a range of possibilities for challenging a society's commonsense assumptions and for analyzing the interface between their own everyday lives and those broader social formations that bear down on them. Authority, at best, becomes both a referent for legitimating a commitment to a particular vision of pedagogy and a critical referent for a kind of auto-critique. It demands consideration of how authority functions within specific relations of power regarding its own promise to provide students with a public space where they can learn, debate, and engage critical traditions in order to imagine otherwise and develop discourses that are crucial for defending vital social institutions as a public good.

Progressive educators need to rethink the tension between the pedagogical and the performative by asking how the performative functions pedagogically. While pedagogy can be understood performatively as an event where many things can happen in the service of learning, it is crucial to stress the importance of democratic classroom relations that encourage dialogue, deliberation, and the power of students to raise questions. Moreover, such relations don't signal a retreat from teacher authority as much as they suggest using authority reflexively to provide the conditions for students to exercise intellectual rigor, theoretical competence, and informed judgments. Thus, students can think critically about the knowledge they gain and what it means to act on such knowledge in order to expand their sense of agency as part of a broader project of increasing both "the scope of their freedoms" and "the operations of democracy."[59] What students learn and how they learn should amplify what it means to experience democracy from a position of possibility, affirmation, and critical engagement. In part, this suggests that progressive educators develop pedagogical practices that open up the terrain of the political while simultaneously encouraging students to "think better about how arrangements might be otherwise."[60]

At its best, critical pedagogy must be interdisciplinary and radically contextual and must engage the complex relationships between power and knowledge, critically address the institutional constraints under which teaching takes place, and focus on how students can engage the imperatives of critical social citizenship. At the same time, critical pedagogy must be self-reflexive about its aims and practices, conscious of its ongoing project of democratic transformation, but openly committed to a politics that does not offer any guarantees. But refusing dogmatism does not suggest that educators descend into a laissez-faire pluralism or an appeal to methodologies designed to "teach the conflicts." On the contrary, it suggests that, in order to make the pedagogical more political, educators afford students with diverse opportunities to understand and experience how politics, power, commitment, and responsibility work on and through them, both within and outside of schools. This, in turn, enables students to locate themselves within an interrelated confluence of ideological and material forces as critical agents who can both influence such forces and simultaneously be held responsible for their own views and actions. Within this perspective, relations between institutional forms and pedagogical practices are acknowledged as complex, open, and contradictory—though always situated within unequal relations of power.[61]

I also want to stress the importance of addressing in any viable theory of critical pedagogy the role that affect and emotion play in the formation of individual identities and social collectivities. Engaging education as a productive and performative force suggests taking seriously those maps of meaning, affective investments, and sedimented desires that enable students to connect their own lives and everyday experiences to what they learn. Pedagogy in this sense becomes more than a mere transfer of received knowledge, an inscription of a unified and static identity, or a rigid methodology; it presupposes that students are moved by their passions and motivated, in part, by the affective investments they bring to the learning process. This suggests, as Paulo Freire points out, the need for a theory of pedagogy willing to develop a "critical comprehension of the value of sentiments, emotions, and desire as part of the learning process."[62] Not only do students need to understand the ideological, economic, and political interests that shape the nature of their educational experiences; they must also address the strong emotional investments they may bring to such beliefs. For Shoshana Felman, this suggests that educators take seriously the role of desire in both ignorance and learning. "Teaching," she explains, "has to deal not so much with lack of knowledge as with resistances to knowledge. Ignorance, suggests Jacques Lacan, is a 'passion.' Inasmuch as traditional pedagogy postulated a desire for knowledge, an analytically informed pedagogy has to reckon with the passion for ignorance."[63] Felman elaborates further on the productive nature of ignorance, arguing, "Ignorance is nothing other than a desire to ignore: its nature is less cognitive than performative . . . it is not a simple lack of information but the incapacity—or the refusal—to acknowledge one's own implication in the information."[64] If students are to move beyond the issue of understanding to an engagement with the deeper affective investments that make them complicitous with oppressive ideologies, they must be positioned to address and formulate strategies of transformation through which their individualized beliefs and affective investments can be articulated with broader public discourses that extend the imperatives of democratic public life. An unsettling pedagogy in this instance would engage student identities and resistances from unexpected vantage points and articulate how they connect to existing material relations of power. At stake here is not only a pedagogical practice that recalls how knowledge, identifications, and subject positions are produced, unfolded, and remembered but also how they become part of an ongoing process, more strategic so to speak, of mediating and challenging existing relations of power.

CONCLUSION

The current cynicism and despair that inform the discourses of many social and educational theorists point to one of the more startling acts of forgetting that has taken place since the 1980s. Increasingly, theorists across the ideological spectrum have either dismissed or ignored the central role that pedagogy has played in foregrounding the connection among teaching and politics, knowledge and power, and learning and social change. Their social amnesia is all the more troubling since pedagogy has a long and critical tradition of defending schooling as a vital public good while promoting the goal of educating students to become socially concerned citizens "who could help determine, through vision and wisdom, the nation's political course."[65] Theorists as different as Frederick Douglas, John Dewey, W. E. B. Dubois, Paulo Freire, and Cornel West have all stressed the crucial link between education and democracy, on the one hand, and pedagogy and the production of critical agents and citizen activists on the other. As a moral and political practice, pedagogy has often been addressed by such theorists as one of the principal means through which to provide students with the knowledge, skills, and experiences that would enable them to understand, engage, and shape the symbolic and institutional conditions that influenced their lives. Within this progressive legacy, education constitutes the ongoing task of being more than a mechanism for social and cultural reproduction. Rather, it is indispensable for understanding public agency and the necessity for creating the democratic identities, values, and relations that provide the conditions for students and others to influence and participate in ongoing conversations about important political and social issues that shape the common good and expand and energize democratic life. In light of the current assault on education and all other aspects of public life by reactionary cultural warriors, heavily financed conservative think tanks, and corporate power, progressives need to rethink both the legacy of education, as a force for democratic social transformation, and pedagogy, as a crucial practice for both understanding and engaging culture as the primary educational force through which agency is shaped, identities are produced, and resistance is constructed. Within this context, pedagogy becomes synonymous with a form of cultural politics that provides an opportunity to expand the sites in which critical pedagogical work takes place (what Raymond Williams called "the sites of permanent education"). This critical work offers new hope for challenging and transforming the politics of despair and cynicism through strategic interventions that offer opportunities for educators to redefine and transform the connections among language, desire, meaning, everyday life, and material relations of power, as part of a broader social movement to reclaim the promise and possibilities of a strong democracy.

5

"SOMETHING'S MISSING"

From Utopianism to a Politics of Educated Hope

NEOLIBERAL HOPES AND PRIVATIZED UTOPIAS

> Any vision of hope that individualizes what is essentially social conjures away a vital dimension of people's being and the chance of living this in a full, rich democratic community.[1]

We live at a time, to paraphrase Fred Jameson, when it has become easier to imagine the end of the world than the end of capitalism.[2] For the left, the militant hope of socialism appears to have collapsed into a century of disastrous betrayals of revolutionary dreams, mass murders, and an endless series of self-deceptions about the promise of a future in which human beings realize their full potential.[3] At the beginning of the new millennium, a combative optimism has given way to a profound pessimism in which it is hard, if not impossible, to imagine a life beyond the "dream world" of capitalism. In short, secular hope, at least in its traditionally leftist versions, appears to have become either an act of bad faith or an illusion.

Historically, utopian thinking has always conjured up a contradictory and contested legacy. While progressive social critics, including Ralph Bellamy, Jacob Riis, John Dewey, Ernst Bloch, and Herbert Marcuse, have embraced it as a basis for challenging existing inequalities and injustices, utopian thinking has received mixed reviews from many notable liberal and progressive thinkers, including Karl Mannheim, Hannah Arendt, Isaiah Berlin, Jacques Derrida, and Vaclav Havel.[4] But tapping into utopian energies has not simply

captured the imagination of some progressive social critics. The call of utopian thinking has also been a driving force of dominant powers, extending
from the Christian church, which proclaims it as one of the three cardinal
virtues, to corporate management teams that use posters, financial incentives,
and other rewards to manipulate workers by fostering a hope that cancels out
forms of despair and resentment that might produce unacceptable levels of
resistance and social criticism. But for most of the latter half of the twentieth
century, many progressives and a large number of cultural activists on the
right have regarded utopianism, though for different reasons, as either a flight
from reality (if not sanity) or as a prelude to state terrorism. For progressives,
utopianism is often denounced for its reliance on grand social schemes that
inevitably lead to the specter of fascism and the legacy of twelve million
slaughtered in the German Holocaust. For many conservatives, utopian idealism bears the burden of legitimating Soviet Communism, with its propensity
for violence and the unprecedented human butchery initiated by Stalin, the
Khmer Rouge, and Mao's Great Leap Forward. Until recently, both the left
and right have viewed utopianism as synonymous with "the major blood-
baths of the twentieth century . . . chalked up to Nazism and Soviet Communism," each representing a different version of utopianism's plunge into massive experiments in social engineering and state control.[5]

The contradictory legacy of utopianism has emerged in full force once
again. Scorned by progressives, and utterly distrusted by cultural conservatives, it has now become a rallying cry for liberal and conservative advocates
of the free market. Within the current historical conjuncture, utopian thinking has narrowed its focus and has become the driving force of neoliberalism,
which argues through its various defenders that utopia has found its ultimate
expression in the latest stage of capitalist democracy. The most famous example of this position can be found in the work of Francis Fukuyama, who
boldly asserts the new vision of hope as the ultimate victory of capitalism
against all other social formations. According to Fukuyama, humankind has
arrived at its final destination, what he terms the "End of History."[6] This is a
period in which capitalism has won a crucial intellectual and political victory,
implying "a common evolutionary pattern for all human societies."[7] In this
view, capitalism has decisively abolished both the need and the necessity for
oppositional notions of hope, not because of a repressive and iniquitous social
and political order, but because the conditions for imagining a better world
no longer exists. Fukuyama is worth quoting at length on this issue:

Today . . . we have trouble imagining a world that is radically better than our
own, or a future that is not essentially democratic and capitalist. Within that

framework many things could be improved. . . . But we cannot picture to ourselves a world that is *essentially* different from the present one, and at the same
time better. Other less reflective ages also thought of themselves as the best, but
we arrive at this conclusion exhausted, as it were, from the pursuit of alternatives we felt *had* to be better than liberal democracy.[8]

Fukuyama's notion of hope represents both the swindle of fulfillment and a
radical deflection from what constitutes a meaningful democracy. As a swindle of fulfillment, it ignores the deep-seated contradictions both within the
United States and outside of its borders in which late capitalism, with its
huge concentrations of power, wealth, and hypercommercialism, furthers instances of exploitation, misery, human suffering, and ecological violence.

Any reference to neoliberal utopianism seems a bit premature in a world
in which, out of a total of six billion human beings, the number of persons
subsisting below the international poverty line rose from 1.2 billion in 1987
to 1.5 billion today and, if recent trends persist, will reach 1.9 billion by
2015." Such figures are exacerbated by the fact that 34,000 children [world-
wide] under age five die daily from hunger and preventable diseases" while,
at the same time, the "world's 200 richest people more than doubled their
net worth in the four years to 1998, to more than $1 trillion. The assets of the
top three billionaires are more than the combined GNP of all least developed
countries and their 600 million people."[9] Moreover, the collapse of democracy into neoliberal capitalism offers up a notion of hope that is utterly personal, displacing grand social and collective hopes with the narrow convic-
tions of the entrepreneurial self unconstrained by the discourse of social
responsibility and public accountability. Neoliberalism offers economic ambition instead of moral idealism and, in the spirit of utopian possibilities,
makes the cash nexus the central feature of social exchange, reinforcing the
presupposition that democracy is compatible with the market-based logic
that all social and public goods are for sale.[10] Autonomy no longer means
developing the capacities for self-development, critical thinking, political
agency, and moral leadership, but has been transformed under the imperatives of the market into a relentless pursuit of personal gain, and an unleash-
ing of brutal self-interests.

As a radical deflection, hope is packaged as the promise of neoliberal capitalism, substituting the celebration of wealth, privilege, and greed for notions
of hope grounded in an opposition to economic injustice, racism, domination, and diverse forms of oppression. Within this discourse, public responsibility is transformed into private gain, and public issues reduced to private
worries. Hope loses its political bearings in this narrative and rewrites social

obligation as the counting up of private gains and rewards. Similarly, hope is abstracted from any notion of social vision and the necessity of keeping social change alive. Mortgaged to the dictates of the global market, the media conglomerates now package hope as either a commodity or as part of a crude survivalist ethic. This is evident in prime time media's offer of hope in the instant fix of game shows such as *Who Wants to Be a Millionaire*. It also finds expression as social Darwinism resurrects itself both as a popular racialized theory of intelligence and as the organizing principle of reality-based television series such as *Mole, Big Brother,* and *Survivor* I & II. Not only do such spectacles celebrate a survival of the fittest ethic, reinforced with large monetary prizes to the lone "survivors," they also relieve viewers of the assumption that they should assume any responsibility for the "weak"—that is, the impoverished and the powerless.

Neoliberalism's dystopian notion of hope is also evident as cultural critics, usually from heavily financed right-wing foundations, endlessly parade in front of the media denouncing any form of social provision that appeals to principles outside of the logic of the market. For example, right-wing cultural critic Dinesh D'Souza, unabashedly condemns social critics who complain about social issues as "self-righteous moralizers" because he imagines that they all share in the wonderful affluence of the society they are criticizing. He points to Mark Petracca, a radical political scientist, who publicly revealed that he has hired a nanny but refused, on principle, to hire a gardener.[11] Petracca's critique of neoliberalism is now cancelled out because he makes enough income to hire a nanny, his hypocrisy as a social critic secured by the fact that he has employed hired-help. D'Souza's tabloidesque exposé is a crude attempt to render Petracca's insightful reminder that beneath capitalism's market-driven utopia are disturbing indications such as the growing divide between the rich and the poor, 13.5 million children living in poverty, unremitting racism, widespread political corruption, and the growth of a horrendously harsh criminal justice system.[12] D'Souza is defensive about the glittering privileges of affluence, but he seems impervious to the fact that such privileges point to vast inequities of power that, as Ellen Willis points out, enable "the rich to dominate politics and policymaking, to defund public goods, to resist regulation, to deny workers job security and benefits, to enforce long hours of work for low wages, to bid up the price of land and housing, to reshape all social institutions on the model of the hierarchical corporation."[13] D'Souza appears indifferent to the fact that Petracca's story about hired help is not a personal lament, but a public intervention against those social and economic forces that produce exploitive dependencies and threaten democracy. Of course, D'Souza has no apologies for his own right-wing policy recommendations and racist ramblings, including the claim that vast civilizational differences exist between blacks and whites or that African Americans are responsible for fostering "black cultural pathology."[14] According to D'Souza's logic, the privileges of corporate global capitalism not only undercut leftist social criticism but also provide a certain legitimacy for the use of racist discourse, especially when it comes from one of capitalism's privileged defenders. For D'Souza, hope resides in the domain of the narrowly personal, while issues regarding crippling poverty, inadequate health care, racial apartheid in the inner cities, and the widening chasm between the classes have been either removed from the inventory of public discourse and social policy or factored into talk-show spectacles. Within this discourse, private gain and unadulterated avarice not only cancel out social criticism, it becomes the only marker of identity, success, and citizenship.

What is most crucial to understand about the rhetoric of hope spewed forth in the breathless rhetoric of the mass media, right-wing free market intellectuals, and governments alike proclaiming the victory of free-market rationality is that it represents both a thinly veiled attack on democratic values and a relentless attempt to undermine and eliminate the public realm as a terrain of deliberation, education, engagement, and social change. Focusing on the growing concentration of wealth and power in the media industry, media analyst Robert W. McChesney lends credence to this position by arguing that neoliberalism produces a culture of hypercommercialism that promotes the "decline, if not the elimination, of notions of public service," and erodes the institutional basis for "having an informed and participating citizenry."[15] Social critic Ronald Aronson rightly argues that the greatest threat coming from models of neoliberal utopianism put forth by conservatives such as Fukuyama and D'Souza lies in their attempts to depoliticize and privatize the public sphere and to reduce ethics and justice to the rules of the market rather than to the democratic imperatives of public life. According to Aronson, market-driven utopias and their conservative ideologues

> have implored us to turn away from the public realm as a terrain for improvement and change, to cut our losses there and limit our involvements, and to instead encourage individual responsibility, personal initiative, and the centrality of people's private activities. Our social order, except where it has tried hard and done too much, may not be perfect but it is good enough. The political realm, at best, provides for essentials of common life, setting rules and providing the absolutely essential infrastructures for private activities, including economic activity. Individual's lives are mostly to be lived in and through these private pursuits.[16]

Complementing Aronson's argument, the esteemed political theorist Sheldon Wolin argues that the distinctiveness of market-driven notions of utopia compared to past theories of utopia is that they no longer preclude the evils of misery, oppression, and dependency. In fact, global capitalism's current appeal to utopia incorporates dystopia as a very condition for its existence. In this accommodating view of utopia, problems can be contained but never eliminated, cleaned up but never purged from the social order. As Wolin points out, "Its opposite is 'inside' because this particular utopia cannot be realized without dystopia, without reproducing it; hence utopia never promises to eliminate dystopia, merely to be allowed to recruit from its meritocratic escapees. The very language used, "the *persistence* of racism," "*generations* of those on welfare," is not meant to call the utopia into question but to state some of its conditions while offering object lessons. . . . A few sacrificial bulls may be offered up but . . . the system could not work without corruption or with republican civic virtue"[17]

Within this dystopian universe, the public realm increasingly becomes an instrumental space "in which substantive private goals of diverse kinds may be pursued."[18] This is evident in the ongoing attempts by many liberals and conservatives to turn commercial-free public education over to market forces, dismantle traditional social provisions of the welfare state, turn over all vestiges of the health care system to private interests, and mortgage social security to the whims of the stock market.[19] Conservatives, such as writer Tom Wolfe, view such moves as integral to what they regard as the triumphalist vision of America.[20]

Liberals are less enamored of the image of the United States as a global haven of democracy, but their tone is more apologetic than critical, more accommodating to the existing social order than resistant. While many liberals may not be ideological cheerleaders for neoliberalism—particularly its more mean-spirited attempts to undermine the most basic safety mechanisms of the welfare state and wreak havoc upon the lives of the poor and dispossessed—they appear *unwilling* to critically engage the assumption that questions set by market forces are the only kind of questions that can be raised about public life. For instance, the philosopher Richard Rorty claims he wants to preserve the discourse of hope while repudiating the self-loathing he ascribes to dissenting left critics who don't share his morally uplifting view of patriotism.[21] Sounding more like a right-wing cultural critic than a liberal, Rorty appears stuck in an odd place politically and theoretically and ultimately links his own version of hope to Harold Bloom's deeply conservative politics of resentment—one that dismisses not only any version of progressive cultural politics, but also rejects any view of pedagogy that suggests that learning is *not* at odds with the imperatives of democratic social change. Rorty wants the university to be a center for social protest, but he has no way of theorizing pedagogy as a political and ethical practice, as an act of resistance aimed at creating the knowledge and skills for students to understand and actively shape, when necessary, the social forces that bear down on their lives. Maybe this is why Rorty has nothing to say about Bloom's reified view of pedagogy as a tool for enlightening the mind or his displacement of education to the realm of pure contemplation.[22] Russell Jacoby believes that Rorty may be suffering from an overdose of irony, and that while "he may believe in liberal ideas and in their future . . . [his] belief lacks conviction." How else to explain Rorty's claim that "I do not think we liberals can now imagine a future of human dignity, freedom, and peace. . . . It is not something we remedy by a firmer resolve, or more transparent prose, or better philosophical accounts of man, truth or history. It is just the way things happen to have fallen out."[23]

Another example of liberal cynicism—with its dystopian belief that ideas can only serve power and that little can be done to imagine or challenge dominant ideological, economic, and political forces—can be found in the recent writings of *New York Times* columnist James Traub. Traub argues that more money will have no effect on schools largely inhabited by the poor, as if lack of basic resources, dilapidated buildings, dysfunctional plumbing, overcrowded classrooms, and underpaid teachers have no bearing on how teachers teach and children learn.[24] Resurrecting a culture of poverty thesis—the underside of the racist social Darwinism theories that have made a comeback under neoliberalism—Traub attributes school failings largely to the cultural capital of the poor and the social relations that inform their everyday life. Missing from this analysis is any reference to either the retrograde public policies that have been put into place by Reagan, Bush (father and son), and Clinton ideologues over the last twenty years or the devastating effects of how power is used in an iniquitous social order, especially in financing public schools, to privilege the children of the rich. The social, as well as the political, drop out of this argument and, in doing so, mimic the discourse of neoliberalism. Of course, there is a certain irony in the fact that many rightwing advocates of the market completely disagree with Traub, calling for the investment of huge sums of money into schools in order to transform them into the primary means for educating children to be workers and consumers. Traub completely ignores this argument in his discussion of public schools. Hence, it comes as no surprise that, in a later article published in the *New York Times Magazine*, Traub practically gloats over the emergence of private, for-profit companies, such as the Global Education Network, that sell college courses over the Internet.[25] Though Traub has some reservations about the corporate leasing of education, it seems that the best way to talk about the meaning, promise, and future of higher education is to examine the way in which the marketplace is combining with the world of the Internet to market online professional education. Within Traub's discourse, ethical, political, and social concerns are displaced for human interest stories in which high-rolling Wall Street financiers, such as Herb Allen, hook up with eccentric faculty, such as Mark Taylor of Williams College (described as a child of '68) to prove that the marketplace is a source of educational innovation and re-form. Traub's celebration of the rise of corporate culture as the new learning culture does more than replay Fukuyama's tired "end of history" mantra, it also offers a conversion story for those who seem to miss the point.

Unsurprisingly, Taylor, the former '60s radical, is transformed into a cor-porate operative who describes his current role within the academy in the following terms: "Insofar as you want to engage in practice responsibly you have to play with the hand you're dealt. And the hand we're dealt seems to me to be one in which the market has certainly won out over other kinds of systems."[26] Taylor now believes that corporate culture and the Internet will change every aspect of the academy. No more tenure, no more unions, no more talk about giving students more control, and no more silly theoretical incursions into the obligations of higher education to link teaching and learn-ing with the demands of critical citizenship, civic courage, and democratic public life. In the end, Traub offers Taylor up as a poster boy for neoliberal-ism and its view of the intellectual as a corporate adventurer who has little interest in producing ideas that are subversive to traditional social orders and absolutely crucial to the political and cultural life of democratic societies. In this scenario, academics become corporate operatives lending their support to neoliberalism's efforts to sweep the globe clean for the investment opportuni-ties of the commanding corporations. Under these circumstances, training replaces education, everyday life becomes standardized and privatized, and capital accumulation becomes the driving force of neoliberal utopianism.

Moral indifference to the suffering of diverse groups, along with a disposi-tion to say little about the role that intellectuals might play as engaged and oppositional social critics, often does more than create apologies and a retreat into a comfortable cynicism parading as the voice of civility; it also reinforces the privileges of a group of intellectuals for whom an accommodation to dominant power appears central to either their sense of professionalism or their entry into the discourse of major media apparatuses. This is cynicism accompanied with a snarl toward those from marginal groups who would dare raise their voice in protest or without fear or embarrassment lay claim to a concrete utopianism. Norman Geras rightly touches on the dialectic of hope and cynicism that weaves through the appeal to utopianism. He writes:

> We should be, without hesitation or embarrassment, utopians. At the end of the twentieth century it is the only acceptable political option, morally speaking . . . irrespective of what may have seemed apt hitherto either inside or outside the Marxist tradition, nothing but a utopian goal will now suffice. The realities of our time are morally intolerable. . . . The facts of widespread human privation and those of political oppression and atrocity are available to all who want them. They are unavoidable unless you wilfully shut them out. To those who would suggest that things might be yet worse, one answer is that of course they might be. But another answer is that for too many people they are already quite bad enough; and the sponsors of this type of suggestion are for their part almost always pretty comfortable.[27]

But if liberals increasingly buy into the new utopianism of the market-place, they do so at a heavy price when it comes to rethinking the role of politics as a mode of critique and oppositional practice. In an age in which the poverty of the social order is increasingly matched by the poverty of intellectual courage, liberal politics becomes dissociated from social movements, cultural power, and policy considerations aimed at promoting collective solutions to collective problems.[28] Divorced from the positive ideals of critical citizenship, the building of democratic public spheres, and the creation of public values that encourage leadership linked to the imperatives of deliberation and the carrying out of social change, politics is now reduced to a hollow myth buttressed by the drama of an ever-changing spectacle. As the realm of politics shrinks in a climate of conservative retrenchment and cultural backlash, academics such as Stanley Fish provide a glimpse of how liberalism abets a devitalized politics in the age of market utopianism. In a *New York Times* op-ed that focuses on the Florida ballot counting controversy, Fish completely ignores the ways in which "the public" is removed from the operations of power that shape an impoverished mode of electoral politics, arguing instead for a notion of politics based almost exclusively on effects, rather than on principles. For Fish, politics is not, in part, about what it means for diverse social actors to inscribe themselves in public struggles in order to shape those cultural and institutional forces that bear down on their lives. On the contrary, politics, for Fish, is given full expression in the willingness of presidential candidates Al Gore and George W. Bush and their supporters to continue to struggle over the ballot controversy as a means to implement their political agendas. Questions regarding what Al Gore or George W. Bush believe, or what the consequences of their actions might mean for society, appear irrelevant in Fish's definition of politics.

This is indeed an example of neoliberal politics without apologies. Reduced to the pragmatics of processes and effects, politics is devitalized as it is removed from broader considerations of justice, compassion, and the ethical imperative to build a better society. Atomized and instrumentalized, politics registers itself as a field of direct action, a reverential embodiment of effects removed from the complexities of context, history, resources, and culture that give it meaning and substance. Politics becomes a metaphor for the entrepreneurial self as the determined, autonomous subject who is able to put his or her practices into effect. Lost in this perspective are important questions about the varied sites, practices, and forms of power that give meaning to how politics is shaped, deployed, and played out on a daily basis. In this view, politics imitates the market to the degree that it highlights the importance of struggle but ignores the ethical implications of such struggles. Politics, in Fish's discourse in particular, has no way of differentiating between struggles based on the narrow imperatives of the market—encapsulated in its relentless appeal to self-interests, its privatized notion of agency, and its obsession with citizenship as an act of consuming—and struggles that call for a restoration of political culture in order to address those social problems that shape everyday life while developing broader movements for social change. What Fish unwittingly promotes is a version of neoliberal politics that consistently works to undermine any attempt to revitalize political culture as an ethical response to the demise of democratic public life. Under such circumstances, liberal and conservative notions of the future increasingly share a view of neoliberal utopianism in which hope is foreclosed around the issue of social justice and expanding democratic relations but entirely open regarding the limitless ability of global capitalism to redefine politics as a function of the market and the good life as the unrelenting pursuit of wealth, material relations of power, and profit.

RETHINKING UTOPIA AS AN
IMAGINED POSSIBILITY

There is a time and place in the ceaseless human endeavor to change the world, when alternative visions, no matter how fantastic, provide the grist for shaping powerful political forces for change. I believe we are precisely at such a moment. Utopian dreams in any case never entirely fade away. They are omnipresent as the hidden signifiers of our desires. Extracting them from the dark recesses of our minds and turning them into a political force for change may court the danger of the ultimate frustration of those desires. But better that, surely, than giving in to the degenerate utopianism of neoliberalism (and all those interests that give possibility such a bad press) and living in craven and supine fear of expressing and pursuing alternative desires at all.[29]

Anti-utopianism now takes a different form and is expressed in neoliberalism's subversion of the critical legacy of utopianism. Feeding into the increasingly dominant view that society *cannot* be fundamentally improved outside of market forces, neoliberalism strips utopianism of its possibilities for social critique and democratic engagement, and, by doing so, it undermines the need to reclaim utopian thinking as both a discourse of human rights and a moral referent for dismantling and transforming dominant structures of wealth and power.[30] To reduce utopian thinking to state terrorism and progressive visionaries to unrealistic, if not dangerous, critics is to come perilously close to adopting what Russell Jacoby calls a "convenient cynicism,"[31] a belief that human suffering, hardship, and massive inequalities in all areas of life are simply inherent in human nature and an irreversible part of the social condition. Within this discourse, hope is foreclosed, politics becomes dull, and resistance is privatized, aestheticized, or degenerated into all forms of hypercommercialized escapism. Against a militant and radically democratic utopianism, neoliberalism not only appears flat; it offers up an artificially conditioned optimism—operating at full capacity in the pages of *Fast Company, Wired Magazine,* and *Forbes* as well as in the relentless entrepreneurial hype of figures such as George Gilder, Tom Peters, and the Nike and Microsoft revolutionaries—in which it becomes increasingly difficult to imagine a life beyond the existing parameters of market pleasures, mail-order catalogues, and shopping malls.[32]

Against the dystopian hope of neoliberalism, I want to argue for the necessity of an oppositional utopianism as a crucial component for those who want to reclaim a notion of ethical advocacy and radically charged politics that provides the basis for reimagining and struggling for a substantive and vital democratic social order "grounded in broad-based civic participation and popular decision making."[33] But recognizing the need to overcome a debilitating pessimism as one of "the most important question[s] that anyone seriously interested in social change must confront"[34] means more than resurrecting an artificially conditioned optimism, it also suggests rethinking the very notion of utopian thinking as central to any viable notion of political agency, pedagogy, and social change.[35]

Since Thomas More first coined the term in 1516, utopianism has barely escaped the original distinction posited by combining the Greek words "good place" and "no place." Defined as an utterly abstract quantity lacking any specificity, utopia as a "no place" was removed from the necessity of a healthy realism capable of identifying ideologies, institutional structures, economic forces, and social formations that provided a historically specific context for change. Utopianism as a "good place" suggested that human beings contained a disposition, capacity, and need for change rooted in the unconscious, elements of fantasy, and desire that was an essential part of human nature. As a "no place," utopian thinking unhinged itself from issues of context, struggle, education, and power, while utopianism as a "good place" fell prey to both essentialist definitions of human needs and human nature and posited the mirage of universal utopia as something that simply had to be discovered.[36] In both definitions, utopianism not only lacks a sense of specificity as a basis for mobilizing diverse resources for better understanding and changing specific historical contexts, it also refuses to recognize that different contexts give rise to diverse alternative visions of the future. As a result, both positions ignore the social gravity of particular relations that articulate between specific discourses, representations, everyday life and structures of power. In addition, neither notion of utopian thinking has any sense of what it might mean to pluralize utopian visions and consequently has little to say about the diverse struggles needed to articulate various utopian interventions to promote strategies aimed at enacting power and changing contexts as part of the wider struggle for a robust and active democracy. Equally important is the failure of both positions to address the pedagogical challenges at work in fashioning those human capacities in which people might recognize the potential they have as political agents capable of imagining new democratic forms of human association in the world and carrying out initiatives necessary to construct them. As illusory as these notions of utopia might be, the greatest dangers facing the twenty-first century do not come from the shortcomings of utopian thinking, but from the wish to refrain from thinking of alternatives to the present—allowing intellectual pessimism to become complicitous with the status quo by degenerating into indifference and quietism. More specifically, the most serious threats come from the increasing prevalence on a global scale of those undemocratic forces that undermine economic, social, and political justice while simultaneously denying the very idea or existence of public spaces that provide the possibility of transforming individual troubles into public issues, private woes into collective struggles.

Utopian thinking matters, but not as a version of privatized hope or as a hope without realism. Within these discourses, possibility gets bad press, collapsing into either a retreat from politics or producing a cynicism in which the "total embrace of the power of reality" is seen as fate or a bad joke.[37] The philosopher Ernst Bloch is instructive here. He counters these notions of utopianism by arguing that hope must be concrete, a spark that not only reaches out beyond the surrounding emptiness of privatization but anticipates a better world in the future, a world that speaks to us by presenting tasks based on the challenges of the present time. For Bloch, utopianism becomes concrete when it links the possibility of the "*not yet*" with forms of political agency animated by a determined effort to engage critically the past and present in order to address pressing social problems and realizable tasks.[38] Bloch believed that utopianism could not be removed from the world and was not "something like nonsense or absolute fancy; rather it is *not yet* in the sense of a possibility; that it could be there if we could only do something for it."[39] As a discourse of critique and social transformation, utopianism in Bloch's view is characterized by a "militant optimism," one that foregrounds the crucial relationship between critical education and political agency, on the one hand, and the concrete struggles needed, on the other hand, to give substance to the recognition that every present was incomplete. For theorists such as Bloch, utopian thinking was anticipatory, not messianic; mobilizing, rather than therapeutic. At best, utopian thinking, as Anson Rabinach argues, "points beyond the given while remaining within it."[40] The longing for a more human society in this instance does not collapse into a retreat from the world but emerges out of critical and practical engagements with present behaviors, institutional formations, and everyday practices. Hope in this context does not ignore the worse dimensions of human suffering, exploitation, and social relations; on the contrary, it acknowledges the need to sustain the "capacity to see the worst and offer more than that for our consideration."[41]

The relevance of the meaning and purpose of utopianism extends beyond a historical legacy of struggle that sought to keep the obstinacy of critical thought alive in the face of the potent forces of brute power, privilege, and indifference. While such legacies are an invaluable resource for critically engaging utopian thinking as a mode of opposition, they also point to the necessity for reinventing the discourse of utopianism as both a referent and a challenge for engaging the debilitating pessimism that currently undermines any progressive notion of social change. The debilitating pessimism in question expresses itself within the current historical conjuncture both as a retreat from the political and an unwillingness on the part of liberals and progressives to produce any real project of transformation.[42] Ellen Willis adds a twist to this logic by claiming that the current collective expression of devalued politics is, in part, due to the anti-utopian belief on the part of many on the right and the left that neoliberal forms of democracy is the best we can do. Willis illustrates this point by criticizing the work of right-wing critic Norman Podhoretz who not only argues the familiar line that utopianism inevitably degenerates into mass terror but goes a step further by concluding that America's best defense against such a fate is to support "democracy as it presently exists in the world."[43] In this logic, democracy is not only anti-utopian, but becomes synonymous with the status quo. Willis responds to this argument by rightly arguing that utopianism has not only produced its negation in communist totalitarianism but has also produced an ideal of democracy. She writes:

> The ideal of democracy as something more than just "what is" is not purely abstract for Americans. It is a dynamic, if often submerged, element in our culture, reflected in the irreverence toward authority and toward one's "betters," the expansive optimism, the surge to transcend limits, the penchant for self-invention, the belief in material pleasure as a human right for which Americans are justly known. That these very impulses, especially in the last mentioned, have often been enlisted in the service of corporate power and profits is also true. The point, though, is this: perhaps America's distinctive contribution to a global democratic politics is the idea of an immanent utopia—a vision of freedom and equality constructed from those democratic tropisms already embedded in our bones, a movement propelled not only by dissatisfaction with what is, but by appreciation of what is incipient.[44]

In Willis's perspective, utopianism registers both a refusal to collapse meaningful democracy into the status quo and an appeal to a spirit of resistance that defines democracy as the very basis for political agency and social change. For Willis, imagining otherwise is part of a long tradition of democratic struggle that should be at the heart of utopian thinking. Ruth Levitas qualifies Willis's remarks by arguing more specifically that liberating the imagination must do more than liberate the desire for pleasure and the impulse of freedom; it must also address the specifics of social change:

> The main reason why it has become so difficult to locate utopia in a future credibly linked to the present by a feasible transformation is that our images of the present do not identify agencies and processes of change. The result is that utopia moves further into the realms of fantasy. Although this has the advantage of liberating the imagination from the constraint of what it is possible to imagine as possible—and encouraging utopia to demand the impossible—it has the disadvantage of severing utopia from the process of social change and severing social change from the stimulus of competing images of utopia.[45]

I want to build upon this defense of utopian thinking by arguing that, for utopianism to become significant as a basis for reclaiming and redefining the value of political agency and struggle, it will have to do more than appeal to lofty social visions or call for changes such as the end of neoliberalism as a permanent feature of the world. Both appeals are important, but are not enough. Within the current social order, it is crucial to go further by resurrecting utopianism's most radical implications. Not only does this include mobilizing social visions that have meaningful connections to the experiences, problems, and material relations of power that constitute the terrain of social change, but also lays claim to the crucial idea that public life is conditioned rather than determined and that the essence of politics and moral responsibility lies in believing that human beings have the capacity to intervene in, influence, and shape the forces that structure their lives. Utopian thinking in this sense consists of the seemingly anachronistic idea that political agency becomes meaningful as an act of intervening in the world, and that such interventions reflect a commitment to an ethical ideal grounded in public struggles.[46] Utopianism, at its best, rejects the corporate colonization of the public sphere while affirming the vital democratic core at the center of politics and in doing so provides a vocabulary of civic-mindedness that focuses on "such values as citizen participation, the public good, political obligation, social governance, and community."[47] Against the notion that the world is fully ordered, rendering notions of judgment and responsibility mute, utopian thinking offers resistance against those ideologies of historical inevitability rooted in the pseudo-authority of extra social forces.[48] In this discourse, human agency is not molded but encouraged.[49] Hence, utopian thinking has to make questions of pedagogy *and* political agency central to its definition of critique and possibility, but it can only do this if it situates such a task within a project that rescues democracy from neoliberalism while at the same time pointing to the promise of a social order that creates the social, political, and economic structures necessary for it to truly turn power over to the people. Zygmunt Bauman captures brilliantly what is at stake when democratic visions fall into disrepute and private satisfactions become the sine quo non of freedom:

> We tend to be proud of what we perhaps should be ashamed of, of living in the "post-ideological" or "post-utopian" age, of not concerning ourselves with any coherent vision of the good society and of having traded off the worry about the public good for the freedom to pursue private satisfaction. And yet if we pause to think why that pursuit of happiness fails more often than not to bring about the results we hoped for . . . we won't get far without bringing back from exile ideas such as the public good, the good society, equity, justice and so— ideas that make no sense unless cared for and cultivated in company with oth-

ers. Nor are we likely to get the fly of insecurity out of the ointment of individual freedom without resorting to politics, using the vehicle of political agency and charting the direction which that vehicle should follow.[50]

To Bauman's credit he defends a notion of utopian thinking and political agency that affirms the need for people to enter the world of politics, invoke social visions of the future, and engage in collective efforts for social transformation. Yet, he also underscores a view of social change that addresses the urgency of creating the political and pedagogical conditions in which people armed with critical forms of knowledge and skills can discover their potential and imagine themselves as social agents struggling to further the ideals of a full and rich democracy.

Contemporary critics, such as Ellen Willis, Ron Aronson, Sharon Welch, Howard Zinn, and David Harvey, do a theoretical service in connecting utopian thinking to the project of radical democracy. In fact, I would argue that one of the central principles for reclaiming utopian thinking is precisely the need to bring political agency and culture back to life as an ethical and critical response to the demise of democratic public life. There are hints of such a position, for example, in the work of a vast array of other cultural critics, including political theorists such as Paul Gilroy, Carl Boggs, and Michael Berube.[51] Utopian thinking becomes evident particularly in their call for progressives to develop a public culture that promotes self- and social development, engages in diverse forms of cultural critique, and attempts to affect public policy. But the leap in these important discourses from critique to action appears a bit slippery, especially since such critics rarely say anything about how it might be possible to create either the pedagogical conditions or the agents who might participate in such a project. The call to politics often appears too abstract because there is no sense in these discourses about what it means pedagogically to provide the conditions for people to actually imagine themselves as agents capable of contesting the very systems they want to change. Recognizing this political lacunae is all the more crucial if cultural studies theorists and progressives are to avoid running the risk of sharing with the enemies of cultural politics both a critique of the rising anti-intellectualism in all facets of American life and a refusal to address the role that intellectuals might play both within and outside of the university in challenging such anti-intellectualism as part of a broader pedagogical project for developing critical modes of political agency. Progressives should take note of the contradiction among social conservatives on the left such as Todd Gitlin, who decries the rising tide of anti-intellectualism in American life while at the same time denouncing the academy as a site of contestation and political education.[52] Against this theoretical lacuna, I want to posit the position that any viable notion of concrete and militant utopianism has to connect issues of politics and power, on the one hand, and ethics and social agency, on the other, to the idea of educated hope.[53]

Educated hope combines the pedagogical and the political in ways that stress the contextual nature of learning, emphasizing that different contexts give rise to diverse questions, problems, and possibilities. In doing so, educated hope underscores the need for progressives to be attentive to the ways in which institutional and symbolic power are tangled up with everyday experience. It also registers politics as a pedagogical and performative act, an act that is the outcome of situated struggles dedicated to creating the conditions and capacities for people to become critically engaged political agents. Educated hope as a form of militant utopianism registers politics as a matter of desire, intervention, and struggle. It also takes seriously the importance of civic education while recognizing that such education takes place within a vast array of pedagogical sites throughout the culture. As a form of utopian thinking, educated hope provides the foundational connection that must be made among three discourses that often remain separated: democracy, political agency, and pedagogy. One instructive example of such a call can be found in the work of Marshall Berman.

Berman has recently argued in the pages of *Dissent* that America at the present historical moment is suffering from the lack of a critical culture, "one that struggles actively over how human beings should live and what our life means"[54] In his call to restore such a culture, Berman urges a revival of the practice of what he terms "jaytalking," a form of resistance marked by the willingness to "talk back . . . to talk outside the designated lines."[55] While Berman, on one level, is lampooning Giuliani-type politicians who value order over living in a critical culture, he is also calling for the emergence of oppositional public spaces in the universities, schools, and mass media along with the creation of neighborhoods capable of sustaining experimental theaters, alternative book stores, and independent coffee shops—all those places that are capable of generating spaces in which a critical culture is nurtured through various forms of pedagogical and community building activity.

While many critics, such as Andrew Delbanco, dismiss Berman's suggestions either as "an uncritical nostalgia for the 1960s" or as a vision without any specificity, the real fear at work in such comments lies in the possibility of linking education to social change, learning to critical consciousness, and pedagogy to the imperative of creating political agents—both individual and collective—capable of producing alternative public spheres.[56] This position is somewhat more honestly stated by Roger Shattuck, who inveighs against the so-called politicization of education while at the same time claiming that its real purpose should be to "socialize the young into the existing culture." Instead of teaching students to recognize anti-democratic forms of power, providing them with knowledge that expands their capacity for participating in and shaping public life, Shattuck wants to substitute engaged dialogue, critical thinking, and the possibility for developing social agency for a form of higher education whose purpose is "the transmission of a precious heritage." As part of this undertaking, Shattuck invokes what may be called the "gonad theory" of education to justify such a passive view of pedagogy and devitalized notion of citizenship. He argues:

> Our gonads represent the most stable and protected element in the body and are usually able to pass on unchanged to the next generation the genetic material we were born with. . . . Except for radiation and a few diseases, the life we live does not affect our gonads. No such biological process is built into cultures. But all cultures have discovered something similar—an activity, sometimes developed into an institution, we call education. By education we pass on to the young the customs, restrictions, discoveries, and wisdom that have afforded survival so far. There is good reason to maintain that, unlike many other institutions—political, social, and artistic—which may criticize and rebel against the status quo, education should remain primarily a conservative institution, like our gonads.[57]

There you have it. Not only do conservatives, such as Charles Murray, now invoke a nineteenth-century version of social Darwinism to justify a racist theory of intelligence, but they inspire ideologues such as Roger Shattuck to invoke the biological law of the male testicles to legitimate reducing the purpose of higher education, and education in general, to the grim role of moral and social reproduction, whose aim is simply to transmit the heritage of knowledge, enshrined by conservatives like Shattuck.

Berman's comments, though overly generalized, not only challenge the pessimism and utterly conservative views of educators as different as Delbanco and Shattuck, they are also important because they gesture toward a notion of utopianism as a form of educated hope, one that views politics as including a critical, vital, and constitutive pedagogical dimension. While Berman's comments do not refer to the specific ideas, visions, and modes of critiques that have informed a long and noble tradition of leftist struggles—a missed opportunity on his part to engage the experiences of memory as a form of public pedagogy—they do raise important questions about the pedagogical conditions, cultural practices, and modes of educated hope necessary for cultural politics and social change.

EDUCATED HOPE AND THE PROMISE
OF DEMOCRACY

> Consuming is the core of the modern identity. I fear this is, in part, because we have lost hope in any alternative. Our imaginations are dimmed. Our hopes for a more equitable society are feeble. . . . If our model of human nature is based only on reciprocity and economic exchange, then we are stuck with just that and no more. We have capacities for much deeper commitments, commitments that can make us good and our lives meaningful, but these stay small and private in an environment that lacks hope for a better society.[58]

> The triumph of democracy has been proclaimed as the triumph of "individualism." But this "individualism" is not and cannot be an empty form wherein individuals "do what they like"—any more than "democracy"can be simply procedural in character. "Democracy procedures" are each time filled by the oligarchical character of the contemporary social structure—as the "individualistic" form is filled by the dominant social imaginary, the capitalist imaginary of the unlimited expansion of production and consumption.[59]

Within the last few decades, a number of theorists have begun to raise fundamental questions about the complex relationships among power and democracy. Cultural studies theorists, such as Stuart Hall, Lawrence Grossberg, and Toby Miller, have provided valuable contributions to our understanding of how culture deploys power and is shaped and organized within diverse systems of representation, production and consumption, and mechanisms of regulation and distribution. Central to such work has been how the entanglement of symbolic and institutional forms of culture and power constitute identities, modes of agency, and the social world itself. Within this discourse is the crucial implication that the production of social meaning is the precondition for all meaningful practices. For instance, Stuart Hall has contended that "Cultural change is constitutive of political change and moral awareness of human consciousness."[60] Cary Nelson and Dilip Parameshwar have argued that cultural studies exhibits a deep concern with "how objects, discourses, and practices construct possibilities for and constraints on citizenship."[61] Refusing to split the academic and the political, cultural studies theorists such as Richard Johnson and George Lipsitz have argued that it is crucial for critical educators to defend public and higher education as significant sites of "real" political struggle while at the same time establishing important connections to popular formations outside of the terrain of schooling.[62]

While I take no issue with these concerns, I want to suggest that for too many cultural studies theorists, pedagogy, when invoked as an important political practice, is either limited to the role that oppositional intellectuals might play within academia or is reduced almost entirely to forms of learning that take place in schools. While pedagogy is often related to issues of democracy, citizenship, and the struggle over the shaping of identities and identifications, it is rarely taken up as part of a broader public politics—as part of a larger attempt to explain how learning takes place outside of schools. Put differently, pedagogy is limited to what goes on *in* schools, and the role of cultural studies theorists who address pedagogical concerns is largely reduced to doing or applying cultural studies within such sites of learning. For instance, within this discourse, cultural studies pedagogues can teach students how to look at the media (industry or texts), analyze audience reception, challenge rigid disciplinary boundaries, critically engage popular culture, produce critical knowledge, or use cultural studies to revitalize the curricula and disciplinary formations within public schools and higher education. One of the foremost cultural studies theorists, Lawrence Grossberg, suggests that the challenge cultural studies presents to critical pedagogues is to produce what he calls a "cultural studies of education."[63] Such a project would be concerned with analyzing "what is actually going on in classrooms," addressing how certain issues such as school violence serve as "articulatory points in larger struggles," using cultural studies as part of teacher training programs, or helping teachers and students to develop more sophisticated theoretical models for "rethinking the relations of power in schooling."[64] Angela McRobbie echoes Grossberg's position by arguing that theory can ground itself pedagogically by recognizing "its own place in the classroom."[65] Drawing upon the work of Gayatri Spivak, McRobbie argues that the only way in which cultural studies can address the politics of its pedagogical practices is through engaging the lived experiences that students bring with them to the classroom. Such positions get written in somewhat reductive ways by a host of cultural theorists. For instance, Shane Gunster has argued that the main contribution that cultural studies makes to pedagogy "is that insistence that any kind of critical education must be rooted in the culture, experience, and knowledge that students bring to the classroom."[66] While this is an important insight, it has been argued in enormously sophisticated terms for over fifteen years by a host of progressive educators. But the problem lies not in Gunster's unfamiliarity with such scholarship, but in his willingness to repeat the presupposition that the exclusive site in which pedagogy becomes a relevant object of analysis is the classroom. If he had crossed the disciplinary boundaries that he decries in celebration of cultural studies, he would have found that theorists such as Roger Simon and others have expanded a definition of pedagogy that extends far beyond the classroom. But the main challenge I wish to address comes from the important work of cultural studies theorists such as Grossberg and McRobbie.

I think Grossberg and McRobbie are both right and wrong. Grossberg is right in emphasizing that cultural studies has an important role to play in helping educators rethink, among other things, the nature of pedagogy, disciplinary formations, the purpose of schooling, and the impact on schools of larger social forces. And, surely, McRobbie repeats a now familiar refrain, if not a cliche, among critical educational theorists about connecting pedagogy to the histories, lived experiences, and discourses that students bring to the classroom. But I think both are remiss in suggesting that pedagogy is primarily about schools and that the intersection of cultural studies and pedagogy has little to do with theorizing the role that pedagogy might play in linking learning to social change outside of traditional sites of schooling.[67] Pedagogy, at its best, implies that learning takes place across a spectrum of social practices and settings in society. As a central element of educated hope, pedagogy points to both the multiplicity of sites in which education takes place and, as Roger Simon points out, emphasizes the importance of various cultural workers

> to comprehend the full range of multiple, shifting and overlapping of sites of learning that exist within the organized social relations of everyday life. This means being able to grasp, for example, how workplaces, families, community and institutional health provision, film and television, the arts, groups organized for spiritual expression and worship, organized sport, the law and the provision of legal services, the prison system, voluntary social service organizations, and community based literacy programs all designate sets of organized practices within which learning is one central feature and outcome.[68]

The concept of educated hope rests on a much more expansive notion of pedagogy. Moreover, it points to broader considerations about the role that education now plays in a variety of cultural sites and how the latter have become integral to producing models of human nature through the pedagogical force of a "capitalist imaginary" based almost "exclusively on economic exchange" as mentioned by Cornelius Castoriadis and Randolph Nesse in the epigraphs that introduce this section. As I have stressed throughout this book, a democratically engaged cultural politics requires that progressives both understand and challenge how neoliberalism undermines meaningful democracy in its relentless attempts to valorize private space over public space, commercial goods over public goods, and a wholly privatized, personal notion of citizenship over public citizenship and social provision. Progressives will have to challenge forcefully the portrayal of public space as simply an investment opportunity as well as the increasing attempt by neoliberals to represent the public good as a metaphor for public disorder. In doing so, they will have to address the profound role that the pedagogical force of the broader culture currently plays in producing public transcripts and modes of political agency that shut down democratic relations, identities, and visions. But if progressives are to develop an oppositional cultural politics, it will require more than simply the language of critique.[69] As important as immanent critique might be, it always runs the risk both of representing power as being in the absolute service of domination and failing to capture the always open and ongoing dynamic of resistance at work in alternative modes of representations, oppositional public spheres, and modes of affective investment that refuse the ideological push and institutional drive of dominant social orders.[70]

Combining the discourse of critique and hope is crucial to affirming that critical activity offers the possibility for change. One option that progressives might make in the service of social transformation might be to develop an oppositional cultural politics that takes on the tasks of engaging basic considerations of social citizenship aimed at expanding democratic rights while developing collective movements that can challenge the subordination of social needs to the dictates of commercialism. Central to such a politics would be a public pedagogy that attempts to make visible in a wide variety of sites alternative models of radical democratic culture that raise fundamental questions about the relationship between political agency and social responsibility. At the very least, such a pedagogy involves using theory as a resource to understand and critically engage dominant public transcripts and values within a broader set of historical and institutional contexts. Making the political more pedagogical in this instance suggests producing modes of knowledge and social practices that not only affirm oppositional cultural work but offer opportunities to mobilize instances of collective outrage, if not collective action, against glaring material inequities and the growing cynical belief that today's culture of investment and finance makes it *impossible* to address many of the major social problems facing both the United States and the larger world. Most importantly, such work points to the link between civic education and modes of oppositional political agency that are pivotal to a elucidating a politics that promotes autonomy and social change, a politics of autonomy that is especially relevant to promoting the rights of immigrants and labor while expanding the social obligations and rights of citizenship beyond the borders of the nation-state.[71] Unfortunately, many progressives have failed to take seriously Antonio Gramsci's insight that "[e]very relationship of 'hegemony' is necessarily an educational relationship"—with its implication that education as a cultural pedagogical practice takes place across multiple sites as it signals how, within diverse contexts, education makes us both subjects of and subject to relations of power.[72] I want to build on Gramsci's insight by exploring in greater detail the connection among democracy, political agency, and pedagogy by analyzing some of the work of French philosopher Cornelius Castoriadis and the English cultural critic Raymond Williams. Both of these theorists have made seminal, and often overlooked, contributions to the discourse of utopian thinking and the role of education central to the regime of political democracy. I focus on this radical tradition in order to reclaim a legacy of critical thinking that combines a concrete and militant sense of utopianism with the imperatives of a participatory civic education designed to enrich and enable the possibility of political agency and its crucial role in struggling for a radical democracy.[73] This tradition of critical thought signals for progressives the importance of investing in the political as part of a broader effort to revitalize notions of democratic citizenship, social justice, and the public good.

Castoriadis and Williams were deeply concerned about what it meant to think about politics and agency in light of the new conditions of capitalism that threatened to undermine the promise of democracy at the end of the twentieth century. Moreover, both theorists, in different ways, argue that education in the broadest sense is a principal feature of politics because it provides the capacities, knowledge, skills, and social relations through which individuals recognize themselves as social and political agents. Linking such a broad-based definition of education to issues of power and agency also raises fundamental questions that go to the heart of any substantive notion of democracy: How do issues of history, language, culture, and identity work to articulate and legitimate particular exclusions? If culture in this sense becomes the constituting terrain for producing identities and constructing social subjects, education becomes the strategic and positional mechanism through which such subjects are addressed, positioned within social spaces, located within particular histories and experiences, and always arbitrarily displaced and decentered as part of a pedagogical process that is increasingly multiple, fractured, and never homogenous.

Cornelius Castoriadis has, in the last thirty years of the twentieth century, provided an enormous theoretical service in analyzing the space of education as constitutive of the site of democratic struggle. Castoriadis pursues the primacy of education as a political force by focusing on democracy as both the realized power of the people and as a mode of autonomy. In the first instance, he insists that "democracy means power of the people . . . a regime aspiring to social and personal" freedom.[74] Democracy in this view suggests more than a simply negative notion of freedom in which the individual is defended against power. On the contrary, Castoriadis argues that any viable notion of democracy must reject this passive attitude toward freedom with its view of power as a necessary evil. In its place, he calls for a productive notion of power, one that is central to embracing a notion of political agency and freedom that affirms the equal opportunity of all to exercise political power in order to participate in shaping the most important decisions affecting their lives.[75] He ardently rejects the increasing "abandonment of the public sphere to specialists, to professional politicians."[76] Just as he rejects any conception of democracy that does not create the means for "unlimited interrogation in all domains," that closes off in "advance not only every political question as well as every philosophical one, but equally every ethical or aesthetic question,"[77] Castoriadis refuses a notion of democracy restricted to the formalistic processes of voting while, at the same time, arguing that the notion of participatory democracy cannot remain narrowly confined to the political sphere.

Democracy, for Castoriadis, must also concern itself with the issue of cultural politics. He rightly argues that progressives are required to address the ways in which every society creates what he calls its "social imaginary significations," which provide the structures of representations that offer individuals selected modes of identifications, provide the standards for both the ends of action and the criteria for what is considered acceptable or unacceptable behavior while establishing the affective measures for mobilizing desire and human action.[78] The fate of democracy for Castoriadis is inextricably linked to the profound crisis of contemporary knowledge, characterized by its increasing commodification, fragmentation, privatization, and turn toward racial and patriotic conceits. As knowledge becomes abstracted from the demands of civic culture and is reduced to questions of style, ritual, and image, it undermines the political, ethical, and governing conditions required for individuals and social groups either to participate in politics or construct those viable public spheres necessary for debate, collective action, and solving urgent social problems. As Castoriadis suggests, the crisis of contemporary knowledge provides one of the central challenges to any viable notion of politics and educated hope. He writes:

> Also in question is the relation of . . . knowledge to the society that produces it, nourishes it, is nourished by it, and risks dying of it, as well as the issues concerning for whom and for what this knowledge exists. Already at present these problems demand a radical transformation of society, and of the human being, at the same time that they contain its premises. If this monstrous tree of knowledge that modern humanity is cultivating more and more feverishly every

day is not to collapse under its own weight and crush its gardener as it falls, the necessary transformations of man and society must go infinitely further than the wildest utopias have ever dared to imagine.[79]

Castoriadis was particularly concerned about how progressives might address the crisis of democracy in light of how social and political agents were being produced in a society driven by the glut of specialized knowledge, consumerism, and a privatized notion of citizenship that no longer supported noncommercial values and increasingly dismissed, as a constraint, any view of society that emphasized public goods and social responsibility. What is crucial to acknowledge in Castoriadis's view of democracy is that the crisis of democracy cannot be separated from the dual crisis of representation and political agency. In a social order in which the production of knowledge, meaning, and debate are highly restricted, not only are the conditions for producing critical social agents limited, but also lost is the democratic imperative of affirming the primacy of ethics as a way of recognizing a social order's obligation to future generations. Ethics in this sense recognizes that the extension of power assumes a comparable extension in the field of ethical responsibility, a willingness to acknowledge that ethics means being able to answer in the present for actions that will be borne by generations in the future.[80] This leads directly to Castoriadis's concern with linking the meaning and purpose of democracy to the project of autonomy.

As a project of autonomy, democracy implies a mode of politics that puts into question a society's "already given institutions, its already established representation of the world."[81] Within this perspective, politics, in part, implies a rejection of all those forms of authority that impute their existence to transcendent and extra social sources, such as God or the market, and, in doing so, produce a notion of authority that refuses to "render an account and provide reasons . . . for the validity of its pronouncements."[82] Autonomy as a project of democracy renders society as a social-historical creation and politics as part of a broader concern with power and justice "to create citizens who are critical thinkers capable of putting existing institutions into question so that democracy again becomes society's movement . . . that is to say, a new type of regime in the full sense of the term."[83] For Castoriadis, the project of autonomy was incompatible with the corporatist emphasis on mastery, "perpetual restlessness, constant change, a thirst for the new for the sake of the new and for more for the sake of more."[84]

Central to Castoriadis's work is the crucial acknowledgment that society creates itself through a multiplicity of organized pedagogical forms that provide the "instituting social imaginary" or field of cultural and ideological representations through which social practices and institutional forms are endowed with meaning, generating certain ways of seeing the self and its possibilities in the world. Not only is the social individual constituted, in part, by internalizing such meanings, but he or she acts upon such meanings in order to also participate and, where possible, to change society. According to Castoriadis, politics within this framework becomes the collective activity whose object is to put into question the explicit institutions of society while simultaneously creating the conditions for individual and social autonomy.[85] In this instance, civic literacy and education are not only about competency, but also about the possibility of understanding and interpretation as an act of ntervention. Castoriadis's unique contribution to democratic political theory lies in his keen understanding that autonomy is inextricably linked to forms of civic education that provide the conditions for bringing to light how explicit and implicit power can be used to open up or close down those public spaces that are essential for individuals to meet, address public interests, engage pressing social issues, and participate collectively in shaping public policy. In this view, civic education brings to light "society's instituting power by rendering it explicit . . . it reabsorbs the political into politics as the lucid and deliberate activity whose object is the explicit [production] of society."[86] According to Castoriadis, political agency involves learning how to deliberate, make judgments, and exercise choices, particularly as the latter are brought to bear as critical activities that offer the possibility of change. Civic education, as it is experienced and produced throughout a vast array of institutions, provides individuals with the opportunity to see themselves as more than they simply are within the existing configurations of power of any given society. Every society has an obligation to provide citizens with the capacities, knowledge, and skills necessary for them to be, as Aristotle claimed, "capable of governing and being governed."[87] A democracy cannot work if citizens are not autonomous, self-judging, and independent—qualities that are indispensable for them to make vital judgments and choices about participating in and shaping decisions that affect everyday life, institutional reform, and governmental policy. Hence, civic education becomes the cornerstone of democracy in that the very foundation of self-government is based on people not just having the "typical right to participate; they should also be educated [in the fullest possible way] in order to be *able* to participate."[88] At stake here, as John Binde writes, is not only the legitimacy of civic education as a cultural practice, but utopian thinking as an ethics of the future:

> The human city represents the ideal context for civic education and the promotion of the value of alterity. But, beyond the political feat involved, the stakes
> . . . are cultural. It is not merely a matter of transforming minds in order to

adapt them to the requirements of our contemporary world. It is also necessary to change attitudes, customs, and lifestyles. Preparing citizens for the future is just as much about giving them the means to think as about giving them the freedom and will to do so. If devoid of the strength of will and the certainty of decision, knowledge is either suffering or sheer bliss. The ethics of the future therefore deserves to be part and parcel of an educational design.[89]

Castoriadis was deeply concerned about the relationship among autonomy, judgment, and critical participation in democratic public life. He recognized that people had to learn from a variety of educational spheres the skills needed to be active citizens. But he never substituted the postmodern emphasis on skepticism and irony for the courage and judgments that were necessary in order for intellectuals and others to take a stand in the face of the current onslaughts against humanity and democracy by both a rapacious neoliberalism and various updated versions of totalitarianism. Skepticism was an element of autonomy, but not an end in itself. Autonomy makes justice and the just society the first resort of its discourse and dialogue, deliberation, and social action its outcome. It rejects postmodern versions of skepticism, which increasingly have little to say about the need to address how one must act in the interest of the greatest possible justice. At the same time, autonomy does not offer up a politics of guarantees as much as it claims, as Jacques Derrida puts it, that "There is no 'politics,' no law, no ethics without responsibility of a decision which, to be just, cannot content itself with applying existing norms or rules but must take the absolute risk, in every singular instant. . . . To that end, one must change laws, habits . . . the entire horizon of 'the political,' of citizenship, of belonging to a nation, and of the state."[90] Autonomy, according to Castoriadis, rejects any notion of skepticism that does not open up the terrain of the political. At stake here is the call not to simply problematize the political, but to take the next step and extend its possibilities by opening up new locations for resistance, struggle, pleasures, and social relations that expand the public culture, social agency, and meaningful democracy. Autonomy, in this instance, is not only about problematizing meaning but also about providing the conditions for reappropriating and resuscitating political culture as an ethical response to the demise of democratic public life.

Raymond Williams also linked questions of culture and democracy to the related issues of political agency, pedagogy, and democratic social change.[91] Williams shared Castoriadis's view that individuals and institutions would have to change together for any notion of meaningful democracy to come into being. This suggested, for Williams, that progressives would have to pay closer "attention to the complex ways in which individuals are formed by the institutions to which they belong, and in which, by reaction, the institutions took on the color of individuals thus formed."[92] Williams also focused on the crucial political question of how agency unfolds within a variety of cultural spaces structured within unequal relations of power.[93] He was especially concerned about the connections between pedagogy and political agency, particularly in light of the emergence of a range of new technologies that both proliferated the amount of information available to people while, at the same time, constricted the substance and ways in which such meanings entered the public domain. The realm of culture for Williams had taken on a new role in the latter part of the twentieth century because the actuality of economic power and its attendant networks of control now exercised more influence than ever before in shaping how identities are produced, desires mobilized, and particular social relations assume the force and meaning of common sense.[94]

Williams clearly understood that making the political more pedagogical meant recognizing that where and how the psyche locates itself in public discourse, visions, and passions provides the groundwork for agents to enunciate, act, and reflect on themselves and their relations to others and the wider social order. Making the political more pedagogical, according to Williams, raised important questions about what it might mean for individuals to grasp the tasks and problems confronting democracy on a global scale, especially within the current dominance of political, cultural, and economic forces that are undermining the very possibility of democracy.

In an effort to bring ethical and political culture back to life, Williams attempted to rearticulate the relationship between political agency, cultural politics, and radical democracy. While it is impossible to do justice to the range and depth of his work, I want to point to three elements in his thinking that, in my mind, articulate a crucial set of referents for reclaiming utopian thinking as a form of educated hope.[95] First, Williams strove to redefine the purpose and meaning of democracy by providing a new vocabulary for modern politics. Democracy was not simply about guaranteeing individual rights and extending democratic ownership and control to all aspects of cultural and economic life; it was also about creating the pedagogical conditions, cultural spheres, and public spaces that allowed people to express and create the public values and practices of a substantive democracy. The meaning of democracy could not be defined simply through the lens of power, but also had to be understood as an ethical, political, and educational relationship. For instance, Williams in his classic book, *The Long Revolution,* made the relationship between education and democracy central to utopian thinking. He writes:

Utopian thinking is that which supposes we shall get an educated and participating democracy. . . . It is a question of whether we can grasp the real nature
of our society, or whether we persist in social and educational patterns . . .
cemented by forces that cannot be challenged and will not be changed. The
privileges and barriers, of an inherited kind, will in any case go down. It is only
a question of whether we replace them by the free play of the market, or by a
public education designed to express and create the values of an educated democracy and a common culture.[96]

Like Castoriadis, Williams believed that democracy was about both dismantling hierarchical and oppressive relations of power and providing the social
provisions for all individuals to have access to the political and cultural resources that enabled them to participate in and shape the larger society.[97]
Cultural critic John Brenkman, argues persuasively that at the heart of Williams' project was an attempt to link democracy with the best ideals of socialism, and that the expansive nature of such a democratic project is evident in
Williams's long-standing call for

a deep, pervasive change in institutions and in the very character of social relationships, from the impersonal relationships through which the society's wealth
is created and distributed down to the personal relationships in which moral
attitudes and mutual obligations are enacted.[98]

Williams's call for a new vocabulary and politics suitable for constructing a
radical democratic social order did more than construct a prophetic vision for
social change. This points to his second important contribution to the notion
of educated hope. Williams reinvented the notion of education as central to
both established forms of public and adult education, but he also articulated
an understanding of pedagogy and education that included a range of cultural
and social institutions outside of the institutional apparatuses of formal learning. Williams forcefully argued that the pedagogical force of the wider culture
was the primary sphere on which learning now took place and that it was
precisely within the highly mediated terrains of the new cultural media and
other "teaching" spheres that the most valuable pressure for social change was
constituted. Williams coined this new development a form of "permanent
education," and rightfully believed that as a mode of cultural politics it could
not be ignored in any viable struggle for radical democracy. He writes:

What it valuably stresses is the educational force of our whole social and cultural
experience. It is therefore concerned, not only with continuing education, of a
formal or informal kind, but with what the whole environment, its institutions

and relationships, actively and profoundly teaches. . . . [Permanent education also refers to] the field in which our ideas of the world, of ourselves and of our possibilities, are most widely and often most powerfully formed and disseminated. To work for the recovery of control in this field is then, under any pressures, a priority.[99]

According to Williams, how people think about social change could not be separated from the way in which their knowledge, identities, and values are shaped by the pedagogical forces at work in the larger spheres of media and popular culture. Williams was clear in his conviction that the notion of "permanent education" presented an important challenge to progressives who had either largely ignored the relationship between learning and social change or had reduced such questions to the politics of formal schooling. But regardless of how progressives had felt about the politics of education, the time had come for them to acknowledge the primacy of pedagogy in constituting any definition of the political. In what appears to be prescient for the time in which it was written, Williams articulates the following concern:

> The need for permanent education, in our kind of changing society, will be met in one way or another. It is now on the whole being met, though with many valuable exceptions and efforts against the tide, by an integration of this teaching with the priorities and interests of a capitalist society, and of a capitalist society, moreover, which necessarily retains as its central principle (though against powerful pressures, of a democratic kind, from the rest of our social experience) the idea of a few governing, communicating with and teaching the many.[100]

Williams's crucial recognition here is that education operates throughout the culture in many different spheres and that it plays a primary role in shaping modes of agency, self-representation, and effective democracy itself. Equally important is his understanding of the role that pedagogy plays as a dominant force for denying particular forms of social agency either through the force of exclusion or of marginalization. Not only does Williams broaden our understanding of pedagogy but he also makes it clear that it must be considered as part of a broader struggle over forms of identification and agency linked to citizenship rights that expand the imperatives of a meaningful and full democracy.

The third contribution that comes out of Williams's work centers around his defense of cultural politics.[101] Williams's work incorporates both a social vision and practical goals regarding what kind of society he wants progressives to help build as well as an astute understanding of how pedagogy is always at the heart of any organizing movement for change. Central to these related considerations is Williams's defense of cultural politics. Culture for Williams is a crucial terrain of struggle and power, one that has assumed unparalleled significance within late modern society. As a result of the electronic technology revolution and the massive changes wrought by the information revolution, culture has become a powerful sphere where questions of ideology, consciousness, affect, and material relations of power intersect with everyday life to construct peoples' perceptions of themselves and the larger world. Most importantly, it is the site where power is deployed on a daily basis and takes hold through the force of language, experience, force, and persuasion, and, as a result, has become one of the most significant forces for global change. Culture for Williams does not suggest the priority of meaning over material relations of power, nor does it suggest that power can be meaningfully engaged outside of meaning. Williams fully agreed with Frankfurt School theorists Theodore Adorno and Max Horkheimer that questions about culture cannot be abstracted from questions regarding economics and politics nor be dismissed as merely superstructural.[102] But Williams goes further in arguing that cultural politics expands the field of the political not only by pluralizing the sites of struggle but also by developing new opportunities for forms of cultural production that expand the form and content of knowledge, experience, and relations that inscribe, articulate, and produce modes of oppositional agency. Cultural politics foregrounds not just the traditional emphasis on power, concrete labor struggles, and workers' movements but also issues of value, ethics, meaning, and affect. Williams does not simply attempt to legitimate the political value of cultural politics; he goes much further by raising questions, such as how cultural politics might be seen as an integral and useful element of any viable attempt to engage in forms of political and social change that further the promise of a radical democracy. Williams is worth repeating on this issue:

> I think that a political strategy which doesn't take account of cultural questions is living in the past. This does not imply that they should take priority over all the other kinds of struggle: the problem is precisely that they are seen as separate sectors—the "economic wing," the "political wing," and the "cultural wing." Only when they are *not* seen as sectors can the effect of the important cultural arguments come through: that there is none of these sectors that does not immediately involve the others; that a lot of the major economic and industrial disputes are about cultural institutions; that culture is involved in politics in quite a new way, especially in the involvement of the media; and conversely that all the questions about culture involve hard economic questions of political

institutions. Whenever there's a move to concentrate on just one sector, it's often understandable in the context of the time, but it's always theoretically wrong.[103]

If one of the characteristics of the present time is a retreat from the political accompanied by a growing disdain, if not cynicism, toward public life, the work of Castoriadis and Williams reminds us of what it means to render hope practical and despair unconvincing. They rightly argue that if utopian thinking is to become concrete, it must be rooted in a social vision that is practical, recognize that changing consciousness and transforming institutions is as much a pedagogical issue as a strictly political one, and acknowledge that any worthwhile notion of politics demands that cultural practices neither be overlooked nor taken up in a trivial manner.[104] Changing the conditions of widespread despair in the United States suggests not only reinventing self-determination as a central feature of social citizenship; such a challenge also points to the necessity of finding ways to articulate democratic notions of individuality with larger considerations of the public good and social responsibility grounded in a moral culture of mutual solidarity and habits of mind based on compassion, respect for differences, and a willingness to work with others. Against the destructive and dehumanizing impulses and practices of neoliberalism, the time has come for progressives to rethink and revitalize cultural politics and social change as part of a broader effort to reclaim ethical responsibility, political will, critical agency, and democratic public life. This demands a better understanding of the world in which we want to intervene, new political projects that take up the challenge of global citizenship, and forms of activist pedagogy that entail "making the world something other than what it is."[105] Maybe the place to begin is with Ernst Bloch's admonition that "to be human really means to have utopias."[106]

Afterword

READING GIROUX

Cultural Studies, Critical Pedagogy, and Radical Democracy

Douglas Kellner

A fter publishing a series of books that many recognize as major works on contemporary education and critical pedagogy, Henry Giroux turned to cultural studies in the late 1980s to enrich education with expanded conceptions of pedagogy and literacy.[1] This cultural turn is animated by the hope to reconstruct schooling with critical perspectives that can help us better understand and transform contemporary culture and society in the contemporary era. Giroux provides cultural studies with a critical pedagogy missing in many versions and a sustained attempt to link critical pedagogy and cultural studies with developing a more democratic culture and citizenry. The result is an intersection of critical pedagogy and cultural studies that enhances both enterprises, providing a cultural and transformative political dimension to critical pedagogy and a pedagogical dimension to cultural studies.

Crucially, Giroux has linked his attempts to transform pedagogy and education with the project of promoting radical democracy. Giroux's earlier work during the 1970s and 1980s focused on educational reform, pedagogy, and the transformation of education to promote radical democracy. In *Border Crossings* (1992:1), Giroux notes "a shift in both my politics and my theoretical work." The move included incorporation of new theoretical discourses of poststructuralism and postmodernism, cultural studies, and the politics of identity and difference embodied in the new discourses of class, gender, race, and sexuality that proliferated in the post-1960s epoch. Giroux criticized those who ignore "the sea changes in social theory" within the field of education and called for a transformation of education and pedagogy in the light of the new paradigms, discourses, and practices that were circulating by the 1990s.

One of the key new discourses and practices that Giroux was henceforth to take up and develop involved the burgeoning discipline of cultural studies. In his initial appropriations of cultural studies, he presented his shift as a "border crossing" that involved transformative transdisciplinary perspectives that overcame the disciplinary abstractions and separations of such fields as education, social theory, and literary studies. In metatheoretical discussions, Giroux presented reasons for the importance of cultural studies in reconstructing contemporary education and the need for new understandings of culture, cultural politics, and pedagogy that went beyond the orthodoxy of both Left and Right, focusing on how the transformation of education and pedagogy could contribute to the project of radical democracy. Giroux thus uses cultural studies to transform and enrich critical pedagogy and to provide new intellectual tools and practices to transform education. In turn, he argues that cultural studies needs to see the importance of pedagogy and to continue its commitment to radical democratic social transformation, rather than to merely indulge in textualist readings or audience studies of how people use and enjoy popular culture, as in some versions of cultural studies that have emerged in the past years.

For over a decade now, Giroux has accordingly focused on developing the relationship among critical pedagogy, cultural studies, and radical democracy in a series of books, including *Border Crossings* (1992); *Living Dangerously: Multiculturalism and the Politics of Culture* (1993); *Disturbing Pleasures: Learning Popular Culture* (1994); *Fugitive Cultures* (1996); *Channel Surfing: Racism, the Media, and the Destruction of Today's Youth* (1997); *The Mouse That Roared: What Disney Teaches* (1999); *Stealing Innocence* (2000); and *Impure Acts. The Practical Politics of Cultural Studies* (2000).[2] This rich and productive corpus crisscrosses the borderlines of educational theory and pedagogy, cultural studies, social theory, and radical democratic politics, promoting a genuinely transdisciplinary and transformative reconstruction of education, theory, society, and politics.

My study will accordingly engage Giroux's writing in these arenas over the past decade, highlighting what I see as the most significant contributions to transforming education and society, as well as some limitations of his work. At stake is developing a critical pedagogy and cultural studies that will help empower the next generation and enliven democracy as we enter a situation perilous to democracy and the public in the new millennium.

GIROUX'S BIG THEMES: YOUTH AS HOPE AND SCAPEGOAT

Giroux's work is important because it takes on many of the "big" issues of the contemporary era. Several of his recent books have focused on the social construction and media representations of youth in explorations of how youth have been both scapegoated for social problems and commodified and exploited by the advertising, consumer, and media industries. Giroux always situates his cultural analyses within a political and historical context so that, for instance, the war against youth is seen as part of an attack on the welfare state, public schooling, and democratic culture during the Reagan-Bush-Clinton-Bush years. Giroux also takes care to contextualize his writings within his own working-class background, his history as a critical educator, and his emergence as a radical critic of existing culture, society, politics, and the educational establishment. Giroux combines the personal and the political, the theoretical and the practical, in taking on the key issues of the day.

In the light of the ongoing attack on youth and youth culture in the contemporary post-Columbine conjuncture, it is interesting to read in Giroux's 1996 *Fugitive Cultures* his analyses of how media were then scapegoating youth, especially youth of color, as the source of social problems and the escalation of violence in society. Giroux cites the disturbing statistic that "close to 12 U.S. children aged 19 and under die from gun fire each day. According to the National Center for Health Statistics, 'Firearm homicide is the leading cause of death of African-American teenage boys and the second-leading cause of death of high school age children in the United States'" (cited in Giroux 1996: 28).

Giroux correctly notes that the proliferating media stories about youth and violence at the time generally avoid critical commentary on the connections between the escalation of violence in society and the role of poverty and social conditions in promoting violence—a blind spot that continues into the present. In addition, he astutely notes that the media scapegoating of youth also neglects dissection of the roles of white men in generating violence and destruction, such as "the gruesome toll of the drunk driver who is typically white" (1996: 37).

At the same time, working-class youth and youth of color are being represented in the media and conservative discourses as predators, as threats to existing law, order, and morality. Most disturbingly, at the very time that poverty and division between the "haves" and the "have nots" are growing, a conservative-dominated neoliberal polity is cutting back the very programs—public education, job training and programs, food stamps, health and welfare support—that provide the sustenance to create opportunities and hope for youth at risk. Giroux correctly rejects the family values and moralistic critique of media culture of such conservatives who lead the assault on the state and welfare programs while supporting prisons, harsher punishment, and a "zero tolerance" for youthful transgressions (ch. 2).

Instead, Giroux targets the corporations who circulate problematic images of youth and the right-wing social forces that scapegoat youth for social programs at the same time as they attack programs and institutions that might actually help youth. Giroux is clearly aware of media culture as pedagogy and calls upon cultural critics to see the pedagogical and political functions of such cultural forms that position youth as objects of fear or desire. In a series of studies, Giroux notes how corporations exploit the bodies of youth to sell products, manufacturing desires for certain products, and constructing youth as consumers.

In a brilliant critique of a series of Benetton fashion ads, Giroux argues that the 1985 United Colors of Benetton campaign used images of racial harmony to sell both its clothing line and a banal view of cultural unity that erased class, racial, gender, and sexual difference, as well as inequalities, oppression, and suffering (1994: 3ff). In his sharp analysis of the 1991 Benetton campaign, which included compelling images of a person with AIDS, poverty, war, and environmental destruction, Giroux argues that the purported social realism of these ads was used to aestheticize suffering and to sell an image of the Benetton corporation as a vehicle of social responsibility. Giroux deconstructs the campaign by disclosing the corporation's commitment to neoliberal antigovernment positions, its hostility to unions, and its attempt to position its fashion line within a global clothing market. Carrying out a detailed analysis of the production and reception of the Benetton campaign, Giroux dissects how a major global corporation uses images as vehicles of ideology and promotion of its wares. His studies demonstrate the need for a visual pedagogy that engages the production and reception of corporate images, as well as providing a hermeneutical reading of the specific images and texts.

Giroux continued his pedagogy of the corporate image and advertising in a critique of 1995 Calvin Klein ads. This advertising campaign deployed photos by Perry Meisel of youthful bodies, posed in provocative sexual displays bordering on the pornographic, to sell high-end clothing (1997, ch. 1). The ironic use of underclass youth to sell expensive clothes underlines what Giroux sees as the dual process of scapegoating youth while objectifying and commodifying them to sell products. Young bodies are positioned in such images not as sources of agency or resistance but as a "site of spectacle and objectification, where youthful allure and sexual titillation are marketed and consumed by teens and adults who want to indulge a stylized narcissism and coddle a self that is all surface" (1997: 21).

Giroux also critically interrogates a Calvin Klein "heroin chic" campaign that portrayed emaciated bodies and covertly romanticized drug use and youth decadence (1999, ch. 2), thus falling in line with conservative attacks on youth as decadent and immoral. His intention, however, is not to engage in a moralistic critique of such ads. Rather, Giroux undertakes to show how they merge fashion and art to shape images of the youthful body in the interests of commodification. This process helps generate corporate profits while providing highly problematic role models and forms of identity for youth. Giroux is concerned that youth are being increasingly driven from the public sphere, active democratic citizenship, and empowering creativity, into privatized spaces where they are positioned as consumers and provided with identities that replicate commodified models and ideals.

Channel Surfing (1997) and his more recent *Stealing Innocence* (2000) provide examples of critical pedagogy that demonstrate that "childhood" and "youth" are social constructions and sites of struggle between opposing political ideologies and forces. "Children" and "youth" in Giroux's view are a complex site of hope and possibility, as well as domination and exploitation. Giroux critically engages the pedagogies in locales ranging from schooling to media culture and everyday life that shape youth. In particular, he provides a sustained critique of representations that scapegoat youth for public problems at the same time that the political and media establishment carry out attacks on public schools and on programs and policies that provide opportunities and hope for youth. Giroux criticizes representations of youth such as are found in Calvin Klein ads, depictions of irresponsible sex and drug use in films like Larry Clark's *Kids* (1996), and a variety of urban films that especially vilify youth of color and help foster public images of youth as decadent, corrupt, and in need of discipline and control.

Against the scapegoating and commercialization of youth, and the promotion of attitudes of despair and hopelessness, Giroux wants to foster an ethic of hope and possibility, conceptualizing youth as a contested terrain, as an arena both of oppression and struggle. Giroux argues that, by criticizing misrepresentations of youth in media culture and the scapegoating of youth through negative media images and discourses, we are combating an attack on youth used to justify cutbacks in education and harsher criminal penalties and other punitive measures that are arguably part of the problem rather than the solution.[3]

Giroux sees culture and the media as forms of pedagogy, every bit as important—and in some cases more so—than schooling. He calls for a cultural studies that provides a counterpedagogy to the teaching that is provided by mainstream schooling and corporate and media culture, noting: "For years, I believed that pedagogy was a discipline developed around the narrow imperatives of public schooling" (1994: x). And yet, he notes that his own identity was largely fashioned on the terrain of popular culture and everyday life that shaped him more significantly than public education. Accordingly, he argues that pedagogy needs to be theorized in terms of a variety of public sites that shape, mold, socialize, and educate individuals. Indeed, Giroux convincingly demonstrates in book after book that it is precisely corporate media culture that is shaping our culture and everyday life, as well as institutions such as schools and cultural sites like museums, theme parks, shopping centers, and the like.

For Giroux, "the politics of culture provide the conceptual space in which childhood is constructed, experienced, and struggled over" (2000a: 4). Culture is both the sphere in which adults exercise control over children and a site where children and youth can resist the adult world and create their own cultures and identities. It is thus important to critically question "the specific cultural formations and contexts in which childhood is organized, learned, and lived" (1994: x).

In a study of child beauty pageants (2000a, ch. 1), Giroux shows how this competitive sphere imposes adults' models on children, promotes restricted and problematic gender roles, and displays provocative sexual displays in young girls. Giroux does not, a la Neil Postman, lament the "adultifying" of the child and the disappearance of childhood (pp. 12ff and 40) but focuses on the exploitation of children in these "nymphet fantasies," in which adults project their desires and impose their models upon girls. Giroux's concern is with how children and youth are exploited and socialized by commercial consumer culture and with the lack of public spaces and sites for the young to develop agency and learn democratic and cooperative social relations and values in an increasingly commodified and privatized culture and society.

Giroux's analysis of the genealogy of child beauty pageants calls attention to an often neglected source of childhood construction that needs to be engaged by a critical cultural pedagogy. As an example of corporate pedagogy, Giroux devoted sustained study to the multiple roles in childhood socialization, ideological indoctrination, and commercialization of the Walt Disney corporation, resulting in a book on Disney and its pedagogies (1999). Giroux's first study of the cultural production "the Wonderful World of Disney"—a slogan that he suggests itself stands as a metonym for the United States—analyzes certain Disney Touchstone films, targeted mainly at teenagers and adults.

HOLLYWOOD PEDAGOGY

Giroux notes how the terrain of Hollywood film provides an important ground of pedagogy and takes on the politics of representation in two Disney

Touchstone films, *Good Morning, Vietnam* (1987) and *Pretty Woman* (1990). Giroux presents Barry Levinson's take on Vietnam as an attempt to recuperate the sense of U.S. loss over the Vietnam war, to establish an ethos of innocence for American memory, and to erase from history the turbulence and violence of the Vietnam era. The suffering and tragedy of Vietnam is displaced by Robin Williams's "comic, manic improvisation" (1994: 35). Williams plays a DJ for an Army radio station in Saigon, circa 1965. Conflict focused on what sort of music the DJ could play. Giroux suggests that cultural struggle over music replaces the dynamic of contestation over the war itself, while the U.S. intervention is clothed in innocence, presenting U.S. soldiers as tourists to an exotic locale.

Giroux also criticizes the racism and sexism in the film, as in the representations of the black sidekick to the DJ, played by Forest Whitaker, who is presented as "a shuffling, clumsy grunt" and is positioned as the obedient servant to the colonial master. Not surprisingly, the representations of the Vietnamese are racist, with women displayed as sexual commodities for U.S. servicemen, while, in general, the Vietnamese are present as exotic Others who are perpetuators of criminality and lawlessness.

Pretty Woman, in Giroux's reading, also presents ideological representations of recent U.S. history, this time in the Cindrella story of a working-class prostitute, played by Julia Roberts, who is groomed and redeemed by a corporate raider (Richard Gere). Assimilating appropriate fashion and style imagery, in the Disney redoing of the Pygmalion myth, the prostitute reconstitutes herself as a suitable corporate trophy wife, and patriarchal relations and family values thus triumph over sordid and inappropriate sex and style. The predatory business practices of the corporate raider are erased in the chivalrous behavior of the businessman, whose questionable business practices are justified when he takes over his father's corporation, redeeming the bad father who had mistreated him and his mother.

The Disney world of innocence and family values is thus able to triumph and redeem even disturbing and base historical and social conditions. Giroux's second sustained critique of Disney ideology involved critical scrutiny of Disney animation cartoons aimed at children (1996: ch. 3 and its continuation in 1999). He notes that, while cultural studies has traditionally focused on youth culture, it has largely ignored children's culture, such as animated films (1996: 89–90). Giroux scrutinizes the narrow gender roles in these films and finds that, although some of the young women portrayed, such as the woman-mermaid Ariel in *The Little Mermaid* (1989) or the young woman in *Beauty and the Beast* (1991), are initially depicted as feisty and active, they are positioned to find true love and happiness in submission to male-dominated romance. Other Disney films, like *Aladdin* (1992), simply portray women as handmaidens to male pleasure, or, like *The Lion King,* (1994) are strictly patriarchal, depicting women in subordinate roles.

Giroux dissects, as well, the stereotyping and covert racism in recent Disney animation films. Arabs are depicted in vile racist representations, and many of the villains in Disney animation "speak through racially coded language and accents" (106). The heroes and heroines in these films, however, speak standardized American and are portrayed in images modeled after idealized American youth. A Disney cultural worker, for instance, admitted that the figure of *Aladdin* was modeled after Tom Cruise (106), and, as Giroux suggests, heroines such as the little Mermaid or Pocahontas are modeled after Southern California nubile teen models. Such representations normalize whiteness and American fashion and style as the ideal for youth, fostering insecurities and feelings of inferiority in youth of color or other nationalities.

In addition, and notoriously, Disney films erase the scars and ugliness of colonial history, as in *Pocahontas* (1995), which shows no trace of the displacement, suffering, and death inflicted indigenous peoples by the European colonists. Moreover, Disney films like *The Lion King* display "deeply antidemocratic social relations" (107), naturalizing authority, hierarchy, structural inequality, and royalty as part of a natural order. Class, gender, and racial inequalities are presented as benign and justified in this world, displaying Disney nostalgia for a simpler and more harmonious world that erases from cultural memory the turbulence and pain of history and the continuation of social inequalities, injustice, and suffering in the present.

Giroux thus critically dissects the sorts of pedagogy involved in the Disney world. He analyzes "what Disney teaches," the implications of a big corporate conglomerate playing such a major role in pedagogy and socialization, and the ways that this influences education, politics, and our cultural and public life, here in the United States and globally. Giroux's book on Disney includes dissection of the structure and power of the Disney corporation and raises questions about the effects of the possession of so much cultural power. Demonstrating the immense range of cultural sites occupied by the Disney corporation, Giroux discloses the diversity of its products in critical analyses of Disney's films, its forays into education and community building, and its extensive marketing operations of toys and merchandise spun off from its films. Critically engaging such a cultural empire requires combining historical, social, and political analysis, textual readings, and studies of cultural effects of a wide range of artifacts. Giroux thus produces a cultural studies that deploys transdisciplinary perspectives, including analyses of political economy and production, cultural artifacts and sites, and their reception and effects.

Giroux, thus, offers a wide-ranging model of cultural studies and greatly expands the domain of pedagogy, demonstrating the importance of critically engaging the pedagogy of a broad spectrum of cultural artifacts often ignored by educators. Since youth today are the subjects of education, critical teachers must understand youth, their problems and prospects, hopes and fears, competencies and limitations. Understanding and productively engaging youth in the context of their everyday lives is clearly one of the big issues for educators, parents, citizens, and those of us concerned about the future. For youth are the future, and the quality of life and the polity of the new millennium depend on educating youth and helping produce generations who can themselves create a better, freer, happier, and more just society. Hence, Giroux constantly argues that educators, parents, and citizens should be deeply concerned with youth. This involves attempting to understand youth culture and problems, combating the ways that young people are being misrepresented in the media and miseducated in the schools, and developing pedagogical strategies and cultural politics that will reform and democratically transform media, education, and society.

Cultural studies is useful here because it provides access to youth culture, to the actual culture that socializes and educates youth—or in some cases miseducates it—and thus potentially increases our understanding of the individuals we are teaching and working with. Clearly, Giroux demonstrates the importance of media education for a reconstruction of schooling and the importance of cultural studies for a transformative critical pedagogy. He also consistently argues that key social phenomena such as the situation of youth can only be grasped through their race, gender, and class configurations and that youth are articulated by these concrete social determinants that must be addressed in any adequate analysis.

THE INTERSECTION OF CLASS, RACE, AND GENDER

For Giroux, culture matters precisely because such constituents of everyday experience as youth, gender, race, class, sexuality, and so on are constructed in and through cultural representations. Often, these representations are invisible and their effects are unperceived. Hence, a critical cultural studies must make visible how representations construct a culture's normative views of such things as class, race, ethnicity, gender, sexuality, place, occupation, and the like, and how these representations are appropriated to produce subjectivities, identities, and practices.

Some of Giroux's first concrete cultural studies of the 1990s involve analysis and critique of how Hollywood celluloid culture constructs a pedagogy of class, race, and gender. He indicates the need for critical media pedagogy to disclose how these texts are constructed and to help enable students to critically dissect and interpret media representations, narratives, and their effects. In a reading of *Dead Poets Society* (1993: 40ff), Giroux tells how his students initially identified with the rebellious teacher, Mr. Keating, played by Robin Williams. Keating set out to reinvigorate education at a conservative boys boarding school, Welton Academy, which functioned to prepare elite males for Ivy League colleges and ruling-class life. At first, Giroux notes, students saw the Williams figure as an ideal of transformative education, passionately committed to teaching, and helping to change his students' life in an emancipatory fashion.

But a closer reading of the film, Giroux remarks, discloses a "politics and aesthetics of nostalgia" that looks back to past cultural forms (e.g., romantic poetry) as privileged cultural texts, thus, in effect, affirming a conservative canon as the heart and soul of pedagogy. Thus, while the film does provide a critique of authoritarian and disciplinary education, it does not go beyond conservative individualism and aestheticism and fails to engage the problems, conflicts, and struggles of the present, to see the past as a contested terrain, or to engage those voices and texts that more radically contest the inequities and injustices of Western civilization. Moreover, when Keating himself is challenged by the authorities for his unorthodox teaching practices and unjustly dismissed over the suicide of a student, he politely and respectfully submits to his fate, rather than exhibiting any critique, resistance, or struggle against the repressive and authoritarian power structure that rules the institution.

Furthermore, Giroux criticizes the representations of women in the film "that are misogynist and demeaning" (1993: 47). Women are positioned primarily to support and provide pleasure to men; they are relegated "to either trophies or appendages of male power" (48). Women are not presented in the film as active subjects with their own dreams and agency, but as "reified object[s] of [male] desire and pleasure" (48).

Of course, race is invisible in *Dead Poets Society*, which "privileges whiteness, patriarchy, and heterosexuality as the universalizing norms of identity" (42). The film takes for granted the equation of whiteness with class privilege and does not trouble its nostalgic narrative with the disruptive dynamics of race and sexuality. Likewise, in another probing cultural study of the period,

Giroux shows how the contemporary conflicts over gender, race, and class are ideologically smoothed and absorbed in the narrative machine of *Grand Canyon* (1993: 104ff). In this film, the white yuppie family of the story come to recognize racial and cultural difference in the present, but in a manner that reassures them that they do not have to surrender power and privilege and that difference can be harmoniously absorbed into the existing order.

Indeed, Giroux has intensely engaged over the past decade the problematics and dynamics of race—clearly one of the major issues of our time—as well as the intersections of race, class, gender, multiculturalism, and the crisis of democracy and public schooling in the United States (see especially Giroux 1993, 1996, and 1997). He enriches these topics with his combination of critical pedagogy, cultural studies, and a sustained political situating of representations and struggles over race within the context of burning issues and conflicts of the day.

In discussing issues of violence in the media and the effects of media violence on youth and society, Giroux argues that discussions of violence and media must include race and class (1997, preface and throughout). In a series of texts, he has carried out sustained critiques of media stigmatizing of youth as the source of social ills through analysis of depictions of violent youth in the media and journalism, cinematic representations of youth in Hollywood film, and political discourses that call for "zero tolerance" of youth indiscretions and crimes (ch. 2).

In particular, Giroux shows how media representations of blacks stigmatize youth and, more broadly, people of color. In *Fugitive Cultures* (1996), Giroux documents the role of media presentations of blacks that have helped promote what he calls "a white moral panic" (1996: 97). During the era of the O. J. Simpson trials in the mid-1990s, major magazines featured threatening black males on their covers with stories like "A Predator's Struggle to Tame Himself" and "The Black Man Is in Terrible Trouble. Whose Problem Is That?" (1996: 97). Giroux points out that the endless repetition of these images "reproduce racist stereotypes about blacks by portraying them as criminals and welfare cheats"; it also "remove whites from any responsibility or complicity for the violence and poverty that has become so endemic to American life" (1996: 66).

Racial coding of violence and the association of crime with youth of color was evident in the attacks on rap music and hip-hop culture that circulated throughout the 1990s.[4] As an example, Giroux cites the hypocrisy, during the 1996 presidential campaign of Bob Dole's attack on rap and Hollywood films' depiction of violence, drugs, and urban terror. For Dole refused to criticize violence in the films of the Hollywood right, such as those of Republicans Bruce Willis and Arnold Schwarzenneger. Moreover, he was a fervent supporter of the NRA and a critic of stricter gun laws, and failed to address the ways that poverty and worsening social conditions generated violence (produced in part by Republican policies that Dole spearheaded). Moreover, Dole had reportedly often not even seen the films nor heard the music he attacked (1996: 67ff).

Always clearly pointing to the political consequences of such cultural and political discourses and representations, Giroux notes that "such racist stereotyping produce more than prejudice and fear in the white collective sensibility. Racist representations of violence also feed the increasing public outcry for tougher crime bills designed to build more prisons and legislate get-tough policies with minorities of color and class" (1996: 67). Hence, racist and brutal depictions of people of color in media culture contribute to intensification of the culture of violence and fuel campaigns by right-wing organizations that stigmatize racial groups. Such representations also promote social and political conditions that aggravate, rather than ameliorate, problems of crime, urban decay, and violence.

Indeed, throughout the 1990s and continuing into the new millennium, there have been copious media spectacles featuring dangerous blacks, including sustained attacks on rap music and hip-hop culture, black gangs and crime, and urban violence in communities of color. Latinos are also stigmatized with political (mis)measures such as Proposition 187 "which assigns increasing crime, welfare abuse, moral decay, and social disorder to the flood of Mexican immigrants streaming across the borders of the United States" (1996: 66). Social scientists contribute to the stigmatization in books like *The Bell Curve,* which assert black inferiority and provide "a respectable intellectual position" for racist discourse in the national debate on race (1996: 67).

Hollywood films and entertainment media contribute, as well, to negative national depictions of people of color. In his discussion of Hollywood cinematic portrayals of inner city youth, Giroux analyzes how communities of color are shown as disruptive forces in public schools, contributing to white moral panic that youth of color are predatory, violent, and are destroying the moral and social fabric of the country. Films like *Boyz N the Hood* (1991), *Juice* (1992), *Menace II Society* (1993), and *Clockers* (1995) present negative representations of African American youth, which Giroux argues, feed into right-wing moral panics and help mobilize support for harsher policing and incarceration of ghetto youth. Against these prejudicial and sensationalistic fictional representations, Giroux valorizes Jonathan Stack's documentary *Harlem Diary* (1996), in which urban youth are themselves provided with cameras and cinematic education to explore their situations and to give voice to their own fears and aspirations (1997: 62).

In addressing the culture of violence in *Fugitive Cultures* (1996), Giroux engages what he calls "hyper-real" violence in the films of Quentin Tarantino: *Reservoir Dogs* (1992) and *Pulp Fiction* (1994). Giroux argues that Tarantino's use of excessive and exaggerated violence in these films aestheticizes the brutality of violence, contributing to a cynical and nihilistic cinema. *Reservoir Dogs* uses a gritty realism and stylized violence to represent extremely ruthless crime in a way that "revels in stylistic excess in order to push the aesthetic of violence to its visual and emotional limits" (1996: 71).

Pulp Fiction, in Giroux's reading, promotes the same cynical ethos of Tarantino's earlier film, but in the register of a more hip, cool, and stylized post-modern idiom. Pastiching the crime genre of "pulp fiction," Tarantino fragments his narrative structure, deploys a sadistic irony and ultra-hip talk and music, and puts on display a misanthropic amorality to promote what Ruth Conniff has called "a culture of cruelty" (1996: 76). Tarantino, in Giroux's reading, deploys violence for shock and schlock effects, playing with cinematic conventions, without critically analyzing, contextualizing, or contesting the patterns of violence in his films. Violence in Tarantino's films is gratuitous, contingent, and ubiquitous, rather than emerging from specific contexts and social conditions. It can erupt anywhere, anytime, to anyone, rather than being generated by specific social causes and conditions. It is aestheticized and used for shock effects rather than to probe into what causes violence and its horrific effects on human beings and communities. Such films thus contribute to promoting a culture of brutality by naturalizing and romanticizing major forces of human suffering and tragedy.

Giroux also critiques the racism and sexism in Tarantino's film, noting the racist language and obsessive use of the "N-word," as well as the highly problematic representations of women and homophobia. Indeed, Giroux suggests that the rape of a black by two white thugs in *Pulp Fiction* combines homophobia with racism (82), presenting at once highly derogatory images of gay sex and positioning the black man as a deserving target of white male rage (he is about to kill the Bruce Willis character for honorably refusing to throw a fight, as the black thug ordered). Giroux also points out how the sociopath Jules (played by Samuel Jackson) misuses the African American tradition of prophetic language in his pretentious use of religious discourse in the context of committing heinous crimes (82).

Giroux insists that such cinematic transgression and irony are not innocent or merely playful, but have harmful political and cultural effects. Yet , Giroux does not himself stigmatize Hollywood films or the media for the alarming escalation of violence in the United States, calling attention instead to conditions of poverty, social injustice, and urban decline that contribute to the larger problems of the contemporary era. Attacking Bob Dole's and other's hypocritical assaults on Hollywood and the media, Giroux argues that it is precisely conservative policies that cut back public institutions that would provide adequate education, welfare, employment, public spaces, and life opportunities for youth that helped generate the alienation, violence, and nihilism that are all too evident in contemporary American life—and not only in communities of color, as we are aware in the post-Columbine epoch.

Hence, a critical cultural studies and pedagogy should, at once, carry out critical discussion of the politics of representation in media culture, focusing on the images and discourses of race, gender, class, and sexuality, but, at the same time, it should contextualize the critique within broader social conditions, discourses, and struggles. While ethical and ideological critique of specific forms and texts of media culture are certainly appropriate, the critical pedagogue avoids moralizing assaults on media culture per se. The focus is instead on how racism, sexism, poverty, political discourses and policies, and the social context, as a whole, produce phenomena like violence and suffering. Although media culture can be contributory, it is not the origin of human suffering, and thus, censoring media images is not the solution to problems like societal violence and injustice. Rather, there is a complex nexus of conditions that causes violence and youth nihilism, and while media culture can be criticized for its representations it should not be scapegoated.

The political contextualization, critique, and focus of Giroux's work, however, sometimes lead his exercises in cultural studies and critical pedagogy to what might be called a political and ideological overdetermination of his readings of specific cultural texts. While Giroux increasingly focuses on the importance of cultivating the ethical dimensions of education and critical pedagogy, his readings of specific cultural texts usually privilege political critique over valorization of positive ethical, aesthetic, and philosophical dimensions to the text. There is in Giroux a perhaps-too-quick collapse of the aesthetic and textual into the political in some of his readings. This procedure is arguably justified in discussions of films like the works of Tarantino or *Fight Club* (ch. 3), which aestheticize violence and, indeed themselves, collapse aesthetics into politics. This is also the case with ad campaigns that Giroux criticizes for their aestheticizing and commodification of youthful bodies, promoting "heroin chic" and other dubious ideals for youth. And Benetton ads or other images that aestheticize urban deprivation and suffering in glossy images also merit sharp critique.

But certain cultural texts have an aesthetic excess, a polysemic overdetermination of meaning, contradictory moments and aspects, that can be read against the ideological grain even of conservative texts and those that aestheticize violence. For instance, although I agree with Giroux that Larry Clark's *Kids* is highly problematic and can be read as part of a set of representations and discourses that demonize youth as nihilistic, decadent, and immoral (1997: 45), the film also provides a cautionary morality tale warning of the consequences of causal drug use and unsafe sex. While visiting at Wake Forest University, I attended a showing of the film, after which a visibly shaken audience seriously discussed the danger of AIDS and unsafe sex. There was also a heated discussion of race and representation provoked by the film. Thus, while *Kids* does depict urban youth as "decadent and predatory," as Giroux argues, it also allows for a diagnostic critique of children going astray without responsible parenting or adequate mentoring. The film shows adults as almost completely absent from children's life and society at large as negligent and failing to provide adequate parenting, supervision, education, and spaces to provide youth the opportunity to develop agency, moral responsibility, and healthy communities.

Thus, in addition to political and ideological critique, films and other media texts can be read diagnostically to provide critical insight into contemporary society (see Kellner 1995). Consequently, on one hand, one can agree with Giroux that, in films such as *Boyz N the Hood* (1991), *Menace II Society* (1993), and *Clockers* (1995), black male youth are framed through narrow representations that fail to challenge and, in effect, reiterate the dominant neoconservative image of "blackness as menace and 'other'" (1997: 45). Yet, a diagnostic critique can also discern how these films provide insights into the constraints that black youth face and the need to fight the injustice of racial oppression and inequality.[5] Hence, in addition to ideological and political critique, a critical cultural studies can read texts to gain critical knowledge of their conjuncture and can valorize oppositional or utopian moments that can work against the grain of their otherwise conservative or hegemonic problematics.

Nonetheless, Giroux is right to call for political critique of cultural texts, to take culture seriously as a site of pedagogy and the construction of our sense of gender, race, class, sexuality, and other potent markers of contemporary experience and practice. His politicizing of cultural studies provides a salutary alternative to depoliticizing or aestheticizing cultural studies that focus on banal consumer use of media artifacts, refuse ideological or hermeneutical critique, or flatten cultural texts into one-dimensional nonsignifying surfaces, as in some "postmodern" versions of cultural studies. By contrast, Giroux's political readings and critique of cultural texts, his contextualizing of media artifacts in the social and political struggles in which they emerge, and his insistent focus on the politics of representation encompassing the full dimensions of class, race, ethnicity, gender, and sexuality provide productive models for cultural studies and critical pedagogy. This work demonstrates the need for their articulation to provide more responsible and responsive theoretical and political models and practice.

CRITICAL PEDAGOGY, RADICAL DEMOCRACY, AND SOCIAL JUSTICE

Throughout his work within cultural studies, Giroux sees "culture as the site where identities are constructed, desires mobilized, and moral values shaped" (2000b: 132). Importantly, culture "is the ground of both contestation and accommodation" and "the site where young people and others imagine their relationship to the world; it produces the narratives, metaphors, and images for constructing and exercising a powerful pedagogical force over how people think of themselves and their relationship to others" (2000b: 133). Hence, culture is intrinsically pedagogical; it forms, shapes, and cultivates individuals and groups and is, thus, an important site for radical democratic politics.

While culture can be conservative and can shape individuals into conforming to dominant modes of thought and behavior, it also presents a site of resistance and struggle. A critical pedagogy and cultural studies thus attempts to give voice to students to articulate their criticisms of the dominant culture and to form their own subcultures, discourses, styles, and cultural forms. Navigating the tricky and treacherous shoals between those who would claim that culture has nothing to do with politics and who would engage in elitist or textualist pedagogy abstracted from concrete political and historical conditions and struggles and those, mostly on the Left, who deny that culture is crucial for politics, Giroux wants to insist that both culture and politics have an important pedagogical dimension. In his recent *Impure Acts. The Practical Politics of Cultural Studies* (2000b), Giroux notes the irony that, in a time of technological and cultural revolution marked by new media, technology, and forms of culture, there is crisis of democratic culture. This era is marked, Giroux argues, by rampant consumerism, the suppression of dissent, corporate conglomerate control of major culture sites, and reduction of schooling to prepare students to get better test scores and fit into the new global economy. In this context, he calls upon teachers, theorists, and cultural activists to perceive that "struggles over culture are not a weak substitute for a 'real' politics, but are central to any struggle willing to forge relations among discursive and material relations of power, theory and practice, as well as pedagogy and social change" (2000b: 7).

In the contemporary conjuncture, Giroux stresses the importance for teachers and other cultural workers to reinvigorate democratic culture and to intervene in the new cultural spaces to revitalize democracy. For Giroux, cultural studies deals with media culture contextually and politically, seeing the ways that media texts either reproduce existing relationships of domination and subordination in relation to gender, class, race, and other hierarchies, or resist modes of inequality, injustice, and domination. Culture can promote democracy by projecting images of a more egalitarian and just social order or by providing more empowering images of youth, women, people of color, and other oppressed groups. Further, media culture can provide useful moral education, critical knowledge of contemporary conditions, and empowering representations, which can help generate more informed, educated, and active subjectivities.

By combining cultural studies and critical pedagogy during the past decade, Giroux took a postmodern turn that saw the potentiality for a reconstructive project democratically transforming education, pedagogy, culture, and society. For Giroux, the new "post" theories provided the resources for new discourses, pedagogy, practices, and politics. It supplied the material and tools for reinventing education and radical democratic politics. Giroux's main focus was the reconstruction of education and pedagogy in the service of radical democracy. This involved a heightened focus on culture in which cultural studies not only engaged contemporary cultural texts but helped to cultivate the ability to retrieve histories and imagine new futures. Giroux's critical pedagogy sought not only new media literacies and ways of reading culture but also ways of reinventing education in the service of a transformative democratic politics.

Thus, while some versions of the postmodern turn took their avatars into the realms of increasingly abstract and pretentious discourse, Giroux sought a new language for critical pedagogy and radical democracy.[6] Whereas some champions of the postmodern turn (especially followers of Baudrillard, Virilio, and some of the more exotic brands of French postmodern theory) fell into a hopeless nihilism and pessimism, perceiving the collapse of Western civilization and modernity in the implosive postmodern realms of new media, technology, and social conditions, Giroux called for a reconstruction of Enlightenment narratives of democracy, emancipation, and social justice and transformation. He sought new subjects for a transformative practice that would help realize the progressive promises of the Enlightenment rather than promoting anti-Enlightenment and anti-rational thought and practice (which themselves, as Habermas constantly reminds us, can be enemies of democracy and social justice).

Avoiding extreme and problematic versions of the postmodern turn, Giroux was able to develop radical critiques of modern theory, pedagogy, and politics, while providing reconstructive alternatives that draw on both modern and postmodern traditions. His reconstructive and radical democratic postmodern politics are evident in his deployment of the categories of identity and difference. Whereas modern theory tends to erase or cover over difference with its emphasis on unified subjects, common culture, universal reason, truth, and values, Giroux defends an affirmation of difference that also articulates shared experiences, goals, and democratic values. Thus, while an extreme postmodern valorization of difference would erase all universals, commonalities, and shared identities, Giroux deploys a dialectic of identity and difference that sees the complexity and multiplicity of social identities and the possibility for producing more democratic and just subjectivities, discourses, and practices.

Likewise, where an extreme postmodern identity politics would verge toward separatism, or reduce politics to construction of highly specific racial, gender, sexual or other identities that often fetishize difference, Giroux calls for a "border politics," where individuals cross over and struggle together for democracy and social justice. Giroux has developed a pedagogy of representation, place, performance, and transformation. His pedagogy of representation and place involves grasping the larger historical contexts that produce various oppressions, resistance and struggle, identity, and differences. His pedagogy of representation involves perceiving how media, education, political discourses and practices, and other institutional forces generate cultural images and discourses that produce and reproduce forms of oppression and domination, but also generate transformative struggles for a freer and more just society. But his pedagogy of representation also involves the construction of subjectivities and practices that would be able to give voice and expression to their own histories, oppressions, and aspirations and to fight against domination and for transformative democracy and social justice. Here Giroux's pedagogy of place cultivates the ability to retrieve hidden or submerged life histories and those of one's groups, to situate these histories in the political context of the present, and to activate them within the political struggles for the future (see, for instance, Giroux 1993, ch. 2 and 4).

Thus, Giroux has promoted a pedagogy that cultivates both a retrospective grasp of one's historical past, a perception of the dominant forces of oppression and resistance in the present, and an anticipation of a better future rooted in historical struggle and vision. The pedagogy of place and representation in Giroux's work involves also cultivating a pedagogy of the popular. For it is the popular forms of media culture that often shape an individual's sense of history, the present, and the future, as well as one's understanding of the dynamics of race, gender, class, sexuality, and so on. Here, cultural studies provides the critical tools to provide competencies that enable teachers, students, and citizens to develop the ability to analyze and criticize cultural representations that promote domination and oppression. It also, as Giroux argues, can help foster resistance and the construction of transformative concepts of history, possibility, and a more democratic and egalitarian configuration of class, gender, racial, and other identities.

But in linking cultural studies with critical pedagogy, Giroux also wants to animate capacities to produce alternative subjectivities and practices in the struggle for radical democracy and social justice. This involves seeing teachers as cultural workers who provide the theory, language, and skills to both dissect the dominant culture and construct a new, more democratic, culture and more empowered and ethical identities. In this vision, intellectuals and teachers are cultural workers engaged in a struggle to represent the present, past, and future. Giroux has a democratic faith in the potential of teachers, students, and citizens to educate themselves and to struggle together for a better world.

Giroux thus sees cultural politics as encompassing education, artistic work, and the pedagogy of social movements. His performative pedagogy (see the introduction to Giroux and Shannon 1997 and Giroux 2000b, ch. 6) attempts to demonstrate how cultural texts enact broader societal and political issues in a pedagogy that makes visible relations of power, domination, and resistance in media culture. For Giroux, educators and radical intellectuals are cultural workers who should struggle to nurture and keep alive democratic culture, educating individuals for democracy, and promoting citizenship and moral education. Giroux has always been steadfastly on the Left, but he has long opposed a form of Marxist orthodoxy that privileges the working class as the primary agent of social change and that privileges economic issues over all other cultural, social, or political issues and struggles. In *Living Dangerously* (1993), Giroux wrote: "Contrary to the conventional left thinking . . . the greatest challenge to the right and its power may be lodged not in the mobilization of universal agents such as the working class or some other oppressed group, but in a cultural struggle in which almost every facet of daily life takes on a degree of undecidability and thus becomes unsettled and open to broader collective dialogue and multiple struggles" (36).

In particular, Giroux has stressed how education, youth, race, gender, and culture in general have been contested terrains. Schooling, in his view, is a site of struggle among conservative, neoliberal, and more democratic forces—and continues to be so as we enter a new millennium. Likewise, youth is a site of contestation with corporate and conservative forces attempting to colonize, commodify, and control youth, while more democratic and emancipatory forces attempt to educate and empower young people, stressing hope, possibility, and the possibility of collectively creating a better world. The intense struggles over race and gender during the past decades bring cultural representations and a wealth of political, cultural, and social issues to the fore; this requires that critical pedagogy, cultural studies, and a radical democratic politics work to struggle for social justice and equality in an environment hostile to such ideals.

As we enter the new millennium, the turbulence of the technological revolution and global restructuring of capitalism creates a volatile situation where established orthodoxies and authorities are becoming questioned, new technologies, discourses, and practices are emerging, and the entire social field is one of contestation between corporate, conservative, neoliberal, and democratizing forces. Giroux's contribution over the past decades has been to always side with radical democratizing forces on the issues of the restructuring of education, political transformation, and a democratization of all forms of social, political, and cultural life. Giroux thus advances forms of radical democratization and social justice that balance support for civil rights, an egalitarian democratic culture, and a revitalized public sphere with respect for difference. This project provides marginal and excluded voices a chance to participate and creates the democratic institutions—schooling, media, cultural forms, public spaces, and so on—that make possible a genuine participatory democracy. It directs critical pedagogy and cultural studies to struggle for democratization and against injustice and not just to provide more sophisticated methods of reading cultural texts. In these ways, Giroux encourages those of us involved in the project of cultural studies not to forget democratic politics and social struggle as we attend to our pedagogical and public performances.

CONCLUDING REMARKS

The essays collected in this book represent some of Giroux's most recent and best work. On the whole, the studies in *Public Spaces, Private Lives: Beyond the Culture of Cynicism* advance Giroux's project of combining a pedagogy of critique with a politics of hope. Providing a contemporary twist to C. Wright Mills's insistence that public policies and hopes must address private problems, Giroux argues for the need to cultivate collective hope and democratic public spaces in an era of private visions marked by a triumphant market capitalism and withdrawal into the spheres of consumerism and individualism by large sectors of the public. Giroux counters this turn to the private sphere with a call for the need to cultivate public visions and practices of a democratic politics, to reinvigorate citizenship, and to develop a cultural politics that aims at social justice and not merely affirming group or individual identity.

In the opening chapter, "Cultural Studies and the Culture of Politics: Beyond Polemics and Cynicism," Giroux stresses the urgency of the need for education and cultural studies to address issues of public importance and to provide a vision of a democratic society and social justice that can be applied to practical efforts to create a more democratic society. Emphasizing the need to overcome cynicism and retreat into the private sphere, Giroux calls for a reconstruction of education and society in the effort to counter the decline of democracy and rise of cynicism. This requires cultural studies to overcome a too narrow textualist approach or a truncated turn to audience-reception of cultural artifacts, and to see how cultural artifacts are articulated with political discourses and struggles, thus bringing cultural studies to bear on crucial social and political problems of the era.

For Giroux, a revitalized cultural studies is an important part of a reconstruction of society and education. Attacking both elitist conservative assaults on cultural studies and a reductive "left materialist" argument that only nitty-gritty economic and political issues are of importance and that culture is secondary and derivative, Giroux argues that culture is central to the construction and reproduction of contemporary society and everyday life. Accordingly, cultural politics, ranging from critical pedagogy to the production of oppositional art and journalism, are an important dimension of contemporary political struggle.

Chapter 2, "Youth, Domestic Militarization, and the Politics of Zero Tolerance," continues Giroux's intense focus on youth, race, class, and culture that have been the fulcrum of several of his recent books. In this chapter, Giroux guides cultural studies and critical social theorists to address changes in the political situation of youth. In particular, Giroux criticizes conservative discourses and policies that villainize youth as the source of contemporary disorder. Since the Bush administration policies on education and "faith-based charity" programs are guided by principles of "zero tolerance," Giroux's critique engages a particularly noxious discourse and politics that contemporary educators and citizens will be confronted with in the years to come. Crucially, Giroux shows how discourses of "zero tolerance" articulate with right-wing policies that support authoritarian education, the prison-industrial complex as the solution to social problems, and punitive punishment for youthful misbehavior, and seeks alternatives to these repressive policies and institutions.

"Private Satisfactions and Public Disorders: *Fight Club,* Patriarchy, and the Politics of Masculine Violence" (chapter 3) shows how Hollywood films can produce a form of public pedagogy that a critical cultural studies should engage. Giroux's study of *Fight Club* reveals how David Fincher's 1999 film combines a sharp critique of consumer culture with a disturbing depiction of masculinized violence and brutality. The characters in the film compensate for the poverty of private life by immersing themselves in a brutalized culture of male bonding and fighting. Thus, the film's critique of capitalism is accompanied by pathological fantasies of violence that articulate with right-wing militia discourse and practice, providing another salient example of the intersection of how cultural texts reproduce political discourses and problematics.

"Pedagogy of the Depressed" (chapter 4) provides a sharp critique of conservative views of education advanced by Harold Bloom, Roger Shattock, Dinesh D'Souza, and others, as well as critically engaging recent assaults on critical pedagogy from the left. Like his discussion in chapter 1 of contemporary critical discourses against cultural studies, Giroux roots these attacks in current struggles over education. Giroux provides a defense of critical pedagogy, arguing that its emphasis on developing educational practices of dissent, critique, and dialogue should be articulated with a politics of possibility and hope. This combination, he suggests, can provide substance to contemporary education that will make it a force of democracy and progressive change and not just social reproduction.

In "'Something's Missing': From Utopianism to a Politics of Educated Hope" (chapter 5), Giroux fleshes out the dimension of "educated hope" that informs his version of critical pedagogy. For Giroux, discourses of democracy, political agency, and pedagogy must be articulated together and directed toward contemporary problems and issues. The study continues his critique of neoliberal politics and educational practices and sketches out how a wide range of contemporary thinkers envisage an alternative culture and society that can nourish a politics of hope and dreams of a better life and society. Giroux points to the need for vision and hope to nourish projects of social transformation. He thus attempts to reinvigorate a radical utopian tradition where utopian perspectives are a guiding force of social transformation and not just a fantasy and escape.

Giroux's studies sharply criticize a wide range of both conservative and left-liberal assaults on critical pedagogy and cultural studies while presenting a positive version of a project that combines cultural studies and critical pedagogy with a radical democratic politics and project of social reconstruction. The inquiries engage a tremendous range of contemporary literature and positions in cultural politics and education and provide an excellent survey of crucial contemporary issues and positions. But they also contain fresh presentations of Giroux's current views on pedagogy, cultural studies, and democratic theory and politics.

In sum, Giroux's recent studies, collected in this volume, renew his call to reconstruct education to cultivate citizenship, social justice, and democracy in a politics of educated hope. For Giroux, mediation of the public and private, of class and culture, and of theory and politics is crucial for a new vision of education and politics. Giroux stresses the importance of articulation of theory and practice, of culture and politics, for a reinvigoration of democratic politics and projects of social transformation. He challenges education to develop new pedagogies and cultural studies to both reconstruct education and provide projects to democratize culture and society. These texts critically engage traditional and contemporary orthodoxies of the right and left and should provoke useful reflection and debate over a wide range of important issues.

REFERENCES

Aronowitz, Stanley, and Henry Giroux. 1985 (2nd edition 1993). *Education Still Under Siege.* Westport, Conn.: Bergin & Garvey.

———. 1991. *Postmodern Education.* Minneapolis: University of Minnesota Press.

Giroux, Henry. 1992. *Border Crossings. Cultural Workers and the Politics of Education.* New York: Routledge.

———. 1993. *Living Dangerously: Multiculturalism and the Politics of Culture.* New York: Peter Lang.

———. 1994. *Disturbing Pleasures. Learning Popular Culture.* London and New York: Routledge.

———. 1996. *Fugitive Cultures.* New York: Routledge.

———. 1997. *Channel Surfing: Racism, the Media, and the Destruction of Today's Youth.* New York: Saint Martin's.

———. 1999. *The Mouse That Roared: What Disney Teaches.* Lanham, Md.: Rowman & Littlefield.

———. 2000a. *Stealing Innocence.* New York: St. Martin's.

———. 2000b. *Impure Acts. The Practical Politics of Cultural Studies.* New York: Routledge.

Giroux, Henry, and Peter McLaren, eds. 1989. *Critical Pedagogy, the State, and the Struggle for Culture*. Albany, N.Y.: SUNY Press.

Giroux, Henry, and Peter McLaren. 1994. *Between Borders: Pedagogy and Politics in Cultural Studies*. New York: Routledge.

Giroux, Henry, Peter McLaren, Colin Lankshear, and Mike Cole. 1994. *Counternarratives*. New York: Routledge.

Giroux, Henry, and Patrick Shannon. 1997. *Cultural Studies and Education: Toward a Performative Practice*. New York: Routledge.

Giroux, Henry, and Roger Simon. 1989. *Popular Culture, Schooling & Everyday Life*. Granby, Mass.: Bergin & Garvey.

Kellner, Douglas. 1995. *Media Culture*. London and New York: Routledge.

———. 2000. "New Technologies/New Literacies: Reconstructing Education for the New Millennium." *Teaching Education* 11, no. 3 (2000): 245–265.

NOTES

INTRODUCTION

1. For some recent sources that have addressed this theme, see Jeffrey C. Goldfarb, *The Cynical Society: The Culture of Politics and the Politics of Culture in American Life* (Chicago: University of Chicago Press, 1991); Joseph N. Capella and Kathleen Hall Jamieson, *Spiral of Cynicism: The Press and the Public Good* (New York: Oxford University Press, 1997); Russell Jacoby, *The End of Utopia* (New York: Basic Books, 1999); William Chaloupka, *Everybody Knows: Cynicism in America* (Minneapolis: University of Minnesota Press, 1999); Zygmunt Bauman, *In Search of Politics* (Stanford, Calif.: Stanford University Press, 1999); Carl Boggs, *The End of Politics: Corporate Power and the Decline of the Public Sphere* (New York: Guilford Press, 2000); Zygmunt Bauman, The Individualized Society (London: Polity, 2001).

2. Zygmunt Bauman, *Globalization: The Human Consequences* (New York: Columbia University Press, 1998), p. 5.

3. Carl Boggs, *The End of Politics* (New York: Guilford Press, 2000), p. ix.

4. Zygmunt Bauman, *Globalization: The Human Consequences* (New York: Columbia University Press, 1998), p. 82

5. On this issue, see Roberto Mangabeira Unger and Cornel West, *The Future of American Progressivism* (Boston: Beacon Press, 1998).

6. Cornelius Castoriadis, "Institution and Autonomy," in Peter Osborne, ed. *A Critical Sense: Interviews with Intellectuals* (New York: Routledge, 1996), p. 8.

7. Gary Olson and Lynn Worsham, "Staging the Politics of Difference: Homi Bhabha's Critical Literacy," *Journal of Advanced Composition* 18, no. 3 (1999): 11.

8. Stuart Hall cited in Les Terry, "Travelling 'The Hard Road to Renewal,'" *Arena Journal*, no. 8 (1997): 55.

9. Sheldon Wolin, "Political Theory: From Vocation to Invocation," in Jason Frank and John Tambornino, eds. *Vocations of Political Theory* (Minneapolis: University of Minnesota Press, 2000), p. 4.

CHAPTER 1

This chapter revisits an argument I began in Henry A. Giroux, "Revitalizing the Culture of Politics: An Introduction," *Impure Acts. The Practical Politics of Cultural Studies* (New York: Routledge, 2000), pp. 1–15.

1. See, for instance, Associated Press, "With Impeachment Over, Lieberman Worries About Public Cynicism, Alienation," 19 February 1999; John M. Broder, "Amid Political Cynicism, Standing Steadfast in Her Faith," *New York Times,* 6 September 1999, sec. A, p. 12; Robert Kuttner, "Clinton's Tokenism on Long-Term Care," *Boston Globe,* 10 January 1999, sec. C, p. 7; Adam Pertman, "The Impeachment Case/On to the Full House/The Historians' Perspective," *Boston Globe,* 16 December 1998, sec. A, p. 41; Brian S. McNiff, "Student Governor Banishes Cynicism for a Day," *Worcester (Mass.) Telegram & Gazette,* 10 April 1999, sec. A, p. 2; Allison Mitchell, "Campaign Overhaul, Again," *New York Times*, 10 September 1999, sec. 4, p. 2. For an excellent analysis of the role the media play in fueling voter cynicism, see Joseph N. Capella and Kathleen Hall Jamieson, *Spiral of Cynicism: The Press and the Public Good* (New York: Oxford University Press, 1997).

2. This theme is taken up in Jeffrey C. Goldfarb, *The Cynical Society: The Culture of Politics and the Politics of Culture in American Life* (Chicago: University of Chicago Press, 1991); Capella and Jamieson, *Spiral of Cynicism;* Russell Jacoby, *The End of Utopia* (New York: Basic Books, 1999); William Chaloupka, *Everybody Knows: Cynicism in America* (Minneapolis: University of Minnesota Press, 1999); Zygmunt Bauman, *In Search of Politics* (Stanford, Calif.: Stanford University Press, 1999); Carl Boggs, *The End of Politics: Corporate Power and the Decline of the Public Sphere* (New York: Guilford Press, 2000). I take the term "culture of antipolitics" from Boggs, p. 21.

3. Robert W. McChesney, *Rich Media, Poor Democracy: Communication Politics in Dubious Times* (Urbana: University of Illinois Press, 1999), p. 6.

4. Boggs, *End of Politics,* p. vii. Boggs argues that a culture of antipolitics has five broad features in common: "an unmistakable retreat from the political realm; a decline in the trappings of citizenship and with it the values of democratic participation; a narrowing of public discourse and the erosion of independent centers of thinking; a lessened capacity to achieve social change by means of statecraft or social governance; and the eventual absence of a societal understanding of what is uniquely common and public, what constitutes a possible general interest amidst the fierce interplay of competing private and local claims" (p. 22).

5. Roberto Mangabeira Unger and Cornel West, *The Future of American Progressivism* (Boston: Beacon Press, 1998).

6. Cited in Alex Kellogg, "Looking Inward, Freshmen Care Less About Politics and More About Money," *Chronicle of Higher Education* (January 21, 2001), p. A 47.

7. Matt Moseley, "Young Americans Volunteer But Don't Vote," *Campaigns and Elections* (April 1999): 35.

8. Nancy Fraser and Linda Gordon, "Contract versus Charity: Why Is There

No Social Citizenship in the United States?" in Gershon Shafir, ed. *The Citizenship Debates* (Minneapolis: University of Minnesota Press, 1998), pp. 113–114.

9. There is a ongoing debate over the meaning and relevance of citizenship for a progressive politics, and I don't want to underplay the problematic nature of my usage of the term. For some recent examples of this debate, see Shafir, *The Citizenship Debates* (Minneapolis: University of Minnesota Press, 1998); also, special issue on citizenship in *Cultural Studies* 14, no. 1 (January 2000).

10. Kevin Mattson, "Talking About My Generation (and the Left)," *Dissent* (Fall 1999): 59.

11. Carl Boggs is exceptionally helpful in this regard and provides a number of recent surveys that chart such a decline. See Boggs, *End of Politics,* pp. 30–34.

12. Bauman, *In Search of Politics,* p. 4.

13. Bauman, *In Search of Politics,* p. 8.

14. Michael Karin, "Where's the Outrage," *New York Times Magazine* (7 June 1998), pp. 78–79.

15. Michael Walzer, "The Big Shrug," *The New Republic,* 2 February 1996, pp. 9–10.

16. Stanley Aronowitz and William Di Fazio, *The Jobless Future: Sci-Tech and the Dogma of Work* (Minneapolis: University of Minnesota Press, 1994).

17. Eric Alterman, "Blowjobs and Snow Jobs," *The Nation* (20 December 1999), p. 10.

18. Jacoby, *End of Utopia,* p. xi.

19. On this issue, see Nina Eliasoph, *Avoiding Politics: How Americans Produce Apathy in Everyday Life* (New York: Cambridge University Press, 1998); Unger and West, *Future of American Progressivism.* On the issue of social citizenship, see Fraser and Gordon, "Contract Versus Charity," pp. 113–127.

20. Robert McChesney, "Introduction," in Noam Chomsky, *Profit Over People* (New York: Seven Stories Press, 1999), p. 11.

21. See, for instance, the stories following the suppression of dissent on Disney-owned ABC, or the increasing corporatization of the university. See also McChesney, *Corporate Media and the Threat to Democracy* (New York: Seven Stories Press, 1997); Henry Giroux, *The Mouse That Roared: Disney and the End of Innocence* (Lanham, Md.: Rowman & Littlefield, 1999); Russell Mokhiber and Robert Weissman, *Corporate Predators: The Hunt for Mega-Profits and the Attack on Democracy* (Monroe, Maine: Common Courage Press, 1999); Chomsky, *Profits Over People.*

22. Cited in Fair Action Alert, "In the Soup at the View: ABC Allows Corporate Sponsor to Buy Talk Show Content," FAIR-L@FAIR-ORG (November 20, 2000), p. 2.

23. For an analysis of this issue, see Eric Alterman, "The 'Right' Books and Big Ideas," *The Nation* (22 September 1999), pp. 16–21.

24. This section on higher education draws from Stanley Aronowitz and Henry A. Giroux, "Higher Education and the Politics of Education," an unpublished paper, 1999, p. 11.

25. This position becomes almost caricature when it is applied to cultural studies by some conservatives. One typical example can be found in Edward Rothstein, "Trolling 'Low' Culture for High-Flying Ideas: A Sport of Intellectuals," *New York Times*, 28 March 1999, sec. A, p. 33. The sixties as the source of most contemporary problems has become a fundamental tenet of right-wing ideology and includes the work of academics such as Harold Bloom to the strident commentaries of former house majority leader, Tom De Lay.

26. David Williams, "Mr. DeLay Had It Right; Absolutism and Relativism Were at the Heart of the Clinton Matter," *Washington Post*, 7 March 1999, sec. B, p. 2.

27. Anthony Lewis, "Self-Inflicted Wound," *New York Times*, 9 February 1999, sec. A, p. 31.

28. This position can be found in the work of Neil Postman. See, for example, Postman, *Technopoly: The Surrender of Culture to Technology* (New York: Knopf, 1992).

29. Some typical examples include: Todd Gitlin, *The Twilight of Common Dreams: Why America Is Wracked by Culture Wars* (New York: Metropolitan Books, 1995); and Alan Sokal and Jean Bricmont, *Fashionable Nonsense: Postmodern Intellectuals' Abuse of Science* (New York: Picador, 1998); Michael Tomasky, *Left for Dead: The Life, Death and Possible Resurrection of Progressive Politics in America* (New York: Free Press, 1996); Jim Sleeper, *The Closest of Strangers: Liberalism and the Politics of Race in New York* (New York: Norton, 1990).

30. Cited in Sherry B. Ortner, "Anthropology in Public," *Dissent* (Fall 1999): 107. See Micaela de Leonardo, *Exotics at Home: Anthropologies, Others, American Modernity* (Chicago: University of Chicago Press, 1998).

31. Alterman, cited in Ellen Willis, *Don't Think, Smile! Notes on a Decade of Denial* (Boston: Beacon Press, 1999), p. xiii.

32. Todd Gitlin, "The Anti-Political Populism of Cultural Studies," *Dissent* (Fall 1997): 77–82.

33. For a brilliant critique of this issue, see Stanley Aronowitz, *The Crisis of Historical Materialism* (Westport, Conn.: Bergin & Garvey, 1981). As Judith Butler points out, the left's call for unity around class "prioritizes a notion of the common" that is not only purified of race and gender considerations, but also "forgets" that those social movements that organized around various forms of identity politics emerged, in part, in opposition to the principles of exclusion in which such calls for class unity were constructed. See Judith Butler, "Merely Cultural," *Social Text* 15, nos. 3–4 (Fall/Winter 1997): 268. Needless to say, there are a number of Marxists who focus on political economy, class, and power in ways that do not fit this description at all and make an enormously important number of theoretical contributions to left issues. See, for instance, the writers associated with the *Monthly Review* and *Against the Current* as representative examples.

34. Willis, *Don't Think, Smile!* pp. x–xi.

35. See note 33, p. x.

36. Lawrence Grossberg, "The Cultural Studies Crossroad Blues," *European Journal of Cultural Studies* 1, no. 1(1998): 65–82.

37. Two that stand out are Tony Bennett, *Culture: A Reformer's Science* (London: Sage, 1998); and Douglas Kellner, *Media Culture: Cultural Studies, Identity and Politics Between the Modern and Postmodern* (New York: Routledge, 1995). For a mix of essays that range from constructive critiques to caricature, see Marjorie Ferguson and Peter Golding, eds. *Cultural Studies in Question* (London: Thousand Oaks, 1997).

38. See, for example, Lawrence Grossberg, *Bringing It All Back Home: Essays on Cultural Studies* (Durham, N.C.: Duke University Press, 1997), especially "Cultural Studies: What's in a Name?" pp. 245–271.

39. Grossberg, "Cultural Studies Crossroad Blues": 78, 66.

40. Willis, *Don't Think, Smile!* p. 192.

41. Jacques Derrida, "Intellectual Courage: An Interview," trans. Peter Krapp, *Cultural Machine* 2 (2000): 7.

42. See, for instance, Tom Cohen, *Ideology and Inscription: "Cultural Studies" After Benjamin, de man and Bakhtin* (New York: Cambridge University Press, 1998).

43. Lawrence Grossberg, Cary Nelson, and Paula Treichler, "Introduction," in Lawrence Grossberg, Cary Nelson, and Paula Treichler, eds. *Cultural Studies* (New York: Routledge, 1990), p. 5.

44. Jeffrey Hart, "How to Get a College Education," *National Review*, 30 September 1986, p. 38.

45. Roger Shattuck, *Candor & Perversion: Literature, Education and the Arts* (New York: Norton, 1999), p. 25.

46. Stanley Aronowitz, "Introduction," in Paulo Freire, ed., *Pedagogy of Freedom* (Lanham, Md.: Rowman & Littlefield, 1998), p. 4.

47. Shattuck, *Candor & Perversion*, p. 25.

48. Susan Bordo, *Twilight Zones: The Hidden Life of Cultural Images from Plato to O. J.* (Berkeley: University of California Press, 1999), p. 82.

49. Shattuck, *Candor & Perversion*, pp. 25–26.

50. Willis, *Don't Think, Smile!* p. 23.

51. Shattuck, *Candor & Perversion*, p. 27.

52. Shattuck, *Candor & Perversion*, p. 32.

53. Shattuck, p. 32, appears particularly disturbed that Cary Nelson and I are chaired professors. He mentions this point incessantly along with the fact that we are hackneyed writers, ideological storm troopers, and unqualified for the positions we hold. These charges have more than a decidedly ideological ring; they also suggest something about the ongoing right-wing attack on academic freedom, often couched in the discourse of apocalyptic decline and moral panic.

54. One version of this argument can be found in Stanley Fish, *Professional Correctness: Literary Studies and Political Change* (New York: Oxford University Press, 1995).

55. For Gitlin's most succinct critique of cultural studies, see Todd Gitlin, "The Anti-Political Populism of Cultural Studies," *Dissent* (Spring 1997): 77–82.

56. Robert W. McChesney, "Is There Any Hope for Cultural Studies," *Monthly Review* 47, no. 10 (March 1996): 3.

57. For two brilliant critiques of the materialist attack on cultural politics, see Robin Kelley, *Yo' Mama's Disfunktional!* (Boston: Beacon Press, 1997), especially chapter 4, and Willis, *Don't Think, Smile!*

58. For an excellent commentary on the mutually important relationship of class and social identity to any viable notion of organized politics, see the range of articles in *Social Text,* no. 61 (1999), especially Patrick McCreery and Kitty Krupat, "Introduction," pp. 1–7.

59. Michel Foucault, "Polemics, Politics, and Problematizations: An Interview with Michel Foucault," in Paul Rabinow, ed. *Ethics: Subjectivity and Truth, the Essential Works of Michel Foucault 1954–1984* (New York: The New Press, 1994), pp. 111–119.

60. Lost from this discourse is any attempt to engage, guide, direct, and stimulate new forms of practice and expression. Rather than being a dynamic, critical force, such discourse becomes a kind of pretense for interviewing oneself, a form of self-aggrandizement. On this issue, see Maurice Berger, "Introduction: The Crisis of Criticism," in Maurice Berger, ed. *The Crisis of Criticism* (New York: The New Press, 1998), pp. 1–14.

61. In this regard, see Jeffrey Wallen's brilliant and chilling analysis: Wallen, *Closed Encounters: Literary Politics and Public Culture* (Minneapolis: University of Minnesota Press, 1998).

62. Chantal Mouffe, cited in Lynn Worsham and Gary A. Olson, "Rethinking Political Community: Chantal Mouffe's Liberal Socialism," *Journal of Composition Theory* 19, no. 2 (1999): 180–181.

63. Foucault, "Polemics," pp. 112–113.

64. Pierre Bourdieu, *Acts of Resistance* (New York: New Press, 1999), pp. 8–9.

65. Elizabeth Long, "Introduction: Engaging Sociology and Cultural Studies: Disciplinarity and Social Change," in Elizabeth Long, ed. *From Sociology to Cultural Studies* (Malden, Mass.: Blackwell, 1997), p. 17.

66. Bauman, *Globalization: The Human Consequences* (New York: Columbia University Press, 1998).

67. See, for instance, Bourdieu, *Acts of Resistance;* McChesney, *Corporate Media;* Giroux, *The Mouse That Roared;* Bauman, *In Search of Politics.*

68. Stuart Hall, "The Centrality of Culture: Notes on the Cultural Revolutions of Our Time," in Kenneth Thompson, ed. *Media and Cultural Regulation* (Thousand Oaks, Calif.: Sage, 1997), p. 209.

69. Lawrence Grossberg, "Identity and Cultural Studies: Is That All There Is?" in Stuart Hall and Paul Du Gay, eds. *Questions of Cultural Identity* (Thousand Oaks, Calif.: Sage, 1996), pp. 99–100.

70. Giroux, *Border Crossings: Cultural Workers and the Politics of Education* (New York: Routledge, 1992).

71. James Young, "The Holocaust as Vicarious Past: Art Spiegelman's *Maus* and the Afterimages of History," *Critical Inquiry* 24 (Spring 1998): 673.

72. For some recent analyses of the corporate attack at higher education, see

Randy Martin, ed. *Chalk Lines: The Politics of Work in the Managed University* (Durham, N.C.: Duke University Press, 1998); Aronowitz, *The Knowledge Factory: Dismantling the Corporate University and Creating True Higher Learning* (Boston: Beacon Press, 2000); Giroux, *Impure Acts;* Giroux, *Corporate Culture and the Attack on Higher Education and Public Schooling* (Bloomington, Ind.: Phi Delta Kappa Educational Foundation, 1999).

73. On the issue of pedagogy, hope, and historical contingency, see Paulo Freire, *Pedagogy of Freedom* (Lanham, Md.: Rowman & Littlefield, 1998); Richard Johnson, "Teaching Without Guarantees: Cultural Studies, Pedagogy, and Identity," in Joyce Canaan and Debbie Epstein, eds. *A Question of Discipline* (Boulder, Colo.: Westview Press, 1997), pp. 42–77; Alan O' Shea, "A Special Relationship? Cultural Studies, Academia, and Pedagogy," *Cultural Studies* 12, no. 4 (1998): 512–527.

74. For one important analysis of what it might mean to theorize the role of culture within such considerations, see Grossberg, "The Victory of Culture, Part I: Against the Logic of Mediation," *Angelaki: Journal of Theoretical Humanities* 3, no. 3 (1998): 3–29.

75. Marquard Smith, "On the State of Cultural Studies: An Interview with Paul Gilroy," *Third Text* 49 (Winter 1999–2000): 15–26.

76. David Theo Goldberg, "Surplus Value: The Political Economy of Prisons," *The Review of Education/Pedagogy/Cultural Studies* (forthcoming).

77. Bourdieu, *Acts of Resistance,* p. 8.

78. Bourdieu, *Acts of Resistance,* p. 27.

79. For an excellent summary of this movement, see Richard Apelbaum and Peter Dreier, "The Campus Anti-Sweatshop Movement," *The American Prospect,* no. 46 (September–October 1999): 71–78; for a report on the strike at the University of California-Berkeley and its resolution, see June Jordan, "Good News of Our Own," *The Progressive* (August 1999): 18–19; for a report on various student-labor activism, see Eli Eduardo Naduris-Weissman, "Student-Labor Activism Advances," *Against the Current,* no. 83 (November–December 1999): 11–13.

CHAPTER 2

1. One excellent source analyzing the various debates over citizenship can be found in Gershon Shafir, ed. *The Citizenship Debates: A Reader* (Minneapolis: University of Minnesota Press, 1998).

2. Jacques Derrida, "Intellectual Courage: An Interview," trans. Peter Krapp, *Culture Machine* 2 (2000): 9.

3. In this respect, one can point to the welfare reform bill signed into law by former president Bill Clinton. The bill cut $55 billion from federal antipoverty programs. Peter Edelman, former under secretary of health and human services, resigned over Clinton's support of the bill, calling it, in an article in *The Atlantic Monthly,* the worst thing that Bill Clinton had done. Not only did the bill produce budget cuts

that affected low-income people, but 10 percent of all families were expected to lose income; moreover, Edelman estimated that the bill would move 2.6 million people, including 1.1 million children, into poverty. The bill also resulted in drastic cuts in child nutrition programs—$3 billion in six years—and support for social services—$2.5 billion in over six years, as well. See Peter Edelman, "The Worst Thing Bill Clinton Has Done," *The Atlantic Monthly* 279, no. 3 (March 1997): 43–58. See also the moving analysis by Deborah R. Connolly of the problems experienced daily by a group of poor women trying their best to negotiate a social service system that is underserved and overburdened. In Deborah R. Connolly, *Homeless Mothers: Face-to-Face with Women and Poverty* (Minneapolis: University of Minnesota Press, 2000).

4. Paul Gilroy, "On the State of Cultural Studies: An Interview with Paul Gilroy," *Third Text* 49 (Winter 1999–2000): 21. There are too many texts to mention on media control of public spaces, but one good example is Robert W. McChesney, *Corporate Media and the Threat to Democracy* (New York: Seven Stories Press, 1997).

5. Zygmunt Bauman, *Globalization: The Human Consequences* (New York: Columbia University Press, 1998), p. 21.

6. Lisa Belkin, "The Backlash Against Children," *New York Times Magazine* (23 July 2000), p. 30.

7. Belkin, "Backlash," 32.

8. Belkin, "Backlash," 34.

9. See note 8.

10. R. J. Smith, "Among the Mooks," *New York Times Magazine* (6 August 2000), p. 38.

11. This refusal of many critics to deal with the social, economic, and cultural conditions that produce gangsta rap is taken up in George Lipsitz, "The Hip Hop Hearings: Censorship, Social Memory, and Intergenerational Tensions Among African Americans," in Joe Austin and Michael Nevin Willard, eds. *Generations of Youth* (New York: New York University Press, 1998), pp. 395–411.

12. I have addressed the right-wing attack on youth in great detail in Henry A. Giroux, *Fugitive Cultures: Race, Violence, and Youth* (New York: Routledge Publishing,1996); *Channel Surfing: Race Talk and the Destruction of American Youth* (New York: St. Martin's Press, 1997); *Stealing Innocence: Corporate Culture's War on Children* (New York: St. Martin's Press, 2000).

13. Smith, "Among the Mooks," p. 39.

14. See note 13.

15. Robin D. G. Kelley, *Yo' Mama's Disfunktional! Fight the Culture Wars in Urban America* (Boston: Beacon Press, 1997), p. 17.

16. What writers such as Belkin and Smith leave out of their accounts of children in American is astonishing. For instance, Marian Wright Edelman reports that "13.5 million children live in poverty, 12 million have no health insurance, 5 million are home alone everyday after school lets out. And more than 4,000 each year pay the ultimate price for adult irresponsibility: they are killed by guns. [Moreover] millions more receive substandard education in crumbling schools without enough books,

equipment, or teachers. Or they are eligible for Head Start programs or child care assistance when parents work, but receive neither. Or they are abused or neglected, or are languishing in temporary foster homes, waiting for adoption." Marian Wright Edelman, "There's No Trademark on Concern for Kids," *New York Times*, 29 July 2000, sec. A, p. 27.

17. Toni Morrison, "On the Backs of Blacks," *Time*, vol. 142, no. 21 (Fall 1993): 57.

18. It is important to stress here that, in arguing that the state is being hollowed out, I am not suggesting that the state is homogeneous, nor am I suggesting that the state is losing its power. On the contrary, rather than losing its power, the state is simply abdicating power by refusing both to curb the excesses of capital and to guarantee those public goods, provisions, and safety nets that offer people a modicum of basic needs and protection. Peter Marcuse rightly suggests "that the importance of state action in enabling the capitalist system of the industrialized world to function is increased, not reduced, as that system spreads internationally." On this issue, see Peter Marcuse, "The Language of Globalization," *Monthly Review* 53, no. 3 (July–August, 2000) <www.monthlyreview.org/700marc.htm>, p.2.

19. Cornel West, "America's Three-Fold Crisis," *Tikkun* 9, no. 2 (1994): 41–44.

20. Zygmunt Bauman, *In Search of Politics* (Stanford, Calif.: Stanford University Press, 1999), p. 166.

21. Pierre Bourdieu, *Acts of Resistance* (New York: Free Press, 1998), p. 102. For an insight into the human toll that such ideologies produce at the level of everyday experiences, see Bourdieu and Allain Accard. *The Weight of the World: Social Suffering in Contemporary Society* (Stanford, Calif.: Stanford University Press, 1999).

22. Stephen Holden, "Can Art and Cinema Survive Cruder Times?" *New York Times*, 1 September 2000, sec. B, p. 8.

23. Paul Gilroy, *Against Race* (Cambridge, Mass.: Harvard University Press, 2000), p. 221.

24. "Behind the Power: An Interview with Ruth Wilson Gilmore," *Colorlines* (Winter 1999–2000): 16–20.

25. For one compilation of such acts, see Jill Nelson, ed. *Police Brutality* (New York: Norton, 2000). Also see Christian Parenti, *Lockdown America: Police and Prisons in the Age of Crisis* (London: Verso, 1999).

26. "Behind the Power," p. 17.

27. For an excellent analysis of the rise of zero tolerance policies and the culture of repression, see Parenti, *Lockdown America*.

28. For an insightful commentary on the media and the racial nature of the war on drugs, see Jimmie L. Reeves and Richard Campbell, *Cracked Coverage: Television News, The Anti-Cocaine Crusade, and the Reagan Legacy* (Durham, N.C.: Duke University Press, 1994).

29. Patricia J. Williams, "An American Litany," *The Nation* (12 October 1998), p. 10.

30. Edward Helmore, "The World: Reverend Al Rises Again: Black Leader Returns to Plague New York's Rudi Giuliani," *The Observer* (4 April 1999), p. 23.

31. "Behind the Power," p. 16.

32. Steven R. Donziger, ed. *The Real War on Crime: The Report of the National Criminal Justice Commission* (New York: Harper Perennial, 1996), p. 19.

33. For specifics on this bill, see C. Stone Brown, "Legislating Repression: The Federal Crime Bill and the Anti-Terrorism and Effective Death Penalty Act," in Elihu Rosenblatt, *Criminal Injustice: Confronting the Prison Crisis* (Boston: South End Press, 1996), pp. 100–107.

34. Anthony Lewis, "Punishing the Country, *New York Times,* 2 December 1999, sec. A, p. 1.

35. For some extensive analyses of the devastating affects the criminal justice system is having on black males, see Michael Tonry, *Malign Neglect: Race, Crime, and Punishment in America* (New York: Oxford University Press, 1995); Jerome Miller, *Search and Destroy: African American Males in the Criminal Justice System* (Cambridge: Cambridge University Press, 1996); David Cole, *No Equal Justice: Race and Class in the American Criminal Justice System* (New York: The New Press, 1999).

36. These figures are taken from the following sources: Gary Delgado, " 'Mo' Prisons Equals Mo' Money," *Colorlines* (Winter 1999–2000): 18; Fox Butterfield, "Number in Prison Grows Despite Crime Reduction," *New York Times,* 10 August 2000, sec. A, pp. 1, 10.

37. Manning Marable, "Green Party Politics," Transcript of speech given in Denver, Colorado, on 24 June 2000, p. 3.

38. Prisoners being held in private facilities make up the fastest growing segment of the jail and prison population in the United States. At the same time, only 7 percent of prisons and jails are privately run. It is worth noting that such prisons have bad track records around human rights and providing decent services. They are also actively opposed by corrections guards unions. Cited in Lisa Featherstone, "A Common Enemy: Students Fight Private Prisons," *Dissent* (Fall 2000): 78.

39. Kelley, *Yo' Mama's Disfunktional!* p. 98.

40. See note 39.

41. Donziger, *The Real War on Crime,* p. xii.

42. Featherstone, "A Common Enemy," p. 78.

43. Featherstone, "A Common Enemy," p. 81.

44. Mike Davis, "The Politics of Super Incarceration," in Elihu Rosenblatt, *Criminal Injustice: Confronting the Prison Crisis* (Boston: South End Press, 1996), p. 73.

45. Cited in Jennifer Warren, "When He Speaks, They Listen, "*Los Angeles Times,* 21 August 2000, <www.mapinc.org/drugnews/v00/n1213/a05.html>, p. 2.

46. Donziger, *Real War on Crime,* p. 102.

47. David Cole, *No Equal Justice: Race and Class in the American Criminal Justice System* (New York: The New Press, 1999), p. 144.

48. Donziger, *Real War on Crime,* p. 101.

49. Cited in Eyal Press, "The Color Test," *Lingua Franca* 10, no. 7 (October 2000): 55.

50. Cited in Marable, "Green Party Politics," p. 4.

51. Cited from Eric Lotke, "The Prison-Industrial Complex," *Multinational Monitor* 17 (November 1996):11, see <www.igc.org/ncia/pic.html>.

52. Even more shameful is that fact that such discrimination against African Americans is often justified from the Olympian heights of institutions such as Harvard University by apologists such as lawyer-author Randall Kennedy, who argue that such laws, criminal policies, and police practices are necessary to protect "good" blacks from "bad" blacks who commit crimes. See Kennedy, *Race, Crime, and the Law* (New York: Pantheon, 1997).

53. In their drive to turn a profit, private prisons often keep their facilities full, "cut costs by trimming prisoner facilities and services [such as training for guards and programs for inmates], and inasmuch as they are paid on a per capita basis, they have a strong financial incentive to retain prisoners in lockup as long as possible." Corrections Corporation of America, one of the nation's leading private prison conglomerates, has seen its stock go through the roof since the late 1990s. In fact, one of its facilities, Wackenhut Corrections, in Florida, was so successful in turning a profit due to its use of cheap prison labor that it was named by *Forbes* magazine as one of the "200 Best Small Companies" in 1996. Both quotes cited in Kelley, *Yo' Mama's Disfunktional!* p. 98.

54. Guy Trebay, "Jailhouse Chic, an Anti-style Turns Into a Style Itself," *New York Times,* 13 June 2000, sec. A, p. 23.

55. For a moving narrative of the devastating effects of the juvenile justice system on teens, see Edward Humes, *No Matter How Loud I Shout: A Year in the Life of Juvenile Court* (New York: Touchstone, 1996).

56. Margaret Talbot, "The Maximum Security Adolescent," *New York Times Magazine* (10 September 2000), p. 42.

57. Louise Cooper, Youth Activists Fight Prop 21," *Against the Current* 86 (May/June 2000): 12.

58. Cited in Evelyn Nieves, "California Proposal Toughens Penalties for Young Criminals," *New York Times,* 6 March 2000, sec. A, p. 1, 15.

59. Cited in Sara Rimer and Raymond Bonner, "Whether to Kill Those Who Killed as Youths," *New York Times,* 22 August 2000, sec. A, p. 16. For a general critique of the death penalty system in the United States, see Robert Sherrill, "Death Trip: The American Way of Execution," *The Nation* (January 8/15 2001), pp. 13–34.

60. Cited in Gary Delgado, "Mo' Prisons Equals Mo' Money," *Colorlines* (Winter 1999–2000): 18.

61. Donziger, *Real War on Crime,* p. 123.

62. When Tom Smith of the National Opinion Research Center at the University of Chicago asked respondents to compare blacks and other minorities "on a variety of personal traits in 1990," he found that "62 percent of nonblack respondents thought that blacks were lazier than other groups, 56 percent felt they were more

prone to violence, 53 percent see them as less intelligent, and 78 percent thought they were less self-supporting and more likely to live off welfare." Cited in Douglas S. Massey and Nancy A. Denton, *American Apartheid* (Cambridge, Mass.: Harvard University Press, 1993), p. 95. I mention this study as simply one example of the widespread racism that permeates American culture. Of course, while blacks are not the only group victimized by stereotypes, unlike many other groups, they often do not have the material resources to fight back and prevent such stereotypes from spreading and influencing individual behavior and social policy. Hence, African Americans, especially black youth, as a group, are more likely to suffer the abuse such stereotypes generate. For a more extensive study of the ongoing presence of racism in American society, see: David K. Shipler, *A Country of Strangers: Blacks and Whites in America* (New York: Vintage, 1998); Ronald Walters, "The Criticality of Racism," *Black Scholar* 26, no. 1 (Winter 1996): 2–8. Of course, one could compile an endless list of sources on the latter subject. I only mention three because of limited space.

63. A typical example can be seen in Talbot, "The Maximum Security Adolescent," pp. 41–47, 58–60, 88, 96. Talbot takes up the "get tough" policies that currently characterize the juvenile justice system, but makes no connections to wider social, economic, or political considerations or, for that matter, to the related assaults on teens taking place in a variety of spheres outside of the criminal justice system. Of course, the right-wingers and reactionary-leaning liberals who call for zero tolerance policies have almost nothing to say about the hypocrisy involved in the contradiction between punishing minorities according to get tough policies and either saying nothing or actively supporting a corporate culture that appears addicted to marketing guns and the imagery and culture of gun violence to young children, teens, and adults. The call for zero tolerance laws, rather than gun control, appears odd in a country in which handguns were used to kill 9,390 people in 1996, while in countries with tough handgun laws, the number of such deaths was drastically reduced. For example, "[H]andguns were used to kill 2 people in New Zealand, 15 in Japan, 30 in Great Britain, 106 in Canada, and 213 in Germany." Cited in Bob Herbert, "Addicted to Guns," Op. Ed. *New York Times on the Web* (1 January 2001), <www.nytimes. com/ 2001/01/01opinion/01Herb.html>, p. 1.

64. A classic example of this type of omission can be found in Gregory Michie, "One Strike and You're Out: Does Zero Tolerance Work? Or Does Kicking Kids Out of School Just Make Things Worse?" *Chicago Reader* 29, no. 49 (8 September 2000): 1, 18, 22, 24, 26, 28.

65. Lewis Lapham, "School Bells," *Harper's Magazine* (August 2000), p. 8.

66. Marable, "Green Party Politics," p. 5.

67. An Interview with Jesse Jackson, "First Class Jails, Second Class Schools," *Rethinking Schools* (Spring 2000): 16.

68. Kate Beem, "Schools Adopting Safety Measures," *Centre Daily Times,* 3 March 2000, sec. A, p. 3.

69. See Brian Moore, "Letting Software Make the Call," *Chicago Reader* 29, no. 49 (8 September 2000): 18.

70. Ellen Goodman, " 'Zero Tolerance' Means Zero Chance for Troubled Kids," *Centre Daily Times,* 4 January 2000, p. 8.

71. Editorial, "Zero Tolerance Is the Policy," *Denver Rocky Mountain News,* 22 June 1999, sec. A, p. 38.

72. Editorial, "Growing Zeal for Zero Tolerance Ignores Needs of Troubled Youth," *USA Today,* 22 November 1999, sec, A, p. 27.

73. "First Class Jails, Second Class Schools," p. 16.

74. See note 70.

75. See note 71.

76. Michie, "One Strike," p. 24.

77. The *New York Times* reported that, in responding to the spate of recent school shootings, the F.B.I. had provided educators across the country with a list of behaviors that could identify "students likely to commit an act of lethal violence." One such behavior is "resentment over real or perceived injustices." The reach of domestic militarization becomes more evident as the F.B.I. not only takes on the role of monitoring potentially disruptive student behavior, but also positions teachers to become adjuncts of the criminal justice system. The story and quotes appear in an editorial, "F.B.I. Caution Signs for Violence In Classroom," *New York Times,* 7 September 2000, sec. A, p. 18.

78. Clare Kittredge, "Penalties No Panacea for Youth Violence, a Specialist Warns; Juvenile Aggression Is Conference Topic," *The Boston Globe.* sec. *New Hampshire Weekly,* 16 May 1999, p. 1

79. Tamar Lewin, "Study Finds Racial Bias in Public Schools," *New York Times,* 11 March 2000, sec. A, p. 14.

80. Libero Della Piana, "Crime and Punishment in Schools: Students of Color are Facing More Suspensions Because of Racially Biased Policies," *San Francisco Chronicle,* 9 February 2000, sec. A, p. 21.

81. Marilyn Elias, "Disparity in Black and White?" *USA Today,* 11 December 2000, sec. D, p. 9.

82. Tirozzi cited and paraphrased in Elias, "Disparity."

83. One example of the effects of this system of punishment has on African American students can be seen in a recent report from the Kids First! Coalition in Oakland, which reported that "local discipline policies resulted in students missing more than 29,000 school days in the 1997–1998 school year alone. Seventy-two percent of these students were African American." Cited in Della Piana, *Crime and Punishment,* 80. For a systematic examination of the effects of racial discrimination in U.S. public schools, see Rebecca Gordon, Libero Della Piana, and Terry Keleher, *Facing the Consequences: An Examination of Racial Discrimination in U.S. Public Schools* (Oakland, Calif.: Applied Research Center, 2000).

84. Andrea Shaw Jefferson, "Zero-Tolerance by Schools Troubling," *Times-Picayune,* 18 April 1999, sec. B, p. 7.

85. Bernie Huebner, "I Refuse: Teachers in Main Revolt Against Fingerprinting," *The Progressive* (August 2000), pp. 23–25.

86. Stanley Aronowitz, *The Knowledge Factory* (Boston: Beacon Press, 2000), pp. 61–62.

87. Della Piana, "Crime and Punishment," sec. A, p. 21.

88. Cited in Anthony Lewis, "Punishing the Country," *New York Times,* 21 December 1999, sec. A, p. 31.

89. William Ayers and Bernardine Dohrn, "Resisting Zero Tolerance," *Rethinking Schools* (Spring, 2000): 14.

90. Goodman, " 'Zero Tolerance.' "

91. Daniel Perlstein, "Failing at Kindness: Why Fear of Violence Endangers Children," *Educational Leadership* (March 2000): 76–79.

92. See, for instance, Henry A. Giroux and Stanley Aronowitz, *Education Still Under Siege,* 2nd ed. (Westport, Conn.: Bergin & Garvey Press 1994); Giroux, *Pedagogy and the Politics of Hope: Theory, Culture, and Schooling* (Boulder, Colo.: Westview/Harper Collins,1997) and *Stealing Innocence* (New York: St. Martin's Press, 2000).

93. Cornelius Castoriadis, "Democracy as Procedure and Democracy as Regime," *Constellations* 4, no. 1 (1997): 4.

94. Gary Olson and Lynn Worsham "Staging the Politics of Difference: Home Bhabha's Critical Literacy," *Journal of Advanced Composition* 19, no. 1 (Fall, 1999): 3.

95. Noam Chomsky, *Profit Over People* (New York: Seven Stories Press, 1999), p. 20.

96. Len Terry, "Traveling 'The Hard Road to Renewal': A Continuing Conversation with Stuart Hall," *Arena Journal* 8 (1997): 56.

97. In this instance, I am not suggesting that education simply be viewed as a way to promote critical consciousness, demystify knowledge, or provide alternative, progressive views of the world. I am also suggesting that pedagogy become performative and be seen as a valuable, if not a crucial, tool in linking theory to action and, in particular, in shaping social policy. On the issue of linking cultural politics and public policy, see Tony Bennett, "Putting Policy into Cultural Studies," in Lawrence Grossberg, Cary Nelson, and Paula Treichler, eds. *Cultural Studies* (New York: Routledge, 1992), pp. 23–37; Michael Berube, *The Employment of English* (New York: New York University Press, 1998), especially the chapter, "Cultural Criticism and the Politics of Selling Out," pp. 216–242.

98. Lynn Worsham and Gary A. Olson, "Rethinking Political Community: Chantal Mouffe's Liberal Socialism," *Journal of Composition Theory* 19, no. 2 (1999): 178.

99. Castoriadis, "Democracy as Procedure," p. 11.

100. For a provocative analysis of the relationship between what Norman Geras calls "the contract of mutual indifference," the Holocaust, and neoliberalism's refusal of the social as a condition for contemporary forms of mutual indifference, see Norman Geras, *The Contract of Mutual Indifference* (London: Verso Press, 1998).

101. For some recent commentaries on the new student movement, see Lisa

Featherstone, "The New Student Movement," *The Nation* (15 May 2000), pp. 11–15; David Samuels, "Notes from Underground: Among the Radicals of the Pacific Northwest," *Harper's Magazine* (May 2000), pp. 35–47; Katazyna Lyson, Monique Murad, and Trevor Stordahl, "Real Reformers, Real Results," *Mother Jones* (October 2000), pp. 20–22.

CHAPTER 3

1. Zygmunt Bauman, *In Search of Politics* (Stanford, Calif.: Stanford University Press, 1999), p. 63. Robert W. McChesney defines neoliberalism as the "defining political and economic paradigm of our time—it refers to the policies and processes whereby a relative handful of private interests are permitted to control as much as possible of social life in order to maximize their personal profit. . . . [It is characterized by] a massive increase in social and economic inequality, a marked increase in server deprivation for the poorest nations and peoples of the world, a disastrous global environment, and unstable global economy and an unprecedented bonanza for the wealthy." Cited in Robert W. McChesney, "Introduction," in Noam Chomsky, *Profit Over People* (New York: Seven Stories Press, 1999), pp. 1–2.

2. While this issue is taken up in too many books to cite, some good general introductions to both the neoliberal indifference to social considerations and the growing indifference to democracy itself can be found in: Russell Mokhiber and Robert Weissman, *Corporate Predators: The Hunt for Mega-Profits and the Attack on Democracy* (Monroe, Maine: Common Courage Press, 1999); Richard Sennett, *The Corrosion of Character* (New York: Norton, 1998); William Greider, *One World, Ready or Not: The Manic Logic of Global Capitalism* (New York: Simon and Schuster, 1997); Robert W. McChesney, *Rich Media, Poor Democracy* (Urbana: University of Illinois Press, 1999); Ellen Willis, *Don't Think, Smile! Notes on a Decade of Denial* (Boston: Beacon Press, 1999); for a deeply personal and moving account of the slide into moral indifference and the collapse of the public sphere and its safety nets for children, see Jonathan Kozol, *Ordinary Resurrections: Children in the Years of Hope* (New York: Crown, 2000).

3. For a recent example of this type of analysis, see John Mueller, *Capitalism and Democracy & Ralph's Pretty Good Grocery* (Princeton, N.J.: Princeton University Press, 1999).

4. Cited in McChesney, "Introduction" in Chomsky, *Profit Over People*, p. 9.

5. Pierre Bourdieu, *Acts of Resistance* (New York: Free Press, 1998), p. 32.

6. Michael Hardt and Antonio Negri argue that this is one of the central features of the bold new order of globalization, which they call empire, that now characterizes the twenty-first century. See Michael Hardt and Antonio Negri, *Empire* (Cambridge, Mass.: Harvard University Press, 2000).

7. Walter Mozley, *Working on the Chain Gang* (New York: Ballantine Publishing Group, 2000), p. 12.

8. I take this issue up in Henry A. Giroux, *Impure Acts* (New York: Routledge, 2000).

9. Bauman, *In Search of Politics,* pp. 40–41.

10. Theodor W. Adorno, *Critical Models* (New York: Columbia University Press, 1993), p. 290.

11. See, for example, Janet Maslin, "Such a Very Long Way from Duvets to Danger," *New York Times,* 15 October 1999, sec. B, p. 14; Amy Taubin, "So Good It Hurts," *Sight and Sound* (November 1999), p. 16; Gary Crowdus, "Getting Exercised Over *Fight Club," Cineaste* 25, no. 4 (2000): 46–48.

12. This genre was an outgrowth of a number of films, beginning with Quentin Tarantino's *Reservoir Dogs.* James Wolcott has labeled this genre as " 'scuzz cinema' . . . which earns its name from the pervasive, in-your-face, foul-mouthed scuzzines of its low-life characters, situations, and atmosphere, all of which convey the bottom falling out of civilization" *Vanity Fair* (April 1998), p. 148. The latter infatuation with violence, cynicism, glitz, and shootouts in diners got a remake by adding a more updated gesture towards social relevance, i.e., a critique of suburban life, consumerism, etc.

13. Eleanor Byrne and Martin McQuillan, *Deconstructing Disney* (London: Pluto Press, 1999), pp. 3–4.

14. Rustom Bharacuha, "Around Aydohya: Aberrations, Enigmas, and Moments of Violence," *Third Text* 24 (Autumn 1993): 56.

15. Needless to say, feminist and gay theorists have been analyzing the politics of masculinity for quite some time. For an important series of theoretical analyses on the changing nature of masculinity in Hollywood cinema that draws on many of these traditions, see Stevan Cohan and Ina Rae Hark, eds. *Screening the Male: Exploring Masculinities in Hollywood Cinema* (New York: Routledge, 1993).

16. Homi Bhabha, "Are You a Man or a Mouse," in Maurice Berger, Brian Wallis, and Simon Watson, eds. *Constructing Masculinity* (New York: Routledge, 1995), pp. 57–65.

17. Susan Faludi, *Stiffed* (New York: Morrow, 1999).

18. Tom Peters adds a new twist in applying the logic of the market to everyday life by arguing that everyone should define himself or herself as a saleable item, a commodity. Specifically, Peters argues that people should come to see and treat themselves as brands. According to Peters, the one sure way of being successful in life is to market yourself as a brand name. Or, as Peters puts it, "It's this simple. You are a brand. You are in charge of your brand. There is no single path to success. And there is no one right way to create a brand called You. Except this: Start today. Or Else." Peters, "The Brand Called You," *Fast Company* (August–September, 1997), p. 94.

19. This paragraph on Operation Mayhem is taken from Henry A. Giroux and Imre Szeman, "IKEA Boy and the Politics of Male Bonding: *Fight Club,* Consumerism, and Violence," *New Art Examiner* (December/January 2000/2001), p. 60.

20. Bill Readings, *The University in Ruins* (Cambridge, Mass.: Harvard University Press, 1996), p. 48.

21. See note 20.

22. Bhabha, "The Enchantment of Art," in Carol Becker and Ann Wiens, eds. *The Artist in Society* (Chicago: New Art Examiner, 1994), p. 33.

23. Both of these quotations are from Bhabha, "Enchantment of Art." See note 23.

24. For some excellent commentaries on the politics of masculinity, see R. W. Connell, *Masculinities* (Berkeley: University of California Press, 1995); Berger et al., *Constructing Masculinities*; Paul Smith, ed., *Boys: Masculinities in Contemporary Culture* (Boulder, Colo.: Westview Press, 1996).

25. Paul Gilroy, " 'After the Love Has Gone': Bio-Politics and Ethepoetics in the Black Public Sphere," *Public Culture* 7, no. 1 (1994): 58.

26. For an interesting commentary on the way in which dominant forms of masculinity work to reproduce particular notions of racism, see Robin D. G. Kelley, "Confessions of a Nice Negro, or Why I Shaved My Head," in Don Belton, ed. *Speak My Name: Black Men on Masculinity and the American Dream* (Boston: Beacon Press, 1997), pp. 15–28.

27. For an interesting analysis of what might be called the dialectic of consumerism, see Robert Miklitsch, *From Hegel to Madonna: Towards a General Economy of "Commodity Fetishism"* (Albany, N.Y.: SUNY Press, 1998).

28. Susan Bordo offers a number of critical insights around the relationship between art and its growing tendency to celebrate and "become more sympathetic of the pathologies of our culture than of exposing them." See Susan Bordo, *Twilight Zones: The Hidden Life of Cultural Images* (Berkeley: University of California Press, 1999), p. 27.

29. Dr. Nadine Hoover is on target in arguing "There is something terribly wrong with our society when abuse becomes a means of bonding." Hoover, cited in Andrew Jacobs, "Violent Cast of High School Hazing Mirrors Society, Experts Say," *New York Times*, 5 March 2000, pp. 27–28.

30. The classic work on the relationship between fascism, male violence, and hatred of women is Klaus Theweleit, *Male Fantasies,* Vols. 1 & 2 (Minneapolis: University of Minnesota Press, 1987, 1989).

31. Paul Gilroy, *Against Race* (Cambridge, Mass.: Harvard University Press, 2000), p. 146.

32. Terry Eagleton, *The Ideology of the Aesthetic* (Cambridge, U.K.: Basil Blackwell, 1990), p. 344.

33. One wonders how Fincher would retheorize the relationship between misogyny and the celebration of violence in *Fight Club* in light of the attack by mobs of young men against a number of women in Central Park after the Puerto Rican Day parade in New York City during the summer of 2000. Of course, it would be fatuous to claim that utterly misogynist films such as *Fight Club* are directly responsible for the incident in which fifty-six women were attacked by roving bands of young men who doused them with water, groped them, and ripped off their clothes. But I don't think it would be unreasonable to argue that misogynist films such as *Fight Club* help

to legitimate such acts, because they exercise a pedagogical force shaped largely by a dominant politics of sexist representations that contributes to an increasing climate of hatred and objectification of women.

34. Commenting on what the kinds of violence that is often ignored in films such as *Fight Club,* Holly Sklar writes, "Imagine [films such as *Fight Club* giving] sustained national attention to the violence waged on the mind, body, and spirit of crumbling schools, [or to] low teacher expectations, employment and housing discrimination, racist dragnets, and everyday looks of hate by people finding you guilty by suspicion." Holly Sklar, "Young and Guilty by Stereotype," *Z Magazine* (July/August 1993), p. 53.

35. For a masterful analysis of the complexities of theorizing violence as well as a critique of its romanticization, see John Keane, *Reflections on Violence* (New York: Verso, 1996).

36. This theme is taken up in a number of recent books. See Jeffrey C. Goldfarb, *The Cynical Society: The Culture of Politics and the Politics of Culture in American Life* (Chicago: University of Chicago Press, 1991); Joseph N. Capella and Kathleen Hall Jamieson, *Spiral of Cynicism: The Press and the Public Good* (New York: Oxford University Press, 1997); Russell Jacoby, *The End of Utopia* (New York: Basic Books, 1999); William Chaloupka, *Everybody Knows: Cynicism in America* (Minneapolis: University of Minnesota Press, 1999); Bauman, *In Search of Politics;* Carl Boggs, *The End of Politics: Corporate Power and the Decline of the Public Sphere* (New York: Guilford Press, 2000).

37. Cited in Carol Becker, "The Art of Testimony," *Sculpture* (March 1997), p. 28.

38. For one of the most popular celebrations of this warrior mentality, see Robert Bly, *Iron John: A Book about Men* (Reading, Mass.: Addison-Wesley, 1990); For a sustained critique of this position, see James William Gibson, *Warrior Dreams: Paramilitary Culture in Post-Vietnam America* (New York: Hill and Wang, 1994).

39. This theme is explored in Tania Modleski, *Feminism Without Women* (New York: Routledge, 1991).

40. Cited from the National Center Victims of Crime website. See: <www:207.222.132.10/index%7E1.htm>.

41. Geoffrey Hartman, "Public Memory and Its Discontents," *Raritan* 8, no. 4 (Spring 1994): 28, 26.

42. On the cult of the warrior mythology and its relationship to male violence, see the exceptionally important work done on this subject by Gibson in *Warrior Dreams.*

43. Maslin, "Duvets to Danger."

44. Taubin, "So Good It Hurts."

45. Taubin, "So Good It Hurts," p. 17.

46. Susan Faludi, "It's *Thelma and Louise* for Guys," *Newsweek* (25 October 1999), p. 89.

47. David Edelstein, "Boys Do Bleed," *Slate* (posted on 15 October 1999 at <www.Slate.com>).

48. Gary Crowdus, "Getting Exercised Over *Fight Club*," *Cineaste* 25, no. 4 (2000): 46.

49. Crowdus, "Getting Exercised," p. 47.

50. See, for example, Bob Strauss, "Actors Defend Ultraviolent Film," *The Arizona Republic*, 15 October 1999, sec. D, p. 1; Gavin Smith, "Inside-Out-on-One with David Fincher," *Film Comment* (Sept/October 1999), pp. 58–67.

51. Edward Norton cited in Barry Koltnow, "*Club*'s Call to Arms Is Not Call to Violence," *Centre Daily Times,* 19 October 1999, sec. C, p. 11.

52. Cited in Benjamin Svtkey, "Blood, Sweat, and Fears," *Entertainment Weekly* (15 October 1999), p. 28.

53. Both quotes come from Svtkey, pp. 26, 31.

54. I take up this issue in Henry A. Giroux, *Fugitive Cultures* (New York: Routledge, 1996), and in *Channel Surfing: Racism, the Media, and the Destruction of Today's Youth* (New York: St. Martin's Press, 1998).

55. This issue is treated brilliantly in Susan Jeffords, *Hard Bodies: Hollywood Masculinity in the Reagan Era* (New York: Rutgers University Press, 1994). Of course, this type of representation is ongoing and can be found in recent films such as *Saving Private Ryan, The Thin Red Line,* and *Three Kings.*

56. Hannah Arendt, "On Violence," in *Crisis of the Republic* (New York: Harcourt Brace Jovanovich, 1972), p. 108.

57. See for example, Martin A. Lee, *The Beast Reawakens: Fascism's Resurgence from Hitler's Spymasters to Today's Neo-Nazi Groups and Right-Wing Extremists* (New York: Routledge, 2000).

58. Paul Gilroy, *Against Race* (Cambridge, Mass.: Harvard University Press, 2000), p. 146.

59. Gilroy, *Against Race,* p. 150.

60. Gilroy, *Against Race,* p. 158.

61. Gilroy, *Against Race,* p. 152.

62. James Snead, *White Screens/Black Images* (New York: Routledge, 1994), pp. 131, 142.

63. Gilroy, *Against Race,* p.5.

CHAPTER 4

1. I address this issue in chapter 1.

2. For an insightful analysis of the breakdown of civic life as a condition for such cynicism, see Robert D. Putnam, *Bowling Alone: The Collapse and Revival of American Community.* (New York: Simon and Schuster, 2000). For an analysis of the relationship between work and the corrosion of community and social values, see Richard Sennett, *The Corrosion of Character* (New York: Norton, 1998) and Paulina Borsook, *Cyberselfish: A Critical Romp Through the Terribly Libertarian Culture of High Tech* (New York: Public Affairs, 2000).

3. Frank Rich, "Don't Worry, Be Happy!" *New York Times,* 29 July 2000, sec. A, p. 27. On the issue of public life and cynicism, see also, Bauman, *In Search of Politics*; Henry A. Giroux, *Impure Acts: The Practical Politics of Cultural Studies* (New York: Routledge, 2000).

4. For systemic and critical accounts of the emptying out of the state and its impact on social services, see Noam Chomsky, *Profit Over People: Neoliberalism and Global Order* (New York: Seven Stories Press, 1999); Frances Fox Piven and Richard A. Cloward, *The Breaking of the American Social Compact* (New York: New Press, 1997); Deborah R. Connolly, *Homeless Mothers: Face to Face with Women and Poverty* (Minneapolis: University of Minnesota Press, 2000). See also the corresponding work going on in Europe on this issue, especially the works of Ulrich Beck, i.e., Ulrich Beck, *Democracy Without Enemies,* Mark Ritter, trans. (Cambridge, U.K.: Polity Press, 1998); Ulrich Beck, *The Reinvention of Politics: Rethinking Modernity in the Global Social Order,* Mark Ritter, trans., (Cambridge, U.K.: Polity Press, 1996).

5. See Karen Birchard, "Bank Makes Deal with U. of Oxford to Gain a Share of Spinoff Profits," *Chronicle of Higher Education* (30 November 2000). I mention the *Chronicle* because it is a model example of a serious academic journal that in the last decade has repeatedly endorsed such corporate ties in its pages, while publishing a range of articles that often support attacks on affirmative action, civil rights, and other progressive attempts to bolster democratic rights and public spaces. For a particularly offensive expression of the latter, see the supposed human interest story, see Leo Reisberg, "A Professor's Controversial Analysis of Why Black Students Are 'Losing the Race,'" a favorable story on the work of conservative educator John H. McWhorter. The *Chronicle* uncritically reports that that "Mr. McWhorter says he came to realize that not only were black undergraduates at Berkeley 'among the worst students on campus,' but that black students in general—from kindergarten to graduate school, and from the ghettos to middle-class suburbia—were the weakest in America." He says that black Americans tend to blame their plight on racism, oppression, poverty, and underfinanced inner-city schools. But Mr. McWhorter argues that "black students of all classes and income levels lag behind their white counterparts, because of a mindset endemic to black culture that discourages learning." That such retrograde racist dribble can be taken seriously in any journal represents more than cause for alarm; it points to the resurgence of a racialized form of Social Darwinism that now drives the racialization and criminalization of social policy, especially as it is aimed at young men of color. From Leo Reisberg, "A Professor's Controversial Analysis of Why Black Students Are 'Losing the Race,'" *The Chronicle of Higher Education* (11 November 2000), at <www.chronicle.com/weekly/v46/I49/49a05101.htm>.

6. Jeffrey Williams, "Brave New University," *College English* 61, no. 6 (July 1999): 44.

7. Bauman, *In Search of Politics,* p. 107.

8. Stanley Aronowitz, *The Knowledge Factory* (Boston: Beacon Press, 2000), p. 61.

9. Excerpt from *How to Read and Why*, cited in Harold Bloom, "In Praise of the Greats," *Brill's Content* (May 2000), p. 102.

10. See note 9.

11. Bloom, "In Praise of the Greats," pp. 102-103.

12. Bloom appears completely unaware of the feminist and postcolonial literature that raises important questions about the normative and political nature of home as a Western and patriarchical construct. See, for example, Biddy Martin and Chandra Talpade Mohanty, "Feminist Politics: What's Home Got to Do with It?" in Teresa de Lauretis, ed. *Feminist Studies/Critical Studies* (Bloomington: Indiana University Press, 1986), pp. 191-212; Jonathan Rutherford, "A Place Called Home: Identity and Cultural Politics of Difference," in Jonathan Rutherford, ed. *Identity, Community, Culture, Difference* (London: Lawrence and Wishart, 1990), pp. 9-27; Caren Kaplan, "Deterritorialisations: The Rewriting of Home and Exile in Western Feminist Discourse," *Cultural Critique* 6 (Spring 1987): 187-198; Abdul JanMohamed, "Worldliness—Without World, Homelessness-as-Home: Toward a Definition of the Specular Border Intellectual," in Michael Sprinker, ed. *Edward Said: A Reader* (Cambridge, U.K.: Basil Blackwell, 1992), pp. 97-123; Hamid Naficy, *Home, Exile, Homeland* (New York: Routledge, 1999).

13. Paul Smith, "The Political Responsibility of Teaching Literatures," *College Literature* 17, no. 23 (1990): 81.

14. I have addressed the political nature of education and pedagogy in a number of books. See, for example, Henry A. Giroux, *Pedagogy and the Politics of Hope* (Boulder, Colo.: Westview, 1998); Giroux, *Impure Acts*.

15. See note 11.

16. See note 9.

17. Bloom, "They Have the Numbers; We Have the Heights," *Boston Review* (April/May, 1998), p. 27.

18. In this sense, Bloom echoes right-wing ideologues such as Stephen H. Balch, the president of the National Association of Scholars. Balch argues that any attempt to critically engage, or, for that matter, even question, what he calls the civilizing mission of academe amounts to an "embrace of radical relativism." Rather than recognizing such forms of inquiry as an attempt to think through the responsibility, rights, and claims made in the name of authority, knowledge, and pedagogy, Balch simply dismisses such inquiry as an affront to academic standards and cultural values. Balch appears totally indifferent to the pedagogical and political implications of suggesting to students that they have no ethical or political right (foundation) to engage the knowledge, values, and meanings that they are asked to learn as a basis for developing a sense of individual and political agency. What kind of agency is being put into place under these circumstances? For Bloom and Balch, knowledge is sacred, leaving little if no room for critical inquiry, and hence pedagogy is rendered to a methodology of transmission, a process that refuses questions and takes no risks. See Stephen H. Balch, "The 'Civilizing Mission' of Academe," *Chronicle of Higher Education* (28 July 2000), p. B13.

19. Pierre Bourdieu, *On Television* (New York: The New Press, 1996), p. 35.

20. Daniel Kaufman, "Notes from Hell," *National Review* (30 September 1996), p. 46.

21. I summarize and extend many of these arguments in *Politics of Hope*.

22. See, for example, Homi Bhabha, *The Location of Culture* (New York: Routledge, 1994), p. 181.

23. sor's Controversial Analysis of Why Black Students Are 'Losing the Race,' " a favorFor a classic example of a polemical educational discourse that substitutes cynicism and critical pragmatism for passionate principle, and, in so doing, banishes hope, if not possibility itself, from the very realm of politics, see Illan Gur-Se'ev, "Toward a Nonrepresentative Critical Pedagogy," *Educational Theory* 48, no. 4 (Fall 1998): 463-486. In fact, the entire issue of *Educational Theory*, in which Gur-Se'ev's piece appears, is filled with the work of a number of theorists who are representative of this position. The equally depoliticized but less cynical work I am referring to can be seen in a recent issue of *The Nation*, organized by Herbert Kohl. Kohl appears to have become a broker for an educational discourse that is hostile to radical versions of critical educational theory and practice. See the special issue of *The Nation*, 5 June 2000. If we were to believe these critics, with few exceptions, schools have little to do with the assault on the welfare state, corporate power, the rise of the right in America, or any other broader political issue. For a representative view of Kohl's acrimonious views toward radical pedagogy, see his interview, "Herb Kohl Interview, NYC, June 2, 1997" at <www.zmag.org/sep/kohlint.htm>. Also see, Stan Karp, "Lesson Plans: The Politics of Education: An Interview with Herbert Kohl," <www.zena.secureforum.com/znet/ZMag/articles/April94Krp.htm>.

24. Kaufman, "Notes from Hell," pp. 47–48.

25. Diane Ravitch, *Left Back: A Century of Failed School Reforms* (New York: Simon and Schuster, 2000). Ravitch is relentless in suggesting that the failure of American education is largely the result of the legacy of critical educators and progressives. Unfortunately, she conveniently forgets that most of the problems with public education are largely about racial and class discrimination, economic inequities, the corporatization and selling of schools, and the relentless refusal to link schools to forms of civic education that prepare students to be critical citizens rather than good consumers—hardly problems caused by progressives or left theorists.

26. Leon Botstein, "Making the Teaching Profession Respectable Again ," *New York Times,* 26 July 1999, sec. A, p. 19. Elaine Showalter, "The Risks of Good Teaching: How 1 Professor and 9 T.A.'s Plunged Into Pedagogy," *The Chronicle of Higher Education* XLV, no. 44 (9 July 1999), sec. B, pp. 4-6.

27. E. D. Hirsch, Jr., *The Schools We Need* (New York: Doubleday, 1996); Nat Gage, *The Scientific Basis of the Art of Teaching* (New York: Teachers College Press, 1978).

28. Needless to say, this debate has been central to the history of a number of educational reform groups arguing for the professionalization of the teaching field. For a brilliant analysis of this history, see David F. Labaree, *How to Succeed In School* (New Haven, Conn.: Yale University Press, 1997).

29. Botstein, "Making the Teaching Profession Respectable Again."

30. See also Botstein, *Jefferson's Children: Education and the Promise of American Culture* (New York: Doubleday, 1997).

31. A typical example of such conditions and how they affect the quality of education for students in such schools can be found in Lynette Holloway, "As Poverty Shifts Students, Getting Lessons to Stick Proves a Tough Task," *New York Time,* 25 May 2000.

32. Botstein, "A Tyranny of Standardized Tests," *New York Times,* 28 May 2000, sec. WK, p. 11. For an excellent recent critique of standardized testing, see Peter Sacks, *Standardized Minds* (Cambridge: Perseus Books, 1999); David Owen with Marilyn Doerr, *None of the Above: Behind the Myth of Scholastic Aptitude* (Lanham, Md.: Rowman & Littlefield, 2000).

33. Showalter, "Risks of Good Teaching," sec. B, p. 4.

34. See Showalter, "Risks," sec. A, p. 4.

35. See Showalter, "Risks," sec. B, p. 5.

36. See note 35.

37. See Showalter, "Risks," sec. B, p. 6.

38. To be fair to Showalter, she is not alone among humanities scholars in refusing to step outside of her discipline in order to gain some theoretical purchase on important work done in critical pedagogy. Another example can be found in Biddy Martin, "Introduction: Teaching, Literature, Changing Cultures," *PMLA* 112, no. 1 (January 1997): 7-25.

39. Showalter, "Presidential Address 1998: Regeneration," *PMLA* 114 (May 1999): 318-325.

40. See Ian Hunter, *Rethinking the School* (New York: St. Martin's Press, 1994). This position is also argued for in Tony Bennett, "Out in the Open: Reflections on the History and Practice of Cultural Studies," *Cultural Studies* 10, no. 1 (1996): 133-153. See also Bennett, *Culture: A Reformer's Science* (Thousand Oaks, Calif.: Sage, 1998). This section of my paper draws heavily from Giroux, "Public Pedagogy as Cultural Politics: Stuart Hall and the 'Crisis' of Culture," *Cultural Studies* 14, no. 2 (2000): 341-360.

41. A particularly telling and theoretically sloppy example of this position can also be found in Maria Koundoura, "Multiculturalism or Multinationalism?" in David Bennett, ed. *Multicultural States* (New York: Routledge, 1998), pp. 69–87. Most of these critics appear to have little or no knowledge of the long history of debates within educational circles in the United States over issues of reproduction, resistance, and the politics of schooling. Koundoura is especially uninformed on this issue, citing one article to defend her attack on "border pedagogy." An interesting critique of the limits of governmentality can be found in Toby Miller, *Technologies of Truth* (Minneapolis: University of Minnesota Press, 1998) and in Alan O' Shea, "A Special Relationship? Cultural Studies, Academia and Pedagogy," *Cultural Studies* 12, no. 4 (1998): 513-527.

42. Ellsworth's work continues to inspire a host of polemical attacks motivated

by the triumph of the just cause and the portrayal of the other as an enemy to be annihilated. Unfortunately, within this mode of discourse, not only does the party line seem intent on processing the suspect, but it does so by both closing down any chance of a reasonable exchange and debate while dissolving questions of politics, theory, and practice into an epistemological privileging of particular social positions whose authority appears to be largely derived from unproblematic gender identities. For a classic example of such an intervention, see Patti Lather, "Ten Years Later, Yet Again: Critical Pedagogy and Its Complicities," in Kathleen Weiler, ed. *Feminist Engagements: Reading, Resisting, and Revisioning Male Theorists in Education and Cultural Studies* (New York: Routledge, 2001), pp. 183-195.

43. Elizabeth Ellsworth, "Why Doesn't This Feel Empowering? Working Through the Repressive Myths of Critical Pedagogy," in Lynda Stone, ed. *The Education Feminism Reader* (New York: Routledge, 1994), p. 301. Originally published in *Harvard Educational Review* 59 (1989): 297-324.

44. Ellsworth, "Empowering?" p. 305. In her most recent book, *Teaching Positions* (New York: Teachers College Press, 1997), Ellsworth has modified her position on authority by embracing what she calls "a pedagogy of manipulation," further defined or defended as a "a paradox that doesn't make sense" (150). Indeed! What is often surprising about the way in which her work is addressed both by critics and supporters is their refusal to examine her representations of the texts she often attacks. I would argue that many of her representations border on pure caricature, a position that Nicholas Burbules reiterates in talking about her treatment of his work. See Nicholas C. Burbules, "The Limits of Dialogue as Critical Pedagogy," in Peter Pericles Trifonas, ed. *Revolutionary Pedagogies* (New York: Routledge/Falmer, 2000), p. 266.

45. Bruce Horner, "Politics, Pedagogy, and the Profession of Composition: Confronting Commodification and the Contingencies of Power," *Journal of Advanced Composition* 20, no. 1 (2000): 130. The initial part of the long quote is worth repeating so as not to lose the point. Horner writes: "This account is troubling because the 'failure' of [her] course seems simultaneously inevitable and therefore indisputable and yet beside the point because that failure arises from her treatment of critical pedagogy as a commodity. Having reduced critical pedagogy to a commodity isolated from the material circumstances of its specific enactments, she then critiques it for its failure, as a commodity, to address just such circumstances" (130).

46. Alan O'Shea, "A Special Relationship? Cultural Studies, Academia and Pedagogy," *Cultural Studies* 12, no. 4 (1998): 513-527. Another challenge to the governmentality model can be found in the brilliant article on pedagogy and cultural studies by Richard Johnson, "Teaching without Guarantees: Cultural Studies, Pedagogy and Identity," in Joyce Canaan and Debbie Epstein, eds. *A Question of Discipline* (Boulder, Colo.: Westview, 1997), pp. 42–73.

47. See Stanley Aronowitz and Henry A. Giroux, *Education Still Under Siege* (Westport, Conn.: Bergin & Garvey Press, 1994).

48. See Bennett, *Culture,* p. 223.

49. Jacques Derrida, "Intellectual Courage: An Interview," trans. Peter Krapp. *Culture Machine,* vol. 2 (2000), p. 9. Online journal at <www.culturemachine.tees.a-c.uk/articles/art_derr.htm>.

50. Williams, "Brave New University," p. 749.

51. Paul Gilroy, *Against Race* (Cambridge, Mass.: Harvard University Press, 2000), p. 69.

52. For a fruitful discussion of the ethics and politics of deconstruction, see Thomas Keenan, *Fables of Responsibility: Aberrations and Predicaments in Ethics and Politics* (Stanford, Calif.: Stanford University Press, 1997), p. 2.

53. Derrida, "Intellectual Courage," p. 9.

54. Terry Eagleton, *The Idea of Culture* (Malden, Mass.: Blackwell, 2000), p. 22.

55. Bill Readings, *The University in Ruins* (Cambridge, Mass.: Harvard University Press, 1996), pp. 11, 18.

56. Bruce Horner, "Politics. Pedagogy, and the Profession of Composition: Confronting Commodification and the Contingencies of Power," *Journal of Advanced Composition* 20, no. 1 (2000): 141.

57. Robert Miklitsch, "The Politics of Teaching Literature: The 'Pedagogical Effect,'" *College Literature* 17, no. 2/3 (1990): 93.

58. This expression comes from John Michael, *Anxious Intellects: Academic Professionals, Public Intellectuals, and Enlightenment Values* (Durham, N.C.: Duke University Press, 2000), p. 2.

59. Cornel West, "The New Cultural Politics of Difference," in Russell Fergusen, Martha Geever, Trinh T. Minh-ha, and Cornel West, eds. *Out There* (Cambridge, Mass.: MIT Press, 1991), p. 35.

60. Jodi Dean, "The Interface of Political Theory and Cultural Studies," in Jodi Dean, ed. *Cultural Studies and Political Theory* (Ithaca, N.Y.: Cornell University Press, 2000), p. 3.

61. O'Shea, "A Special Relationship?" 513–527.

62. Paulo Freire, *Pedagogy of Freedom* (Lanham, Md.: Rowman & Littlefield, 1999), p. 48.

63. Shoshana Felman, *Jacques Lacan and the Adventure of Insight: Psychoanalysis in Contemporary Culture* (Cambridge, Mass.: Harvard University Press, 1987), p. 79. For an extensive analysis of the relationship between schooling, literacy, and desire, see Ursula A. Kelly, *Schooling Desire: Literacy, Cultural Politics, and Pedagogy* (New York: Routledge, 1997); Sharon Todd, *Learning Desire: Perspectives on Pedagogy, Culture, and the Unsaid* (New York: Routledge, 1997).

64. Felman, *Jacques Lacan,* p. 79.

65. Carol Becker, "The Artist as Intellectual," *The Review of Education/Pedagogy/Cultural Studies* 17, no. 4 (1995):388.

CHAPTER 5

Ernst Bloch claims that the term "something's missing," taken from Bertolt Brecht's *The Rise and Fall of the City of Mahagonny,* is one of the most profound sentences that

Brecht ever wrote because it offers a provocative referent regarding the importance of utopian thinking. See Ernst Bloch, "Something's Missing: A Discussion Between Ernst Bloch and Theodor W. Adorno on the Contradictions of Utopia Longing," in Ernst Bloch, *The Utopian Function of Art and Literature: Selected Essays* (Cambridge, Mass.: MIT Press, 1988), p. 15.

1. Ronald Aronson, "Hope After Hope," *Social Research* 66, no.2 (Summer 1999): 489.

2. Jameson's exact and much more eloquent quote is: "It seems to be easier for us today to imagine the thoroughgoing deterioration of the earth and of nature than the breakdown of late capitalism." Fredric Jameson, *The Seeds of Time* (New York: Columbia University Press, 1994), p. xii.

3. For an excellent discussion of this issue, see Aronson, "Hope After Hope," pp. 471–494; Leo Panitch and Sam Gindin, "Transcending Pessimism: Rekindling Socialist Imagination," in Leo Panitch and Sam Gindin, eds. *Necessary and Unnecessary Utopias* (New York: Monthly Review Press, 1999), pp. 1–29.

4. There are too many sources to cite on the history of utopianism that have emerged in the last decade, but an excellent representative source includes: Krishan Kuman, *Utopia and Anti-Utopia in Modern Times* (Malden, Mass.: Blackwell Publishers, 1987); for some excellent sources on the new scholarship on utopia, see: Ruth Levitas, *The Concept of Utopia* (Syracuse, N.Y.: Syracuse University Press, 1990); Jamie Owen Daniel and Tom Moylan, eds. *Not Yet: Reconsidering Ernst Bloch* (London: Verso Press, 1997); Andrew Benjamin, *Present Hope* (New York: Routledge, 1997).

5. Russell Jacoby, "A Brave New World: Looking Forward to a Nineteenth-Century Utopia," *Harper's Magazine* (December 2000), p. 78.

6. Francis Fukuyama, *The End of History and the Last Man* (New York: The Free Press, 1992).

7. Fukuyama, *End of History*, p. 48.

8. Fukuyama, *End of History*, p. 46.

9. Thomas W. Pogge, "The Moral Demands of Global Justice," *Dissent* (Fall 2000): 37–38.

10. Michael Walzer, "Pluralism and Social Democracy," *Dissent* (Winter 1998): 4.

11. Dinesh D' Souza, "The Moral Conundrum of Success," *Chronicle of Higher Education*, sec. 2 (10 November 2000), pp. B9–B10.

12. On figures on the growing racial and economic divide, see the Millennium Breach Report, cited in an editorial, "Racial Divide Among Americans Is Worsening Foundation Finds," *Baltimore Sun*, 1 March 1998 p. 1. For some recent figures on child poverty, see Marian Wright Edelman, "There's No Trademark on Concern for Kids," *New York Times*, 29 July 2000, sec. A, p. 27.

13. Ellen Willis, "Buy American," *Dissent* (Fall 2000): 109.

14. Denish D' Souza, *The End of Racism* (New York: Free Press, 1995), p. 24.

15. Robert McChesney, *Rich Media, Poor Democracy* (Urbana: University of Illinois Press, 1999), pp. 2, 16.

16. Aronson, "Hope After Hope," p. 480.

17. Sheldon S. Wolin, "Political Theory: From Vocation to Invocation," in Jason A. Frank and John Tambornino, eds. *Vocations of Political Theory* (Minneapolis: University of Minnesota Press, 2000), p. 18.

18. Perry Anderson, *A Zone of Engagement* (London: Verso, 1992), p. 335.

19. I take up these issues in great detail in Henry A. Giroux, *Stealing Innocence: Youth, Corporate Power and the Politics of Culture* (New York: St. Martin's Press, 2000).

20. For a grand display of this triumphalist vision of America, see Tom Wolfe, *Hooking Up* (New York: Farrar, Straus & Giroux, 2000).

21. Richard Rorty, *Achieving Our Country* (Cambridge, Mass.: Harvard University Press, 1997).

22. See Rorty, *Achieving Our Country,* especially pp. 32–37, 127.

23. Both quotations are from Russell Jacoby, *The End of Utopia* (New York: Basic Books, 1991), p. 126.

24. James Traub, "What No School Can Do," *New York Times Magazine* (16 January 2000), pp. 52–57, 68, 81, 90–91.

25. Traub, "The Campus Is Being Simulated," *New York Times Magazine* (19 November 2000), pp. 88–93, 113–114, 118, 125–127.

26. Traub, "Campus Is Being Simulated," p. 93.

27. Norman Geras, "Minimum Utopia: Ten Theses," in Panitch and Gindin, eds. *Necessary and Unnecessary Utopias* (New York: Monthly Review Press, 1999), p. 42.

28. John Binde touches on what it might mean to link politics to a realistic utopianism. He writes: "To achieve this, a third path is required, namely, that of realistic utopianism. Accordingly, the ethics of the future rests on a renewed dialogue between the present and the future. It involves neither foretelling nor prescribing the future but preparing for it. Preparing for the future has very concrete implications. Do we wish to prepare the global information society? Then make it possible: Give access to electricity, through the development of solar and alternative energies, to the two billion individuals who do not have access to an electric grid; give access to basic means of telecommunications to the over 4.5 billion individuals who do not have access to them; give access to education to those who are denied it. In this way, it should be possible to achieve a representation of the desired future born out of the observation of possible futures." John Binde, "Toward an Ethic of the Future," *Public Culture* 12, no.1 (2000): 65.

29. David Harvey, *Spaces of Hope* (Berkeley: University of California Press, 2000), p. 195.

30. Jacoby, "Brave Old World," pp. 72–80; Geras, "Minimum Utopia," pp. 41–42; Panitch and Gindin, "Transcending Pessimism," pp. 1–29; Harvey, *Spaces of Hope;* Jacoby, *End of Utopia.*

31. Jacoby, "Brave Old World," p. 80.

32. For a critique of entrepreneurial populism of this diverse group, see Thomas

Frank, *One Market under God: Extreme Capitalism, Market Populism and the End of Economic Democracy* (New York: Doubleday, 2000).

33. Carl Boggs, *The End of Politics: Corporate Power and the Decline of the Public Sphere* (New York: Guilford Press, 2000), p. 7.

34. Panitch and Gindin, "Transcending Pessimism," p. 2.

35. For an important contribution to such a project, see Sharon D. Welch, *Sweet Dreams in America: Making Ethics and Spirituality Work* (New York: Routledge, 1999).

36. This issue is taken up brilliantly in Ruth Levitas, *The Concept of Utopia* (Syracuse, N.Y.: Syracuse University Press, 1990).

37. Anson Rabinach, "Benjamin, Bloch, and Modern German Jewish Messianism," *New German Critique* 34 (Winter 1985): 124.

38. Bloch's great contribution in English on the subject of utopianism can be found in his three-volume work, *The Principle of Hope,* [originally published in 1959] trans. Neville Plaice, Stephen Plaice, and Paul Knight (Cambridge, Mass.: MIT Press, 1986).

39. Bloch, "Something's Missing: A Discussion Between Ernst Bloch and Theodor W. Adorno on the Contradictions of Utopia Longing," in Ernst Bloch, ed. *The Utopian Function of Art and Literature: Selected Essays* (Cambridge, Mass.: MIT Press, 1988), p. 3.

40. Anson Rabinach, "Ernst Bloch's *Heritage of Our Times* and the Theory of Fascism," *New German Critique* 11 (Spring 1977): 11.

41. Thomas L. Dunn, "Political Theory for Losers," in Jason A. Frank and John Tambornino, eds. *Vocations of Political Theory* (Minneapolis: University of Minnesota Press, 2000), p. 160.

42. Chantal Mouffe, "Which Ethics for Democracy?" in Marjorie Garber, Beatrice Hanssen, and Rebecca Walkowitz, eds. *The Turn to Ethics* (New York: Routledge, 2000), pp. 85–94.

43. Willis, "Buy American," p. 109.

44. Willis, "Buy American," pp. 110–111.

45. Levitas, *Concept of Utopia,* p. 265.

46. For two brilliant, though different, sources on the notion of ethics as a basis for a performative and public politics, see Jeffrey T. Nealon, *Alterity Politics: Ethics and Performative Subjectivity* (Durham, N.C.: Duke University Press, 1998) and Welch, *Sweet Dreams.*

47. Boggs, "*End of Politics,*" p. ix.

48. Cornelius Castoriadis, "The Greek Polis and the Creation of Democracy," in *Philosophy, Politics, Autonomy: Essays in Political Philosophy* (New York: Oxford University Press, 1991), pp. 81–123.

49. This issue is taken up in great detail in Paulo Freire, *Pedagogy of Freedom* (Lanham, Md.: Rowman & Littlefield, 1998).

50. Zygmunt Bauman, *In Search of Politics* (Stanford, Calif.: Stanford University Press, 1999), p. 8

51. Paul Gilroy, *Against Race* (Cambridge: Harvard University Press, 2000); Gilroy, of course, acknowledges the pedagogical role of visual culture in producing commodified images of blackness, but he exhibits little understanding of pedagogy as a form of resistant possibility; Michael Berube, *The Employment of English* (New York: New York University Press, 1998), especially chapter 10, "Cultural Criticism and the Politics of Selling Out," pp. 216–242; Carl Boggs, *The End of Politics* (New York: Guilford Press, 2000).

52. On the rising anti-intellectualism in American life, see Todd Gitlin, "The Renaissance of Anti-Intellectualism," *Chronicle of Higher Education* (8 December 2000), pp. B7–B9. Gitlin's critique of cultural studies and leftist politics in higher education, see Todd Gitlin, *Twilight of Our Common Dreams* (New York: Metropolitan Books, 1995); Todd Gitlin, "The Anti-Political Populism of Cultural Studies," *Dissent* (Spring 1997): 77–82.

53. Educated hope as both a pedagogical and philosophical notion draws in part from the work of Paulo Freire, especially his *Pedagogy of Hope* (New York: Continuum Press, 1994) and *Pedagogy of Freedom* (Lanham, Md.: Rowman & Littlefield, 1998). I have also explored this idea in highly specific terms in *Schooling and the Struggle for Public Life* (Minneapolis: University of Minnesota Press, 1988).

54. Marshall Berman, "Blue Jay Way: Where Will Critical Culture Come From?" *Dissent* (Winter 2000): 31.

55. See note 55.

56. Andrew Delbanco, "Symposium," *Dissent* (Winter 2000): 36. It is interesting how many of the responses to Berman seem to fall entirely within a language of despair parading as a dose of realism. The responses can be found in the same issue, pp. 34–44. See Berman's response to his critics in "Marshall Berman Replies," *Dissent* (Winter 2000): 44–46.

57. See Roger Shattuck, *Candor and Perversion* (New York: Norton, 1999), pp. 7–8.

58. Randolph M. Nesse, "The Evolution of Hope and Despair," *Social Research* 66, no. 2 (Summer 1999): 462–463.

59. Cornelius Castoriadis, "Culture in a Democratic Society," in David Ames Curtis, ed. *The Castoriadis Reader,* (Malden, Mass.: Blackwell, 1997), p. 347.

60. Stuart Hall, "Subjects in History: Making Diasporic Identities," in Wahneema Lubiano, ed. *The House That Race Built* (New York: Pantheon, 1997), p. 295.

61. Cary Nelson and Dilip Parameshwar Gaonkar, "Cultural Studies and the Politics of Disciplinarity: An Introduction," in Cary Nelson and Dilip Parameshwar Gaonkar, eds. *Disciplinarity and Dissent in Cultural Studies* (New York: Routledge, 1996), p. 7.

62. For instance, see Richard Johnson, "Reinventing Cultural Studies: Remembering for the Best Version," in Elizabeth Long, ed. *From Sociology to Cultural Studies* (Malden, Mass.: Blackwell, 1997), pp. 452–488; George Lipsitz, "Academic Politics and Social Change," in Jodi Dean, ed. *Cultural Studies and Political Theory* (Ithaca, N.Y.: Cornell University Press, 2000), pp. 80–92.

63. Lawrence Grossberg cited in Handel Kashope Wright, "Pressing, Promising, and Paradoxical: Larry Grossberg on Education and Cultural Studies," *The Review of Education/Pedagogy/Cultural Studies* 22, no.1 (2000): 21.

64. Grossberg cited in Wright, "Pressing, Promising, and Paradoxical," pp. 18, 23.

65. Angela McRobbie, "The Es and Anti-Es: New Questions for Feminism and Cultural Studies," in Marjorie Ferguson and Peter Golding, eds. *Cultural Studies in Question* (London: Sage Publications, 1997), p. 178.

66. Shane Gunster, "Gramsci, Organic Intellectuals, and Cultural Studies," in Jason Frank and John Tambornino, eds. *Vocations of Political Theory* (Minneapolis: University of Minnesota Press, 2000), p. 253.

67. I am not suggesting that Grossberg does not understand the more extended role that pedagogy plays as part of a broader notion of cultural studies as much as indicating that he still largely talks about pedagogy through the discourse of schooling.

68. Roger Simon, "Broadening the Vision of University-Based Study of Education: The Contribution of Cultural Studies," *The Review of Education/Pedagogy/Cultural Studies* 12, no. 1 (1995): 109.

69. For an example of how the language of critique, absent any sense of possibility, can degenerate into a total dismissal, if not cynical indifference, of the multiple spheres at which politics and social struggle take place, see Carol Stabile, "Pedagogues, Pedagogy, and Political Struggle," in Amitava Kumar, ed. *Class Issues* (New York: New York University Press, 1997), pp. 208–220. For an extensive critique of this type of pedagogy, see Stanley Aronowitz and Henry A. Giroux, *Education Still Under Siege* (Westport, Conn.: Bergin & Garvey, 1993); Giroux, *Pedagogy and the Politics of Hope: Theory, Culture, and Schooling* (Boulder, Colo.: Westview, 1997).

70. Cornelius Castoriadis, "Power, Politics, and Autonomy," in *Philosophy, Politics Autonomy: Essays in Political Philosophy* (New York: Oxford University Press, 1991), pp. 143–176.

71. The work of Toby Miller is especially constructive on this issue. See Miller, *The Well-Tempered Self: Citizenship, Culture, and the Postmodern Subject* (Baltimore: Johns Hopkins Press, 1993) and *Technologies of Truth* (Minneapolis: University of Minnesota Press, 1994).

72. Antonio Gramsci, *Selections from the Prison Notebooks* (New York International Press, 1971), p. 350.

73. I purposely have not drawn in this case upon the work of Paulo Freire because I have discussed his notion of utopianism and education in great detail in *Stealing Innocence*.

74. Castoriadis, "The Problem of Democracy Today," *Democracy and Nature* 8 (April 1996): 19.

75. Castoriadis, "The Nature and Value of Equity," in *Philosophy, Politics, Autonomy,* pp. 124–142.

76. Castoriadis, *The World in Fragments,* ed. and trans. by David Ames Curtis (Stanford: Stanford University Press, 1997), p. 91.

77. Both quotations are taken from Castoriadis, "Culture in a Democratic Society," in *The Castoriadis Reader,* pp. 343, 341.

78. Castoriadis, "The Crisis of the Identification Process," *Thesis Eleven* 49 (May 1997): 87–88.

79. Castoriadis, "The Anticipated Revolution," *Political and Social Writings,* vol. 3, edited and translated by David Ames Curtis (Minneapolis: University of Minnesota Press, 1993), pp. 153–154.

80. Binde, "Toward an Ethic of the Future," *Public Culture* 12, no. 1 (2000): 65.

81. Castoriadis, "Nature and Value of Equity," p. 136.

82. Castoriadis, "Democracy as Procedure and Democracy as Regime," *Constellations* 4, no.1 (1997): 4.

83. "Democracy as Procedure," p. 10.

84. Castoriadis, " Crisis of the Identification Process," p. 88.

85. Castoriadis, "The Greek Polis and the Creation of Democracy," in *Philosophy, Politics, Autonomy,* p. 102.

86. Castoriadis, "Power, Politics, and Autonomy," in *Philosophy, Politics, Autonomy,* pp. 144–145.

87. Castoriadis, "Democracy as Procedure," p. 15. It is crucial here to note that Castoriadis develops both his notion of democracy and the primacy of education in political life directly from his study of ancient Greek democracy.

88. Castoriadis, "Problem of Democracy Today," p. 24.

89. Binde, "Ethic of the Future," p. 71.

90. Jacques Derrida, "Intellectual Courage: An Interview," trans. Peter Krapp, *Culture Machine,* vol. 2 (2000), p. 7.

91. See especially, Raymond Williams, "Preface to Second Edition," *Communications* (New York: Barnes and Noble, 1967); Raymond Williams, *What I Came to Say* (London: Hutchinson, 1989); Raymond Williams, *Television: Technology and Cultural Form* (New York: Schocken Books, 1975; Alan O'Connor, ed. *Raymond Williams on Television* (New York: Routledge, 1989). Both Castoriadis and Williams provide important models of educational reform. Castoriadis draws much of his inspiration from ancient models of democracy, while Williams develops his educational theories from his extensive work in adult education. For a brilliant analysis of the crisis of the humanities that draws on these two traditions, see Susan Searls, "Rhetorical and Cultural Studies: Beyond the Crisis of the Humanities" (unpublished manuscript, 2001).

92. Williams, "Preface," p. 14.

93. See especially, Williams, *Marxism and Literature* (New York: Oxford University Press, 1977); *The Year 2000* (New York: Pantheon, 1983).

94. Williams, *Marxism and Literature.*

95. For an interesting commentary on how Williams addresses the notion of hope in the context of his on life, see Raymond Williams and Terry Eagleton, *The Politics of Hope: An Interview* (Boston: Northeastern University Press, 1989), pp. 176–183. Also note Williams's comments on utopia in "Utopia and Science Fiction," *Problems in Materialism and Culture* (London: Verso, 1980), pp. 196–212.

96. Williams, *The Long Revolution: An Analysis of the Democratic, Industrial, and Cultural Changes Transforming Society* (New York: Columbia University Press, 1961), p. 155

97. Williams, *The Long Revolution.* See also, Williams, *Resources of Hope: Culture, Democracy, Socialism,* ed. Robin Gable (London: Verso, 1989); also note Williams' important exchanges on matters of culture and politics in Raymond Williams, *Politics and Letters: Interviews with New Left Review* (London: New Left Books, 1979).

98. John Brenkman, "Raymond Williams and Marxism," in Christopher Prendingast, ed. *Cultural Materialism: On Raymond Williams* (Minneapolis: University of Minnesota Press, 1995), p. 263

99. Williams, "Preface," pp. 15, 16.

100. See note 97, p. 15.

101. See, in particular, Williams, *Marxism and Literature: What I Came to Say* (London: Hutchinson, 1989); *Problems in Materialism and Culture.*

102. I take this issue up in detail in *Border Crossings; Cultural Workers and the Politics of Education* (New York: Routledge, 1992).

103. Williams, "Television and Teaching: An Interview with Raymond Williams," *Screen Education* (Summer 1979): 14.

104. I am paraphrasing Cornel West here. See Cornel West, "In Memoriam: The Legacy of Raymond Williams," in *Cultural Materialism: On Raymond Williams,* pp. ix–xiii.

105. David Harvey, "Cosmopolitanism and the Banality of Geographic Evils," *Public Culture* 12, no. 2 (2000): 558.

106. Bloch cited in Aronson, "Hope After Hope," p. 471.

AFTERWORD

1. For his first sustained presentation of the importance of cultural studies for critical pedagogy and the reconstruction of education, see Giroux 1992: 161ff; on the need for a richer understanding of culture, cultural politics, and pedagogy than in conventional orthodoxies, see Giroux 1992; 180ff; some of the positions in his cultural turn were anticipated in Giroux and Simon 1989. For my own takes on media culture and cultural studies, see Kellner 1995.

2. Giroux also coedited a series of books on critical pedagogy and cultural studies, signaling the collaborative nature of the enterprise; see Giroux and Simon 1989; Giroux and McLaren 1989 and 1994; Giroux, McLaren, Lankshear, and Cole 1994; and Giroux and Shannon 1997. One might also cite Giroux's collaborations with Stanley Aronowitz who also worked to combine cultural studies, critical pedagogy, and radical democratic politics (1991 and 1994).

3. For an excellent study of the ongoing and escalating war against youth, see Giroux's recent paper, "Zero Tolerance and Mis/Education: Youth and the Politics of Domestic Militarization" (forthcoming).

4. For my own analysis of the political attack on rap in the early 1990s, see Kellner 1995, ch. 4.

5. Giroux's reading of *Juice* is more nuanced and provides a better context for productive engagement with contemporary films dealing with black urban youth (1996: 39ff). While Giroux is rightfully concerned that the film could help promote "white panic" and negative images of black youth, he notes the critique of violence in the film. While I would agree with Giroux (1996: 44) that one needs to go beyond mainstream Hollywood films to texts like Julie Dash's *Daughters of the Dust* or Leslie Harris's *Just Another Girl on the IRT* to find more progressive and complex representations of African Americans, I would argue that even films that have negative representations can be engaged by a critical cultural studies to produce productive discussions and insights into contemporary social conditions and the dynamics of race, gender, class, and other sites of representation.

6. For Giroux's defense of theoretical language, see 1993, ch. 6 and 1994, ch. 6. In retrospect, I would agree with Giroux on the usefulness of theory and the need for new theoretical languages to describe new social, cultural, and political conditions and to develop more complex discourses to capture the turbulence, intense changes, and novelties of the present. But in the present conjuncture, I would want to mediate between those who call for clarity and accessibility in discourse and writing contrasted to those who defend high theory and complexity. Hence, while I believe it was salutary to appropriate and deploy the new theoretical discourse of the past decades, and have done so myself, I think in the contemporary era, it is important to try to become as clear and accessible as possible. Moreover, I would argue that a virtue of Giroux's recent work is that it is indeed more lucid and accessible to a broader public than his late 1980s and early 1990s work when he was himself, as were many of us, learning new languages and developing new theories and pedagogies. Finally, I would suggest that engaging the new cyberculture and transformations of education and everyday life brought on by new technologies requires complex theoretical language and analysis, as well as new pedagogies and a democratic restructuring of education; see Kellner, 2000.

INDEX

ABOUT THE AUTHOR

Henry A. Giroux is the Waterbury Chair Professor of Education at Penn State University. He is the author of several books, including *The Mouse That Roared: Disney and the End of Innocence; Stealing Innocence: Corporate Culture's War on Children;* and *Impure Acts: The Practical Politics of Cultural Studies.*